Vocabulary
for College

Vanguard Edition
with Analogies

Vocabulary for College

Vanguard Edition
with Analogies

Paul B. Diederich
Sydell Terris Carlton
June Springford Papale
Napoleon J. Papale

 HARCOURT BRACE JOVANOVICH, PUBLISHERS

Orlando   San Diego   Chicago   Dallas

The Authors

Paul B. Diederich took his bachelor's and master's degrees at Harvard University and his doctorate at Columbia. He taught in private and public schools for many years, was an associate professor in English and Examiner in English at the University of Chicago, and was a member of the Research Division of Educational Testing Service in Princeton, New Jersey, until his retirement. With Osmond E. Palmer he coauthored a book of instructional tests for college freshmen, *Critical Thinking in Reading and Writing.*

Sydell T. Carlton received her bachelor's degree from the University of Connecticut and her master's degree from Indiana University, where she taught freshman and sophomore English classes. She has also taught at Rider College and has been a member of the Research and Test Development Divisions of Educational Testing Service.

June Springford Papale was educated in Great Britain and holds a University of London Teaching Certificate. She was a Fulbright Exchange Teacher to the United States and has since received a bachelor's degree from Fairleigh Dickinson University and a master's degree from Seton Hall University.

Napoleon J. Papale took his bachelor's and master's degrees at Montclair State College and did postgraduate work at Rutgers University. Formerly Head of the English Department at Bernards High School in Bernardsville, New Jersey, he has taught at Fairleigh Dickinson University and has served as Director of Teacher Placement at Seton Hall University.

Acknowledgment

The authors wish to thank Osmond E. Palmer for his collaboration in the vocabulary study that yielded the list of words treated in these exercises.

Contents

Vocabulary for College

Vanguard Edition
with Analogies

Introduction

The senior author of *Vocabulary for College* spent more than twenty-five years as a member of the Research Division of Educational Testing Service, which prepares the tests used by the College Entrance Examination Board. The latter is a voluntary association of school and colleges which, ever since 1901, have agreed to accept scores on a common set of examinations as one basis for admission to college.

Before that year, most colleges that required tests for admission made their own and gave them on their own campuses. The time and expense involved in travel and the difficulty of preparing for so many different tests led to the establishment of a common examining agency, controlled by representatives of both schools and colleges. Scores on its tests were accepted as one basis for admission to all colleges that became members of this association, now commonly known as the College Board.

The test that is taken by more than one million students annually has been known since 1926 as the Scholastic Aptitude Test. It is a three-hour test of developed verbal and mathematical abilities. In the verbal section, about one-half of the time is devoted to reading comprehension: passages from books like those that will be assigned in college, not just in literature but in all subjects, followed by multiple-choice questions on what these passages mean. Such a test is one of the best predictors of success in all fields of study in college, since all disciplines require the ability to understand fairly difficult books.

One problem, however, is that reading-comprehension questions take a lot of time: time for reading the passages and then time for going back to figure out the points raised in the questions. This process must not be hurried, because a speeded test of reading comprehension loses much of its predictive power.

It takes, however, a large number of verbal items to work up to a *reliable* score. That is a score that would not change very much if the students were given another test of the same kind the following day. One way to get in enough verbal items without speeding or extending the length of the test is to fill the other half of the verbal section with three types of vocabulary items: *analogies, antonyms,* and *sentence completions.* Following are examples of these vocabulary items.

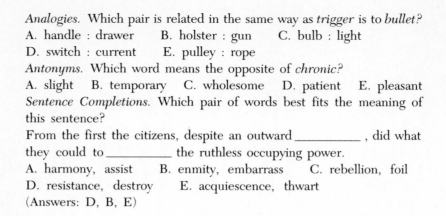

Analogies. Which pair is related in the same way as *trigger* is to *bullet?*
A. handle : drawer   B. holster : gun   C. bulb : light
D. switch : current   E. pulley : rope
Antonyms. Which word means the opposite of *chronic?*
A. slight   B. temporary   C. wholesome   D. patient   E. pleasant
Sentence Completions. Which pair of words best fits the meaning of this sentence?
From the first the citizens, despite an outward _____ , did what they could to _____ the ruthless occupying power.
A. harmony, assist   B. enmity, embarrass   C. rebellion, foil
D. resistance, destroy   E. acquiescence, thwart
(Answers: D, B, E)

Vocabulary items can be used in this way because they are more closely related to reading comprehension than anything else subject to testing. The most obvious reason is that students cannot understand a difficult reading passage if they do not know the meaning of the important words. Besides, students who start with a good vocabulary find reading easier and do more of it than students with a poor vocabulary, and wide reading extends their vocabulary still further. When testing time is very short, as in screening tests for various occupations, vocabulary tests are often used in place of reading tests, since they yield approximately the same scores.

Still, genuine reading ability does not mean a showy acquaintance with a large number of unusual words. Someone has said that reading ability is the reality and vocabulary, its shadow. When it is hard to measure the height of a tree, try measuring the length of its shadow. Extending the length of a shadow will not make the tree grow faster or higher. Knowledge of vocabulary in itself is not the same as reading ability, but measuring vocabulary has become an acceptable substitute for testing reading.

This series of vocabulary books was not written for the purpose of improving a score on any test, whether the Scholastic Aptitude Test, other college entrance and scholarship tests, IQ tests, or screening tests for positions in business, industry, civil service, or the armed forces. Genuine vocabulary development cannot be hurried, and for that reason the authors have provided much more practice with a larger number of important words than you will find in any supposed shortcut method to a large vocabulary. The building and retention of a large vocabulary takes place over a period of time. It does not come about by a sudden feat of memorization. Besides, it would be unethical for the authors to use their special knowledge of College Board tests to coach directly the words used in these tests.

The authors made their own word list by testing approximately 6,000 high school juniors and college freshmen to find out which of the 20,000 most common words in general reading they did not know. The words covered in these text-workbooks are those that were missed by 30 to 60 percent of these students. The authors tried out various types of exercises and selected those that led to genuine understanding and permanent retention of these words. The key to success was to show each word in a large number of complete sentences and to get any type of response that showed whether students understood the word. The simplest way—one that gave the largest amount of practice with each word in the shortest time and allowed students to check their own work—was to have students indicate whether the word was used correctly or incorrectly in each sentence. The bulk of the practice on each word is provided in this way, but other types of items are also used for variety and to make sure that the meaning is clearly understood. This edition has a section that includes approximately 200 analogies. These analogies provide practice in using words from each section in a new context and help students develop critical-thinking skills.

The main purpose of these exercises is to enable the student to read and understand more difficult books. The authors hope everyone will read as many books as possible. The experience of a large testing organization over a long period of time suggests that this is one excellent way to become informed, articulate, and successful.

Paul B. Diederich

How to Use This Book

1. Each entry word in the book receives a half-page treatment, which includes a pronunciation guide, definition, example sentence, sometimes a headnote, and nine exercise items. Eight of these exercise items are sentences using the entry word correctly or incorrectly. Insert either *r* (*right*) or *w* (*wrong*) in the blank at the end of each sentence. The ninth item in each exercise requires you to choose among four or five brief definitions of the entry word. Then you are to write a sentence of your own using the entry word correctly. At the end of each section is a review exercise with sentences containing blanks in which the words you have studied are to be inserted. Following this exercise is a list of words for dictionary study. Below is a model entry with labels identifying the recurring elements. Entry words are reinforced in an analogy section at the back of the Vanguard Edition.

entry word

dissent   *definition*   *example sentence*

pronunciation guide — (di·sent′) | To object, disagree, or differ. | He *dissents* each time we make a new proposal.

etymology — [Latin *dis–*, apart, and *sensus*, feeling.] The opposite of *dissent* is *assent*, which you have encountered in Section 3. *Dissent* is often followed by *from*. A *dissenter* (or *dissentient*) is one who disagrees; a *Dissenter* is an English or Scottish Protestant who refuses to accept the doctrines of the Church of England. The noun form of *dissent* is *dissent* or *dissension;* the adjective form is *dissenting* or *dissentient*.   — *headnote*

right or wrong sentences —
Although Lynn hated to be the only dissenter, she felt that she had to stand by her principles. 1 _____
The proposed new highway led to dissension among the residents of the area. 6 _____   It takes a long time to change customs that have been established by common dissent. 2 _____   The dissenting element in the audience tried to shout the speaker down. 4 _____   Dissenting from the proposal to return to work, the members left the union meeting. 5 _____   The removal of a familiar landmark caused dissent in the town. 9 _____   They found some unusual plants and insects on their pleasant dissent down the mountain. 8 _____   You have the right to dissent, but not before studying the facts.
7 _____ | **Dissent:** 1 respectable   2 downward movement   3 agree   4 differ 3 _____ | — *"tag" definition*

space for original sentence — YOUR SENTENCE: _____
_____

[1:r   2:w   3:4   4:r   5:r   6:r   7:r   8:w   9:r] — *answer key*

2. Before reading further, glance through Section 1 and see whether you have any questions about what you are to do. The following suggestions should answer most questions and your teacher will answer any others.

3. Pay attention to the title and introductory page of each section. These provide a unifying concept that ties together the words to be studied in that section. You may already know some of the words, but it is wise to glance through the exercises and try some of the sentences for each word to make sure. You may know a word in a different sense from the one developed in its exercise.

4. Pronounce the words that you study. A pronunciation guide is printed in parentheses below each word. The symbols are explained inside the back cover of this book. If there is anything tricky about the spelling, spell the word aloud and then write it down to make sure you have it right. This first impression is very important. If you get the word wrong now, you will probably have trouble with it later.

5. Try to remember the definition. This is not a dictionary definition, giving all possible shades of meaning. The definitions in this book try to give the core meaning (or meanings) from which other meanings may be inferred. The definition is followed by an example sentence illustrating the core meaning. If there are two distinct core meanings, two definitions are given and each is followed by an example sentence. It was not found necessary to give more than two core definitions for any word except *capital*, in text-workbook B, which has six. If a word has other meanings that are either too well-known or too technical to be worth learning, they usually are mentioned in the headnote.

6. Headnotes, printed in smaller type below the definition and example, add interest, variety, and useful information. They may touch on such matters as distinctions in meaning, tips on usage, and word origins. These brief etymologies, or word histories, are enclosed in brackets. They may not agree completely with the ones given in a dictionary. The reason for this is that dictionary-makers, in the interest of uniformity, may adhere to rules that can obscure a clear explanation of how the root contributes to the present meaning. A good example of this is found in the headnote for the entry word *vestige* in text-workbook C of *Vocabulary for College*. Some dictionaries just state that *investigate* comes from Latin *investigatus*, meaning investigate. Although that piece of information is true, the typical approach of the authors of this book is more helpful. They go back one step further and inform you that *investigate* is derived from Latin *vestigium*, footprint. That hint at the original meaning of *investigate*, to track something down, gives you an understanding about our English word. The etymology which merely gives *investigatus* tells nothing other than that the word was originally Latin.

7. After the headnote (if there is one) your real work begins. There are eight practice sentences that use the entry word either correctly or incorrectly. You are to mark each sentence either *r* (*right*) or *w* (*wrong*) in the numbered blank at the *end* of the sentence. If you are uncertain, glance back at the definition and example and try to decide whether the sentence is enough like them to be counted as right. If you cannot decide, look at the number of the blank you are trying to fill. Then find this number in the answer key, which is printed at the bottom of the exercise. It shows the authors' answer to this sentence. If their answer surprises you, look up the word in a dictionary. If you are still puzzled, note your objection in the margin and take it up with your teacher privately or with your classmates in the next class discussion of the lesson.

8. You may wonder why the blanks at the ends of the sentences have been numbered in a scrambled order. If the answers were numbered in an ordinary ascending order, and you checked the answer to sentence 1, you would be able to see the next answer, the answer to sentence 2, ahead of time. With the answers in scrambled order, seeing the next answer will do you no good because it probably does not refer to the next sentence. You can still cheat by glancing at the answer key before trying to decide for yourself whether a sentence is right or wrong, but there is no point in doing that, since you are not graded on these exercises. Credit is given only for scores on the tests, which have no right answers in sight and which use sentences that do not appear in the exercises. The easiest, quickest, and most interesting way to prepare for the tests is to do the exercises honestly. Make up your own mind about each sentence, put down your answer, and then check with the key before going on to the next sentence. If you cannot make up your mind about a sentence, do not hesitate to use the key. You will soon find out how much use you can make of the key and still get high scores on the tests.

9. Ingenious students often think of rather farfetched situations in which the wrong sentences could be right. For example, take the sentence "Lawrence of Arabia crossed the desert on an apothecary." If you know that *apothecary* is an old word for *druggist,* the sentence is ridiculous. On second thought, however, the body of a druggist *might* be shipped across a desert for burial, and if there were no other seat on the plane, a man *might* sit on the coffin and thus "cross the desert on an apothecary." But that would be a test of your imagination, not of your vocabulary. If you want to learn the usual meaning of a word, mark a sentence wrong if the word would not ordinarily be used in such a context.

10. A possible situation very similar to that mentioned in paragraph 9 concerns sentences that state facts, such as "The Capitol of the United States is in Washington, D.C." Just as your common sense determined which contexts were clearly too fanciful for the purposes of this book, so

should it determine which words are reasonable in sentences that lend themselves to "true" and "false" interpretations. In the *capitol* example, the word is used in a reasonable context, and you need not question the factual accuracy of the statement. But consider the sentence "Piety is out of place in church." The authors are dealing in vocabulary learning, and since you know that *piety* means devotion, reverence, or holiness, it would clearly *not* be reasonable to use the word in this sentence, and the sentence should be marked *w*.

11. A few headnotes refer you to a dictionary for other, usually technical or rare, definitions of the entry word. However, the sentences in the exercise following such a headnote will not use the word in one of these unmentioned dictionary meanings. In the exercise, correct sentences use the word only in the senses given or implied in the text-workbook definition and headnote.

12. An effort was made to include in each exercise common variant forms of the entry word. In text-workbook B, for example, the sentences on *disparage* use *disparaging, disparagingly,* and *disparagement.* When such variants introduce a new meaning, it is mentioned in the headnote. Otherwise, students translate the definition of the entry word to fit the variant forms.

13. The last item in each exercise usually offers a choice among four brief definitions of the entry word. However, when the entry word has been introduced by two definitions and two examples, you are to choose two out of five brief definitions. In the blank following these items, write the number or numbers of the correct definition(s) and check your answer with the key below. Do not expect these brief definitions to include everything that the word can mean. They are only tags to help you remember the core meaning.

14. At the bottom of each exercise are two lines for you to write a sentence of your own using the entry word correctly. Try to make your sentence different from those given in the exercise, and try to make it show what the word means. For example, "I saw an advocate" is not helpful because the *advocate* might be anything. "She has always been a strong advocate of healthful exercise" is better because it indicates that you know that an *advocate* is one who supports something. Do not expect your teacher to check all these sentences, for that would create a mountain of paperwork that this kind of book aims to avoid. Instead, your teacher will have various students read only the sentences that use words missed on the tests by a large percentage of students. Since you will never know which sentences you may be called upon to read, you should write all of them carefully.

15. At the end of each section, there is a *Review Exercise* with the entry words listed in alphabetical order at the top of the page. Below this list are sentences with blanks to indicate a missing word. You are to choose the entry word that best fits each sentence, using each word only once. If you cross out each word you use in the list at the top of the page, it will make the remaining choices easier. You may make any change in the form of the word that is needed to fit the sentence: for example, add *-s, -ed, -ing,* or some common suffix. When two words fit a sentence equally well, the answer key allows you to count either one as correct. But if there is a slight difference in meaning and one word has already been used, you should use the other in the next appropriate sentence, on the principle that each word may be used only once. This will be the hardest exercise in each section but also the most valuable, since it shows beyond any question whether you know how to use these words. It is so important that a similar exercise, using other sentences, is included in the test on every section. After you complete the *Review Exercise,* you might want to do the analogies for that section. The analogies, located at the back of the book, are further explained in paragraph 18.

16. Following the *Review Exercise* is a list of related words with the caption *For Dictionary Study.* When you read the section introduction, you may find that you already know most of the words. You can make sure by trying a few sentences for each word and checking the answer key. This may take no more than ten minutes. Then, if you do not need to take the time allotted for vocabulary study, you can look up in a dictionary any of the related words. There is room on each page for you to write down a definition and use each word in a short sentence. Be prepared to explain to the class the meaning of any word you have looked up and to illustrate its meaning with your sentence. You may want to divide this work with several classmates, each taking a part of the list. You should be able to answer any questions the other students raise about the words.

17. Throughout the four books of *Vocabulary for College,* a number of key terms are used in the discussions of the entry words. Since it is important that you know the meanings of these terms, they are defined below.

Archaic is an adjective that describes language that is old-fashioned and no longer in common use except in poetry, church ritual, and so forth.

EXAMPLE: *Brethren* is an *archaic* word for members of a society or sect.

Colloquial is an adjective that describes language that is conversational and informal. *Colloquial* words are not typically used in formal writing.

EXAMPLE: *Pal* is a *colloquial* word for a close friend or comrade.

Connotation refers to the idea suggested by or associated with a word or phrase in addition to the actual meaning of the word or phrase. The verb form is *connote.*

>   EXAMPLE: If you are thin, you can be called either *slender* or *skinny.* *Slender* has a positive *connotation* (that is, it is favorable to be called *slender*), but *skinny* has a negative or unfavorable *connotation* (that is, one might be insulted to be called *skinny*).

Imply means to hint, suggest, or indicate indirectly.

>   EXAMPLE: She didn't actually say she would attend the conference, but her answer *implied* that she would.

A *prefix* is a syllable, group of syllables, or word placed at the beginning of a word to form a new word that may change in meaning.

>   EXAMPLE: In the word *inability, in-* is the *prefix.*

A *root* is either a word from which other words are derived or the core of a word to which prefixes and suffixes may be added.

>   EXAMPLE: Latin *habilis* (which means able) is the *root* of *ability.*

>   EXAMPLE: In the word *inability, abil-* is the *root.*

A *suffix* is a syllable or group of syllables placed at the end of a word or word core to change its meaning or to make it a different part of speech.

>   EXAMPLE: In the word *inability, -ity* is the *suffix.*

A *synonym* is a word that has the same or nearly the same meaning as another word. The adjective form is *synonymous.*

>   EXAMPLE: *Keen* is a *synonym* of *sharp,* and *glad* is a *synonym* of *happy.* (Or *keen* is *synonymous* with *sharp,* and *glad* is *synonymous* with *happy.*)

18. Ten analogies for each section are at the back of the text-workbook. Analogies were added to the Vanguard Edition in response to the recommendations of teachers. Analogies are word comparisons that are similar to ratios in mathematics. As a matter of fact, analogies are set up with colons, just as ratios are. You will remember that a simple mathematical ratio is 2 : 4 :: 4 : 8. A simple word analogy is NEAR : FAR :: HOT : COLD. The single colon (:) stands for *is to* and the double colon (::) for *as.* This means, NEAR *is to* FAR *as* HOT *is to* COLD. In this analogy, each pair of words has an antonymous relationship. Each analogy in the text-workbook shows an entry word (capitalized) that is compared with another word (also capitalized). You are then given five pairs of words, each two words related to one another in some way. You are asked to choose the pair that has the same relationship as the capitalized pair. Here is an analogy for you to try.

POLISHED : SHINY ::

    A. sad : happy

    B. one : few

    C. fast : rapid

    D. viral : feverish

    E. warmed : boiling

This analogy is fairly easy. The capitalized pair are two synonyms. There is only one pair of synonyms among the five examples. (C) Another, more difficult, kind of analogy requires you to take several steps to find the correct answer. Try this one.

BOOT : SANDAL ::

    A. sock : stocking

    B. suit : scarf

    C. coat : hat

    D. mitten : glove

    E. belt : buckle

Boot and *sandal* are both items that are worn. But so are all the other things named in this exercise. *Boot* and *sandal* are both worn on the same part of the body. So are pair A, *sock* and *stocking,* and pair D, *mitten* and *glove.* Ask yourself what further relationship there is between *boot* and *shoe.* They are both worn on the feet. The correct answer is the pair that is closest to the capitalized example. (A) There are different kinds of relationships used in the analogies in this book. Here is a list of the analogy categories with an example for each.

    antonym: down : up

    cause and effect: tickle : giggle

    characteristic: bird : flies

    classification: bush : rose

    different degrees: month : year

    function: pencil : write

    grammatical: think : thought

    place: penguin : Antarctica

    part and whole or **whole and part:** keyboard : computer

    synonym: rot : decay

In the analogies in this text-workbook, the meaning used for the entry word is taken directly from the definition(s) and headnote found earlier in the text-workbook. For the meaning of any other words in the exercises, consult your dictionary. Keep in mind that the entry word is always on the left of the capitalized pair. Within each exercise, all the examples to the left of the colon are the same part of speech, and all the words to the right of the colon are, likewise, the same part of speech. As you do the analogies, you will soon realize that they do more than test vocabulary. They require analytical and critical thinking. For these reasons, most standardized verbal tests include analogies.

1 Goodness, Happiness

In these introductions the words to be studied in each section are printed in italics and are listed at the bottom of the page. They are woven into a connected explanation or story to give you a general idea of their meaning. Some are followed by a brief definition in parentheses; others are not—if their meaning can be guessed from the context.

The first three words relate to good character: *benevolence* (goodwill), *exemplary* (deserving imitation), and *reputable* (held in esteem). The next two are more concerned with politeness: *gentility* (refinement) and *decorum* (good taste). The next three are connected with truth: *punctilious* (extremely careful), *candid* (frank, outspoken), and *veracity* (habitual truthfulness). The next word, *feasible* (possible, able to be done), is connected with goodness only in the sense that if a plan is not *feasible*, it can hardly be called a good plan.

The next six words all relate to states of mind: *solace* (to comfort or console), *elation* (joy), *avidity* (eagerness), *preoccupy* (to absorb the attention), *morale* (mental condition or spirit), and *wary* (cautious). The last word, *impunity*, refers to freedom from punishment or other bad consequences of an act.

Remember that these brief definitions are only hints at the central meanings of the words. Other meanings are brought out in the exercises.

---

benevolence, exemplary, reputable, gentility,
decorum, punctilious, candid, veracity, feasible,
solace, elation, avidity, preoccupy, morale,
wary, impunity

---

benevolence

(bə·nev′ə·ləns) Goodwill or the disposition to do good; or an act of kindness or charity. As an act of *benevolence*, members of the club would visit hospitalized patients every week.

[Latin *bene*, well, and *volens*, wishing.] The opposite of *benevolence* is *malevolence*, which contains the same root but a different prefix: *male*, badly, ill.

The attack on the embassy caused a benevolence of diplomatic relations. 3_____ The doctor removed the benevolent tumor that was endangering the patient's life. 6_____ Some philosophers have wondered whether the benevolence of humankind has actually done more harm than good. 9_____ When we shook hands, his face glowed benevolently. 4_____ We were asked to contribute to the Orphans' Benevolent Fund. 8_____ Her acts of benevolence won her many friends. 1_____ We attended a benevolent function given by the Y.M.C.A. 7_____ We considered her happy smile a true reward for our benevolence. 2_____ **Benevolence: 1** kindness or goodwill **2** rupture **3** healthfulness **4** danger or evil 5_____

YOUR SENTENCE: _____

_____

[1:r 2:r 3:w 4:r 5:1 6:w 7:w 8:r 9:r]

---

exemplary

(eg·zem′plə·ri) Serving as a model, deserving imitation, or commendable; or serving as an example or illustration. The preacher referred to the *exemplary* lives of the saints.

Although *exemplary* most often has a positive connotation, it can occasionally mean serving as a warning to others, as in "The *exemplary* punishment kept the rioters from committing acts of violence." The noun form of *exemplary* is *exemplar*, someone or something that serves as a model.

Pilar's exemplary loyalty and conscientiousness made her an effective physician. 9_____ The fine for speeding was imposed with exemplary severity. 3_____ One who lives an exemplary life should have many friends and few enemies. 8_____ The speaker quoted a few exemplary poems to illustrate the point she was trying to make. 6_____ The exemplary changed color when water was added to the flask. 5_____ His topic was so exemplary that only a few people in the audience understood him. 7_____ Harriet Tubman is an exemplar of a courageous woman. 2_____ Brenda was an exemplar of community parks. 4_____ **Exemplary: 1** commendable **2** difficult to understand **3** chemical **4** supporting 1_____

YOUR SENTENCE: _____

_____

[1:1 2:r 3:r 4:w 5:w 6:r 7:w 8:r 9:r]

reputable

(rep'ū·tə·bəl) Respectable or held in esteem. Libraries are a *reputable* source of information.

> One who is *reputable* is in good *repute;* that is, she or he has a good *reputation.*

Our houseguest refused to open the door to the disreputable-looking tramp. 2_____ Although it didn't move, the squirrel kept a reputable eye on all that was going on. 1_____ No one ever doubted the reputability of the attorney. 3_____ The *New York Times* is considered a reputable newspaper. 8_____ News of the hurricane was reputable throughout the area. 6_____ Unless you behave reputably, you will be asked to leave the meeting. 7_____ Only reputable lawyers should be considered for the Supreme Court. 9_____ Clara, a budding zoologist, kept tanks for such reputables as snakes and lizards. 5_____ **Reputable:** 1 observing 2 cold-blooded animal 3 respectable 4 notorious 4_____

YOUR SENTENCE: _____

_____

[1:w 2:r 3:r 4:3 5:w 6:w 7:r 8:r 9:r]

gentility

(jen·til'ə·ti) Refinement, politeness, or respectability; or members of the upper class. The faculty members were impressed by the *gentility* of the college's new president.

> Although *gentility* usually has a positive connotation, it is occasionally used sarcastically or ironically to refer to overrefinement or excessive regard for conventional morality. The adjective form of *gentility* is *genteel.*

Television programs dramatizing the lives of the British gentility have been popular in America. 3_____ I'll drive the gentility to the garage for a tune-up. 2_____ Many old-fashioned symbols of gentility—in dress and in manners—have disappeared from modern life. 8_____ Do you take vitamin C or gentility to guard against colds and flu? 6_____ The light in the gentility glowed softly in the late-afternoon sun. 1_____ Our genteel upbringing did not prepare us for the realities of life. 5_____ True gentility is more than good manners: it is thoughtfulness and generosity as well. 7_____ She came late to the gentility and missed the beginning of the speech. 4_____ **Gentility:** 1 medicine 2 parlor 3 refinement 4 old car 9_____

YOUR SENTENCE: _____

_____

[1:w 2:w 3:r 4:w 5:r 6:w 7:r 8:r 9:3]

decorum

(di·kô′rəm) Propriety and good taste in action, speech, or dress. Maria had a fine sense of *decorum*, bearing herself with grace and ease.

[Latin *decor*, ornament, thing of beauty.] The same root appears in *decorate*.

In early days the rules of decorum were stricter than they are now. 5_____ Decorum dictates that I send a thank-you note for the gift. 8_____ She returned the calculator she had bought because it was indecorous. 4_____ The students smiled decorously when they were introduced to the president of the university. 6_____ She signed her name to the legal decorum. 1_____ The radio station apologized for the indecorous remarks the announcer had made. 3_____ Rude behavior is not merely indecorous; it can be hurtful to other people. 9_____ The macrame planter is decorous and charming. 2_____ **Decorum:** 1 broken 2 official paper 3 good taste 4 attractive 7_____

YOUR SENTENCE: _____

_____

[1:w 2:w 3:r 4:w 5:r 6:r 7:3 8:r 9:r]

punctilious

(pungk·til′i·əs) Careful, meticulous, or very exact. The officer insisted upon *punctilious* execution of his commands.

[Latin *punctillum*, little point, from *pungere*, to prick.] The same root appears in *punctuate*, *punctual*, *punch*, and *point*. One who is *punctilious* carefully obeys *punctilios*, details or procedures of conduct, manners, or ceremony. Do not confuse *punctilious* with *punctual*, prompt, on time.

Working punctiliously, the medieval monks produced many beautiful manuscripts. 6_____ Only a punctilious person could leave the room in such disorder! 4_____ Because of his punctiliousness, no one ever questioned the accuracy of his work. 5_____ Ida's punctilious attention to detail led to her success as an accountant. 2_____ The judge demanded punctilious observance of all the rules of legal behavior. 7_____ They enjoyed a lazy afternoon on the river drifting in a punctilious. 8_____ The jokes the entertainer told lacked any punctiliousness. 1_____ Many punctilious calculations were necessary to ensure the project's success. 9_____ **Punctilious:** 1 careless 2 easygoing 3 pleasure boat 4 careful 3_____

YOUR SENTENCE: _____

_____

[1:w 2:r 3:4 4:w 5:r 6:r 7:r 8:w 9:r]

4

candid

(kan'did) Honest, frank, outspoken, or sincere; or impartial or fair in statement. In their report the board members tried to be as *candid* as possible.

> [Latin *candidus*, brilliantly white, from *candere*, to glow white.] The same root appears in *candidate*, since candidates for office in ancient Rome always wore white togas. *Candid* implies an honesty and a sense of fairness that make deceit impossible even when lack of deceit might be embarrassing to the listener. The noun form is *candidness* or *candor*.

In Adina's candid view, the speaker was an impostor. 8_____   She spoke candidly about her reasons for entering politics. 1_____   Since they are inclined to be candid, I do not believe them. 4_____ From the brink of the canyon, the tourist could enjoy a candid view. 7_____   Butter turns candid if it is exposed to warm air. 6_____   Since you asked for a candid opinion, you should accept the judgment of your critics. 3_____   Despite the consequences he always spoke with candor. 2_____   A look at his candid eyes assured us that he was being truthful. 9_____   **Candid:** **1** stale-smelling **2** photographic **3** frank **4** deceitful 5_____

YOUR SENTENCE: _____

_____

[1:r 2:r 3:r 4:w 5:3 6:w 7:w 8:r 9:r]

---

veracity

(və·ras'ə·ti) Habitual honesty or truthfulness; or accuracy or precision. The editor's passion for *veracity* made her check each detail in the manuscript.

> [Latin *versus*, true.] The same root appears in *verify* and *verdict*. Although *veracity* most often refers to the characteristic of habitual truthfulness, it can occasionally refer to a statement that is true or accurate.

Since we had doubts about the veracity of the witness, we did not know what to believe. 8_____   The audience had the veracity to leave before the performance had ended. 4_____   The critic's veracity was mistaken for rudeness; the authors did not want to hear of their faults. 6_____   Some animals become veracious when they are teased. 1_____   She has too much veracity to be bored. 3_____ He is such a convincing speaker that even his lies sound like veracities. 2_____   A less veracious lecturer would have exaggerated the anecdote for the sake of effect. 7_____   No one ever dared to question the writer's veracity. 9_____   **Veracity:** **1** bold daring **2** resourcefulness **3** fierceness **4** truthfulness 5_____

YOUR SENTENCE: _____

_____

[1:w 2:r 3:w 4:w 5:4 6:r 7:r 8:r 9:r]

feasible

(fē′zə·bəl) Practicable, possible, or capable of being done. Of all those present, it was the treasurer who proposed the most *feasible* plan for raising money.

[French *faisant*, making, doing, from *faire*, to make, or Latin *facere*, to make.]

Although it was a little rocky, the land could feasibly be used for cultivation. 3 _____ Would it be feasible for you to sell fifty tickets? 7 _____ Their suggestions were clever but hardly feasible. 8 _____ Because of a feasibility, the athlete could not lift the heavy bundle. 6 _____ The large fresco was perfect except for a crack in its feasible. 5 _____ It is completely unfeasible to pack one hundred people into this small room. 2 _____ We questioned the feasibility of starting the trip before dawn. 1 _____ You are quite unfeasible; you will never listen to the other side of an argument. 4 _____ **Feasible:** 1 in poor health 2 possible 3 carving 4 impossible 9 _____

YOUR SENTENCE: _____

_____

[1:r 2:r 3:r 4:w 5:w 6:w 7:r 8:r 9:2]

solace

(sol′is) To give comfort to, console, or lessen grief. After his dog's death, friends tried to *solace* Peter.

[Latin *solatus*, comforted.] The same root appears in *console*.

Students volunteered to solace for the Heart Fund. 2 _____ A lollipop was some solace to the child for a visit to the dentist. 1 _____ In times of trouble you may find a book of meditations a great solace. 8 _____ The governor hoped that her sympathetic words would have a solacing effect upon the grieving family. 5 _____ If you solace the stew with just a touch of garlic, you will be quite pleased with the results. 3 _____ A parent's smile can provide solace to an unhappy child. 4 _____ The recipe calls for one cup of solaced apples. 7 _____ The doctor's solacing comments helped the patient to accept his injuries. 9 _____ **Solace:** 1 comfort in grief 2 add to 3 collect funds 4 cut or chop 6 _____

YOUR SENTENCE: _____

_____

[1:r 2:w 3:w 4:r 5:r 6:1 7:w 8:r 9:r]

6

elation

(i·lā'shən) Happiness or joy. Victory over the opposing high school team was cause for *elation*.

[Latin *e–*, out of, and *latus*, carried; hence, carried out of oneself because of joy.]

Those tires need to be elated; they look very soft. 5_____ Finding a guitar at half price at the sale elated Jean. 4_____ It will be necessary to open the question to public elation before a decision can be made. 3_____ The mayor was elated by the city's favorable response to her plan for a larger education budget. 8_____ The announcement that she had won the college's prize for poetry filled Carol with elation. 9_____ Elated by his victories in the field, Napoleon ordered double rations to be issued to the soldiers. 6_____ A feeling of elation came over the young playwright as she read the critic's favorable review of her play. 1_____ The doctor may elate you if you do not take the medicine. 7_____ **Elation:** 1 debate 2 reprimand 3 joy 4 expansion 2_____

YOUR SENTENCE: _____

_____

[1:r 2:3 3:w 4:r 5:w 6:r 7:w 8:r 9:r]

avidity

(ə·vid'ə·ti) Eagerness, great enthusiasm, yearning, or greed. Many people desire power, but only a few long for it with *avidity*.

[Latin *avidus*, desirous, greedy.]

He had a strong avidity to all insects; they made his flesh crawl. 4_____ Whenever she was upset, she escaped to the avidity of her garden. 2_____ You could have passed the examination if you had shown greater avidity for study. 6_____ She picked up the injured bird and returned it to the avidity. 7_____ Lillian Nordica's avid devotion to music eventually led her to the concert stage. 1_____ He gulped down the food with the avidity of a starving man. 9_____ The explorer studied the maps avidly for a clue to the buried treasure. 8_____ Elaine sprang into action with great avidity; she would show them how to win a race. 5_____ **Avidity:** 1 eagerness or enthusiasm 2 distaste or horror 3 birdhouse 4 pleasantness 3_____

YOUR SENTENCE: _____

_____

[1:r 2:w 3:1 4:w 5:r 6:r 7:w 8:r 9:r]

preoccupy

(prē·ok′ū·pī) To absorb or engross mentally. Since they were *preoccupied* by their work, they did not hear us arrive.

Elizabeth Seaman—who wrote under the name Nellie Bly—was a journalist by preoccupation. 2 _____ The youngsters' preoccupation with television led them to neglect their chores. 8 _____ Preoccupied by the soccer game, we didn't notice that it had started to rain. 6 _____ The surgeon used her sharpest preoccupation to cut the heart tissue. 3 _____ A new family will preoccupy our home after we leave it. 1 _____ Helen was preoccupied with thoughts of her upcoming trip to Spain. 7 _____ Noting Bill's preoccupation with his tropical fish, George did not disturb him. 5 _____ Visitors will preoccupy Felipe and keep his mind off his illness. 9 _____ **Preoccupy: 1** sharp instrument **2** engross **3** choose **4** locate 4 _____

YOUR SENTENCE: _____

_____

[1:w 2:w 3:w 4:2 5:r 6:r 7:r 8:r 9:r]

morale

(mə·ral′) Mental condition or frame of mind. After the major victory the *morale* of the troops was excellent.

> Do not confuse *morale* with the adjective *moral* (môr′əl), which means conforming to generally accepted standards of goodness or rightness in conduct. *Morale* refers to a mental condition of courage, confidence, enthusiasm, ability to endure hardships, etc.

The leader felt that if the group could keep up its morale, the hikers would scale the peak before nightfall. 1 _____ One player's morale was so low that the tennis match was practically lost before it had begun. 4 _____ The sad news left us feeling depressed and morale. 9 _____ Because they neither drank nor smoked, everyone considered them to be morale. 2 _____ Morale on the raft was low until a puff of smoke from a ship appeared on the horizon. 8 _____ The class play was a failure, but Sarah applauded loudly to keep up her classmates' morale. 3 _____ Although his paintings were rejected by the museum, his morale remained high. 6 _____ The boss issued a morale that canceled all vacations. 7 _____ **Morale: 1** pronouncement **2** pure in mind **3** mental condition **4** unhappy 5 _____

YOUR SENTENCE: _____

_____

[1:r 2:w 3:r 4:r 5:3 6:r 7:w 8:r 9:w]

8

wary

(wār′i) Cautious, reluctant to proceed rashly, or on guard against danger. I shall keep a *wary* eye on all that happens.

> *Wary* derives from an Old English word for *attention*. *Aware* comes from the same root, as does *beware*, which was originally *be wary*. The expression *wary of* means suspicious of, cautious of.

We were told to be wary of what we said at the meeting. 2_____   Unwary of the danger, they wandered too far into the forest. 8_____   Because he was so wary, we feared that he would start an argument after the game. 1_____   They are too wary to take any precautions. 6_____   Do not be wary if you cannot come to the movies tonight. 3_____   The members of the truce mission viewed the other members of the meeting warily. 4_____   Just before they reached camp, he could hardly lift his wary feet. 9_____   Although descended from wolves, domestic dogs have lost some of the wariness of their wild ancestors. 7_____   **Wary:** 1 courageous 2 inclined to fight 3 tired 4 cautious 5_____

YOUR SENTENCE: _____

_____

[1:w   2:r   3:w   4:r   5:4   6:w   7:r   8:r   9:w]

impunity

(im·pū′nə·ti) Exemption or freedom from punishment, harm, or loss. Growing children seem able to eat green apples with *impunity*.

> [Latin *im–*, not, and *punitus*, punished, from *poena*, penalty, punishment.] The same root appears in *subpoena, pain, penalty, repent,* and *punish*. *Impunity* is almost always preceded by *with*.

Can you come late to class every day with impunity? 8_____   I do not think you can make that unkind statement with impunity. 5_____   When Caroline was offered a job as sales manager, she accepted with impunity. 7_____   Many people cannot watch late-night television with impunity; they become extremely tired the following day. 1_____   The operation was performed with impunity; there were no complications. 6_____   She read the book with impunity, finding it interesting and enjoyable. 2_____   A lawyer assured us that we could enter the agreement with impunity; we would face no risk. 9_____   The work has been done with impunity, and there are several errors in it. 4_____   **Impunity:** 1 eagerness 2 freedom from punishment 3 pleasure 4 carelessness 3_____

YOUR SENTENCE: _____

_____

[1:r   2:w   3:2   4:w   5:r   6:r   7:w   8:r   9:r]

9

1 REVIEW EXERCISE

In each blank write a form of one of the words listed below. Use each word only once.

avidity	elation	impunity	reputable
benevolence	exemplary	morale	solace
candid	feasible	preoccupy	veracity
decorum	gentility	punctilious	wary

Her refined way of speaking and her good manners suggested her 16_____.

Carlos was so 2_____ when he heard the good news that he telephoned his parents across the country.

Pauline was too 13_____ with her work to hear what we were saying.

When asked to give her 15_____ opinion, she had to admit that she thought the boy guilty of the crime.

After his business failed, he had to rely on the 10_____ of his family for support.

He threateningly declared that no one could bully his little brother with 6_____.

In times of trouble he 5_____ himself by playing the piano.

Sociable persons are inclined to observe the rules of 1_____.

A person with a 3_____ background need not fear false accusations.

Since he was not always truthful, we could not depend on the 11_____ of his statements.

She will be an executive soon if she continues to show such 7_____ for hard work.

Larry's 14_____ conduct served as a guide for the young children.

Jan's assistant admired her 12_____ working habits.

Although he admitted that the trip was 4_____, he still refused to go.

They kept a 8_____ eye for large crowds of people and avoided groups of excited talkers.

The 9_____ of the troops improved at the sight of the reinforcements.

1: *decorum*   2: *elated*   3: *reputable*   4: *feasible*   5: *solaces* 6: *impunity*   7: *avidity*   8: *wary*
9: *morale*   10: *benevolence*   11: *veracity*   12: *punctilious*   13: *preoccupied*   14: *exemplary*   15: *candid*
16: *gentility*

altruism

animated

ardor

authenticity

benignity

bountiful

buoyant

chary

circumspect

courtly

creditable

debonair

discreet

ecstatic

engross

enrapture

esprit de corps

estimable

exhilarate

exultant

fastidious

forthright

gallant

humane

humanitarian

immunity

ingenuous

integrity

jaunty

jubilant

meticulous

munificent

paradigm

paragon

practicable

probity

propriety

rapturous

scrupulous

seemly

transported

verisimilitude

vigilant

zeal

2 Unhappiness, Distress

The first three words in this section indicate different states of unhappiness: someone is *despondent* who feels utterly discouraged; one who feels gloomy or sullen is *morose;* and a *downcast* person feels depressed. If our views are *austere* (severe, dedicated to stark simplicity), we may be relatively indifferent to *privations* (hardships, losses) and even to *tribulation* (suffering, trouble, or misery). But most of us would have *misgivings* (doubts, suspicions) about any indifference to suffering. If such an attitude became widespread, we would *rue* (regret) it and *recoil* (shrink back) from it. We doubt that it is wise to be *languid* (weak, lacking vigor or spirit) in facing even the minor *mischances* (misfortunes) in our lives.

Most of us have never seen an actual *melee* in its extreme sense of a confused, general, hand-to-hand fight; we know only its milder forms: a confused struggle or a pushing together. In such situations we are likely to be *disconcerted* (upset or confused). If we were blamed for the disturbance, we might be *abashed* (embarrassed, feeling inadequacy and shame). We might think the accuser was *deranged* (insane), but we would still feel *harassed* (troubled, tormented) by the accusation.

---

despondent, morose, downcast, austere, privation, tribulation, misgiving, rue, recoil, languid, mischance, melee, disconcert, abash, derange, harass

---

despondent

(di·spon′dənt) Despairing, utterly discouraged, or extremely dejected. When his debtors began to clamor, he became more and more *despondent*.

I watched the bereaved people despondently wringing their hands. 1_____ Do not despond; the situation will soon improve. 3_____ She tried to get rid of the despondent thoughts that filled her mind. 4_____ The executive secretary was expected to handle all company despondence. 2_____ The men sat in despondent silence, unable to think of any way to help. 5_____ Her despondence at winning the English prize caused her to sing and whistle. 6_____ I asked you a question, and I expect you to despond promptly. 8_____ A feeling of despondence overcame us all when we heard the bad news. 9_____ **Despondent:** 1 elated 2 replying 3 communication 4 despairing 7_____

YOUR SENTENCE: _____

_____

[1:r 2:w 3:r 4:r 5:r 6:w 7:4 8:w 9:r]

---

morose

(mə·rōs′) Gloomy, glum, sullen, surly, or in bitter ill humor. Despite the good fortune that surrounded her, she always appeared *morose*.

The moroseness that often results from a serious illness never seemed to touch Candice. 1_____ Her morose expression can only mean she has won the scholarship she has been longing for. 9_____ The Christmas festivities were spoiled by Uncle William and his morose disposition. 3_____ Sandra is a morose writer: it takes her some time to get to the point. 7_____ A morose personality will endear you to no one. 2_____ After his wife's death he became silent and morose. 4_____ He sat there morosely, saying hardly a word. 8_____ The pilgrims prayed at the morose before starting on their journey. 6_____ **Morose:** 1 wordy 2 gloomy 3 cheerful 4 difficult 5_____

YOUR SENTENCE: _____

_____

[1:r 2:r 3:r 4:r 5:2 6:w 7:w 8:r 9:w]

14

downcast

(doun′kast′) Depressed, dispirited, dejected, or very discouraged. *Downcast* because he could not attend the baseball game, Steve moped in his room all day.

> *Downcast* may also be used to describe looks that are cast downward out of embarrassment, bashfulness, guilt, etc.

Because the actress had been ill, she was downcast to a minor role in the next play. 6_____ We became aware of his bashfulness when we looked at his downcast eyes. 4_____ Don't be downcast; happier days must be ahead. 8_____ A downcast expression is one that is lacking in confidence or cheer. 5_____ After a downcast of rain, the air seemed pure and sweet. 7_____ Although her books were downcast, they were in neat rows on the shelves. 9_____ Downcast at the news, she felt she would never smile again. 3_____ His daughter's downcastness brought a tear to John's eye. 2_____ **Downcast:** 1 dejected 2 not new 3 cheerful 4 lower 1_____

YOUR SENTENCE: _____

_____

[1:1 2:r 3:r 4:r 5:r 6:w 7:w 8:r 9:w]

---

austere

(ôs · tēr′) Severe, stern, or harsh; morally strict; or simple or lacking ornament. The Puritans are remembered for their *austere* ways.

> *Austere* is usually applied to the habits and modes of life adopted by people and to the environments people create. It often has the connotation not only of severity or stark simplicity but also of restraint, self-denial, or economy.

Because of her austere way of life, the young woman's inheritance lasted only a short while. 8_____ In order to preserve his dwindling food supply, he ate austerely. 7_____ They practiced the austerities one expects to find only among the most dedicated people. 6_____ Emily Dickinson left a wealth of poetry to austerity. 3_____ Her dark leather briefcase and simple outfit gave her an austere appearance. 9_____ To improve the economy, the government adopted an austerity program. 1_____ The speaker was overwhelmed by an austerity of questions from the audience. 5_____ We expected them to be gentle, not austere. 4_____ **Austere:** 1 future generations 2 enthusiastic 3 luxurious 4 severe or simple 2_____

YOUR SENTENCE: _____

_____

[1:r 2:4 3:w 4:r 5:w 6:r 7:r 8:w 9:r]

privation

(prī·vā′shən) Hardship or want, or the loss or absence of a quality. Those who do not have regular work often endure many *privations*.

> [Latin *privatus*, deprived of.] Although *privation* can refer to the lack of any quality (e.g., Cold is a *privation* of heat), its most common meaning is the lack of usual necessities or comforts. In this sense it is usually used in the plural form.

Many privations were heaped upon the fortunate children by their parents. 3_____   Despite the privations they had to suffer, they remained cheerful. 8_____   During the winter, many animals may suffer severe privations. 4_____   Such general privations as darkness and silence can be both good and bad. 2_____   In spite of our numerous privations, we were given no help. 9_____   Unable to undergo the privations of wilderness life, the family returned to Boston. 6_____   Since he had an essay to write, the student hoped to find privation in the library. 1_____   The delegate was not included as a privation in the council meetings. 5_____   **Privation: 1** secrecy **2** confidante **3** hardship or lack **4** privilege or benefit 7_____

YOUR SENTENCE: _____

_____

[1:w   2:r   3:w   4:r   5:w   6:r   7:3   8:r   9:r]

tribulation

(trib′ū·lā′shən) Distress, suffering, trouble, or misery. To some people, life itself seems a burden and a *tribulation*.

> *Tribulation* often occurs in the phrase "trial and *tribulation*," as in Winston Churchill's speech during World War II: "Out of this time of trial and *tribulation* will be born a new freedom and glory for all mankind."

The mighty Mississippi River is fed by numerous small tribulations. 8_____   The reward will be a tribulation for the many hours you have given to this work. 1_____   All those in tribulation were offered comfort by the minister. 3_____   In times of tribulation we often long for a companion. 9_____   A sad and tired face may speak of a life of tribulation. 5_____   The tribulation of the bells heralded the first day of the new year. 4_____   Wars often bring trial and tribulation. 6_____   My illness caused my parents much tribulation. 2_____   **Tribulation: 1** distress **2** ringing sound **3** consolation **4** body of water 7_____

YOUR SENTENCE: _____

_____

[1:w   2:r   3:r   4:w   5:r   6:r   7:1   8:w   9:r]

16

misgiving

(mis·giv′ing) A feeling of doubt, fear, or suspicion. In the middle of my speech I had a *misgiving:* would my message offend the audience?

> *Misgive* can occasionally be used as a verb meaning to cause or feel fear or suspicion, as in "His heart *misgave* him when he saw his foe."

Ronnie finally agreed to go with us, although with some misgiving. 2_____   When she entered medical school, Margarita had no misgivings about the big step she was about to take. 4_____   Have you any misgivings at all about lending money to a stranger? 7_____   Whenever I apologize, my sister is willing to be misgiving of me. 6_____   Yvette, an experienced guide, eased their misgivings about the danger of the journey. 3_____   Had it not been for her teacher's misgivings, Lydia would never have found the courage to continue. 5_____   Her parents agreed misgivingly to allow Carmen to use the family car. 1_____   The clerk misgave me change for a dollar: I had given him only fifty cents. 9_____   **Misgiving:** 1 confidence or support 2 excuse 3 feeling of doubt 4 mistake 8_____

YOUR SENTENCE: _____

_____

[1:r 2:r 3:r 4:r 5:w 6:w 7:r 8:3 9:w]

rue

(rü) To feel remorse, repentance, or regret. He lived to *rue* the day he had acted so foolishly.

> The adjective form *rueful* can mean either (1) expressing sorrow or pity (his *rueful* expression) or (2) deserving pity (their *rueful* surroundings). A far less common meaning of *rue* is a perennial herb with yellow flowers and a bitter taste.

Thank you, but I cannot rue the gift. 8_____   The teacher rued the child for having knocked over a glass of milk. 5_____   The travelers were moved by the rueful poverty of the region. 9_____ Take him away before I rue the day I saw him. 6_____   Avoid green plums, or you will rue the results. 4_____   Her rueful expression told us to expect the worst. 3_____   When the governor saw the results of the flood, she shook her head ruefully. 2_____   The rueful twinkle in his eye indicated his joy at the appointment. 7_____   **Rue:** 1 rejoice 2 regret 3 act rashly 4 reprimand 1_____

YOUR SENTENCE: _____

_____

[1:2 2:r 3:r 4:r 5:w 6:r 7:w 8:w 9:r]

17

recoil

(ri·koil') To fall or draw back, or to shrink back suddenly. I so dread examinations that I *recoil* at the thought of one!

> *Recoil* usually implies drawing back through fear, shock, or disgust. In technical contexts, *recoil* refers to a gun's springing back after it has been fired.

The small band of exhausted soldiers recoiled under the fierce attack of the enemy. 4_____ Although she had tried to stay neutral, she became recoiled in the argument. 1_____ Recoiling at the thought of war, they registered as conscientious objectors. 7_____ The trainer spoke recoilingly to the monkey to try to get it out of the tree. 8_____ Use a thinner recoil to lubricate that bearing. 2_____ Some people recoil at the sight of snakes. 9_____ From the recoil of the fortress, the lookout sighted the approaching armies. 6_____ Bystanders recoiled in horror as they witnessed the accident. 3_____ **Recoil:** **1** tower **2** involve **3** shrink from **4** plead with 5_____

YOUR SENTENCE: _____

_____

[1:w 2:w 3:r 4:r 5:3 6:w 7:r 8:w 9:r]

languid

(lang'gwid) Weak, sluggish, dull, or lacking vigor or spirit. A day of vigorous campaigning left her feeling *languid*.

> [Latin *languere*, to feel faint or overrelaxed.] The same root appears in *lax*, *relax*, and *slack*. It also appears in two other words closely related to *languid*: *languor*, fatigue or sluggishness, and *languish*, to become dull, to lose strength.

The look of languish on the victim's face told us that he was in pain. 6_____ His recent illness caused him to move about languidly. 7_____ Because of the intense heat of the Tropics, we felt too languid for sightseeing. 1_____ She bounded into the room with vigorous and languid steps. 3_____ The stock market was extremely languid today; it is usually far more active. 2_____ The plants languished in the drought. 8_____ The pale looks and languishing manner of the twins worried their parents. 5_____ Feeling languorous, she was unable to attend the scheduled meeting. 4_____ **Languid:** **1** vigorous **2** bestowing **3** deeply sorrowing **4** spiritless 9_____

YOUR SENTENCE: _____

_____

[1:r 2:r 3:w 4:r 5:r 6:w 7:r 8:r 9:4]

18

mischance

(mis·chans′) Misfortune, bad luck, or an unfortunate accident. Most of his financial problems arose from *mischance* rather than from his incompetence.

By mischance the rain stopped just as the parade began. 8_____   Mischance had followed him all his life. 7_____   By mischance the traffic was heavy, and he missed the last train home. 4_____   It was not mischance; it was lack of foresight. 9_____   By happy mischance both girls wanted to see the same movie. 2_____   After his accident we tried to console him by explaining that such a mischance had happened to many other people. 6_____   The mirror was cracked by mischance. 5_____   A pleasing mischance of household items will be offered for sale at the fair. 1_____   **Mischance:** 1 misfortune 2 coincidence 3 mixture 4 good luck 3_____

YOUR SENTENCE: _____

_____

[1:w   2:w   3:1   4:r   5:r   6:r   7:r   8:w   9:r]

melee

(mā′lā or mā·lā′) A confused fight or struggle; or a confused mingling together. Inmates and guards were injured in a *melee* at the prison.

[French *mêlée*, fight, scuffle.] A variant spelling of *melee* is *mêlée*.

Marked fatigue and melee are often symptoms of an oncoming illness. 3_____   His fiery speech turned the peaceful meeting into a wild melee. 7_____   The broker forced a passage for herself through the melee on the floor of the stock exchange. 6_____   How could you make sense out of that melee of misinformation? 1_____   When they arrived at the Tower of London, they had to make their way through a melee of peddlers and tourists. 9_____   He was lucky to escape alive from the melee. 2_____   Each melee represented a well-organized, disciplined group. 4_____   The leader took a secure stance and served as a melee to the climbers following her. 8_____   **Melee:** 1 discomfort 2 harmony 3 confusion 4 anchor 5_____

YOUR SENTENCE: _____

_____

[1:r   2:r   3:w   4:w   5:3   6:r   7:r   8:w   9:r]

19

disconcert

[dis′kən·sert′) To confuse, disturb, frustrate, upset, or embarrass. They *disconcerted* the enemy by a sudden attack.

> One usually *disconcerts* people rather than things. Someone who is *disconcerted* has lost his or her self-possession and thus is in a state of confusion or mental disorganization. A colloquial synonym of *disconcert* is *rattle*.

The bad news we heard disconcerted all of us. 8 _____   An unfortunate accident disconcerted him and made him alter his plans. 6 _____   The scientist refused to publish her results until they had been thoroughly disconcerted as accurate by another researcher. 1 _____   The chess player's unexpected move disconcerted his opponent. 2 _____   A disconcerting stare can cause other people to feel uneasy. 7 _____   We watched the members of the band disconcerting just before the music festival began. 3 _____   For failing to keep in training, I was disconcerted from the track team. 9 _____ Such disconcerting changes of policy will prevent our finishing on time. 5 _____   **Disconcert:** 1 reject or dismiss 2 tune up 3 confirm 4 disturb or upset 4 _____

YOUR SENTENCE: _____

_____

[1:w   2:r   3:w   4:4   5:r   6:r   7:r   8:r   9:w]

abash

(ə·bash′) To embarrass, make ashamed, or make uneasy; or to disconcert or discomfort. He was a man whom nothing could *abash*.

> *Abash* is very similar in meaning to *disconcert*, but *abash* usually implies causing a lack of self-confidence or a feeling of inadequacy or shame, whereas *disconcert* implies causing confusion or disorganization.

Do not try to abash me by pointing out my mistake. 8 _____   Eve was abashed by her cousin's lack of generosity. 5 _____   The fender of the car was abashed in the accident. 3 _____   Abashed by her parents' criticism, she felt it was necessary to defend her actions. 6 _____   As the storm abashed, the dog trembled and hid under the sofa. 1 _____   Her schedule was abashed by a sudden thunderstorm. 9 _____   His abashment was evident when he blushed. 7 _____   Unabashed by the trouble he had caused, he sat there smiling. 2 _____   **Abash:** 1 demolish 2 make uneasy 3 improve 4 reassure 4 _____

YOUR SENTENCE: _____

_____

[1:w   2:r   3:w   4:2   5:r   6:r   7:r   8:r   9:w]

derange

(di·rānj′) To disarrange, upset, or throw into confusion or disorder. The arrival of visitors *deranged* our plans.

Although *derange* most often refers to throwing someone into confusion, it can occasionally refer to disarranging physical objects, as in "He ran into the room with his tie *deranged*." If one speaks of a *deranged* person, one means that he or she is mentally ill.

War deranged the lives of the French farmers. 2_____ Any slight damage to that delicate apparatus might derange its functioning. 5_____ The candidates held a debate in order to derange their prospects. 9_____ Lady Macbeth's mind was deranged by ambition. 8_____ The deranger on the gun determines the elevation necessary to hit the target. 3_____ The suspect was deranged into court to answer the charges that had been made. 7_____ The unexpected snowstorm deranged our travel plans. 6_____ In his derangement he claimed that he was Napoleon. 4_____ **Derange:** 1 adjust 2 bring into court 3 free from blame 4 disarrange 1_____

YOUR SENTENCE: _____

_____

[1:4 2:r 3:w 4:r 5:r 6:r 7:w 8:r 9:w]

harass

(har′əs or hə·ras′) To trouble, worry, annoy, or torment; or to attack an enemy repeatedly. Do you feel *harassed* when you have too much work to do?

After learning to spell *embarrass* with two *r*'s and two *s*'s, you may have trouble with *harass*, which has one *r* and two *s*'s. When you try to remember the spelling, think of the second pronunciation of *harass*, with the accent on the second syllable. This may remind you that it does not follow the spelling of *embarrass*.

An employee who is under a great deal of pressure may feel harassed. 5_____ The enemy harassed the civilians in a sudden attack. 3_____ Reading a comic strip can be a harassing experience. 1_____ Landlords may harass tenants who neglect to pay their rent. 7_____ The woman who won the track event was greeted with cries of harassment. 2_____ David telephoned the newspaper and threatened to harass the editor. 4_____ You may feel harassed by constant complaints from a supervisor. 9_____ The senator felt harassed after she read the telegrams of support from the voters. 6_____ **Harass:** 1 identify 2 horrify 3 trouble or torment 4 respond 8_____

YOUR SENTENCE: _____

_____

[1:w 2:w 3:r 4:r 5:r 6:w 7:r 8:3 9:r]

21

2 REVIEW EXERCISE

In each blank write a form of one of the words listed below. Use each word only once.

abash	disconcert	melee	privation
austere	downcast	mischance	recoil
derange	harass	misgiving	rue
despondent	languid	morose	tribulation

Dick 8_____ what he had done when he saw the unfortunate consequences of his action.

Those near him begged him not to 4_____ over the bad news he had just heard.

By the time the police arrived, six people had been injured in the 12_____.

Gentle by nature, he 10_____ at the thought of having to kill the duck.

In order to save money, the young couple lived quite 6_____.

Soon after he had made his difficult decision, he had many 14_____ about how wise he had been.

By 13_____ she became lost and missed her appointment.

The high humidity today makes me feel too 3_____ to take part in any vigorous exercise.

Although her friends are usually cheerful, she is sometimes full of gloom and 1_____.

As we looked at their 5_____ eyes, we could almost feel their sadness.

We are constantly pestered and 2_____ by bill collectors.

The mountain climbers described the trials and 11_____ of their difficult journey.

The band of soldiers suffered from hunger and other 9_____.

When his mind became 7_____, he was taken to a mental hospital for treatment.

The unexpected news he heard 16_____ him and threw him into a state of total confusion.

He was so 15_____ by what he had done that he was too embarrassed to face us again.

1: *moroseness* 2: *harassed* 3: *languid* 4: *despond* 5: *downcast* 6: *austerely* 7: *deranged* 8: *rued*
9: *privations* 10: *recoiled* 11: *tribulations* 12: *melee* 13: *mischance* 14: *misgivings* 15: *abashed*
16: *disconcerted*

FOR DICTIONARY STUDY

adversity	listless
affliction	lugubrious
apprehension	malcontent
ascetic	melancholy
chagrin	mopish
confound	nettle
crestfallen	nonplus
demented	oppression
discomfit	perturb
discommode	phlegmatic
disheartened	plague
disquiet	plaintive
distraught	repine
doldrums	roil
dour	saturnine
enervated	scruple
fracas	sullen
harry	torpor
infliction	vapors
inquietude	vex
lackadaisical	visitation

3 Positive Judgments, Agreement

The words in this section refer to various ways of praising or agreeing with other people or their views. The *plaudits* (applause) of audiences are the most emphatic expression of positive judgment and agreement, but how much *credence* (belief) can we give to audiences that applaud a contrary view just as loudly? A really thoughtful person will not *covet* (desire greedily) the fame of a popular speaker. His or her experience will *attest* (bear witness) that audiences are fickle. They may seem to *assent* (agree) to contradictory views in the same meeting but remember neither of them afterward. They may applaud any view that seems to be in *concord* (agreement) with any of their beliefs, and they are not worried by the fact that some of these beliefs are not *consistent* (compatible, holding to the same principles) with others. Hence, a crowd may present an appearance of *solidarity* (unity) when it is only confused. One must not expect *fidelity* (loyalty, faithfulness) to the principles discussed in such meetings.

The remaining three words in this section are *liaison* (a close bond or connection), *palaver* (a conference, discussion, or conversation), and *accost* (to approach and speak to).

---

plaudits, credence, covet, attest, assent, concord, consistent, solidarity, fidelity, liaison, palaver, accost

---

plaudits

(plô′dits) Openly expressed approval, or a round of applause.   Long after the concert he could hear the *plaudits* of the audience still echoing in his ears.

[Latin *plaudere*, to strike hand against hand.] The same root appears in *applaud* and *explode*.

We could not help but give plaudits to such a magnificent production. 2_____   An accountant plaudits the books before issuing a financial statement. 1_____   It's enough for me to earn the king's plaudits—I don't care about the rest of the court. 3_____   Her unselfish gesture earned her the plaudits of her friends. 8_____   The wild plaudits of the audience told Judy Garland that she had captured Broadway. 4_____   He searched the sky for a glimpse of the plaudits. 5_____   The librarian was in plaudits about the noise that came from the reading room. 7_____   Do the plaudits of the crowd mean that she has won the election? 9_____   **Plaudits:** 1 expression of approval 2 inspection 3 pale stars 4 state of alarm 6_____

YOUR SENTENCE: _____

_____

[1:w   2:r   3:r   4:r   5:w   6:1   7:w   8:r   9:r]

---

credence

(krē′dəns) Belief or acceptance; or trustworthiness or reliability. We could not place much *credence* in the story he told.

[Latin *credens*, believing.] The same root appears in *creed, incredible, credit,* and *credentials.*

We give credence too easily to what we see in print. 5_____   I refused to give credence to the unkind stories about my friend. 9_____   Such an obvious lie deserves our credence. 3_____   When you reach the rapids, proceed with extreme credence or you will encounter trouble. 7_____   This photograph certainly lends credence to your story. 2_____   The chorus had no difficulty with the credence at the end of the song. 1_____   We must give credence to this warning; our safety may depend upon it. 6_____   Your aunt has left you some investments in a credence to her will. 8_____   **Credence:** 1 belief 2 addition 3 doubt 4 musical passage 4_____

YOUR SENTENCE: _____

_____

[1:w   2:r   3:w   4:1   5:r   6:r   7:w   8:w   9:r]

26

covet

(kuv′it)   To wish or crave for, or to desire greedily.   The wealth they had *coveted* was willed to various charities.

> *Covet* implies greedily desiring that which belongs to someone else. The most famous use of this word appears in the last of the Ten Commandments: "Thou shalt not *covet* thy neighbour's house, thou shalt not *covet* thy neighbour's wife. . . ."

The old dog coveted the affection given the new puppy. 4 _____   The Simons cast covetous eyes on their neighbor's flourishing farm. 1 _____   Coveting the ground at great speed, he managed to catch the train. 5 _____   As soon as I learned that I had passed the exam, I coveted the fact to everyone I knew! 7 _____   The invaders took everything that they coveted. 8 _____   He did not covet the captain's position because the job entailed too much responsibility. 6 _____   The youngsters playing in the fields built covets among the bushes. 9 _____   Although the little boy has plenty of his own toys, his covetousness of his friends' toys is obvious. 2 _____   **Covet: 1** make known **2** move swiftly **3** shelter **4** desire greedily 3 _____

YOUR SENTENCE: _____

_____

[1:r   2:r   3:4   4:r   5:w   6:r   7:w   8:r   9:w]

attest

(ə·test′)   To bear witness to or certify; or to demonstrate or declare as true.   I *attested* to the accuracy of her report.

> [Latin *testari*, to bear witness to.] The same root appears in *test, testify, testament, contest, detest,* and *protest.* When *attest* means to bear witness, it is usually followed by *to*.

The youthful demonstrators attested behind police lines. 8 _____   By voting in elections, we attest our faith in democracy. 4 _____   The popularity of this product attests to its quality. 6 _____   He was willing to attest to his friend's claim of innocence. 7 _____   The expert's attestation assured us that the painting was a genuine masterpiece. 2 _____   I can attest to her reliability, for I have known her for many years. 9 _____   The starter asked the attestants in the race to get on their marks. 5 _____   He is an attestable man and is very easily irritated. 3 _____   **Attest: 1** compete **2** loathe or despise **3** adore **4** bear witness 1 _____

YOUR SENTENCE: _____

_____

[1:4   2:r   3:w   4:r   5:w   6:r   7:r   8:w   9:r]

assent

(ə·sent′) To consent to or agree with. She graciously *assented* to our wishes.

> [Latin *ad*, toward, and *sensus*, feeling.] The same root appears in *sense, nonsense, sensible,* and *consent.* The opposite of *assent* is *dissent.*

Assenting to the top of the ladder, the painter was able to reach the ceiling. 2_____   Assenting to the proposal, we wished them luck in their endeavor. 6_____   He was made king by assent of all the Britons. 4_____   The police assented the accident to fast driving. 5_____   Sweeney was the only assenter to the plan we proposed. 1_____   He stubbornly assented that he was right and that everyone else was wrong. 7_____   When the final member of the club had assented, the annual dues were raised. 3_____   For answer, I nodded assentingly. 8_____   **Assent: 1** insist **2** agree or consent **3** give as a cause **4** rise or climb 9_____

YOUR SENTENCE: _____

_____

[1:r 2:w 3:r 4:r 5:w 6:r 7:w 8:r 9:2]

concord

(kon′kôrd) Agreement or harmony; or friendly and peaceful relations. They lived in peace and *concord* until the warring tribe invaded their tiny nation.

> [Latin *concordia*, agreement, from *con–*, with, together, and *cor*, heart.] *Concord* can also refer to a treaty between two or more nations to establish peaceful relations. In grammar, *concord* refers to agreement between words in case, number, person, and gender. In music, *concord* refers to a combination of harmonious tones. Its opposite is *discord.* Two or more ideas, results, commands, etc. that are in agreement with each other are said to be *concordant.*

Edwin's translation of the sentence was incorrect; the subject and verb were not in concord. 3_____   Since the two sets of instructions from headquarters were not concordant, the soldiers did not know exactly what to do. 1_____   Concord became discord when the soprano sang off-key. 5_____   Your action is not concordant with the general policy of this company. 9_____   She wrote a sympathetic concord to the grieving widow. 6_____   Considering the differences in their personalities, we were surprised that the two roommates lived in concord. 4_____   Let us concord the party by singing "Auld Lang Syne." 8_____   Because we are all in concord with one another, we have been arguing bitterly all afternoon. 2_____   **Concord: 1** disagreement **2** agreement **3** expression of sympathy **4** completeness 7_____

YOUR SENTENCE: _____

_____

[1:r 2:w 3:r 4:r 5:r 6:w 7:2 8:w 9:r]

consistent

(kən·sis'tənt) Compatible or in agreement; or changeless, regular, or keeping to the same principles or actions.   Harry's statements were *consistent* with each other.

> [Latin *con*–, with, and *sistens*, causing to stand.] The same root appears in *assist, resist, consist, exist,* and *persist*. The noun form *consistency* usually means agreement or uniformity (the *consistency* of his actions); but when it refers to liquids, it means degree of firmness or thickness, as in "The *consistency* of the frosting was perfect for spreading."

He risked his life by joining the consistent movement during World War II. 9_____   His actions were not consistent with his words. 7_____   Gwendolyn is consistently disagreeable in the morning. 3_____   The chef inspected the consistency of the sauce. 5_____   Since the reports given by the two witnesses were inconsistent with each other, we did not know what to believe. 8_____   He was a consistent supporter of high tariffs. 4_____   You can depend upon the consistency of her behavior; she always acts in exactly the same manner. 1_____   Since the two statements are consistent, one statement must be wrong. 6_____   **Consistent: 1** in agreement or changeless **2** precise or accurate **3** rebellious **4** contradictory 2_____

YOUR SENTENCE: _____

_____

[1:r 2:1 3:r 4:r 5:r 6:w 7:r 8:r 9:w]

---

solidarity

(sol'ə·dar'ə·ti) Cooperation and loyalty based on unity of interests and beliefs.   It is hard to achieve *solidarity* when each of you thinks only of yourself.

> [Latin *solidus*, firm, solid.] The same root appears in *solid, consolidate,* and *soldier*. The term *solidarity* was first widely used in communist propaganda urging the working class to unite.

There is more solidarity among the police than among criminals. 5_____   With complete solidarity the townspeople took their grievances to the mayor. 7_____   When he is in a mood of solidarity, nobody can cheer him. 1_____   The venture could not succeed without solidarity of purpose. 6_____   Throwing solidarity to the winds, they leaped across the gaping hole. 8_____   Unless our committee achieves solidarity, we will be unable to accomplish our plans. 2_____   Although the serfs of the Middle Ages had common problems, they had no solidarity as a group. 9_____   During his period of solidarity, the prisoner was not allowed to see anyone. 4_____   **Solidarity: 1** group unity **2** caution or carefulness **3** deep depression **4** aloneness 3_____

YOUR SENTENCE: _____

_____

[1:w 2:r 3:1 4:w 5:r 6:r 7:r 8:w 9:r]

fidelity

(fĭ·del′ə·ti or fə·del′ə·ti)   Loyalty or devotion to duty.   He was a man of unquestionable *fidelity*.

> [Latin *fidelis*, faithful.] Many dogs are called *Fido* because of the dog's loyalty and devotion. *Fidelity* can also mean accuracy of reproduction, as in "He copied the manuscript with *fidelity*." *High-fidelity* phonographs are so called because they reproduce sound with great accuracy.

The ballet student always had trouble executing a fidelity. 5 _____   I have great respect for fidelity to the truth. 3 _____   The artist was able to copy the painting with amazing fidelity. 6 _____   After taking the vitamin tablets, she felt full of fidelity. 7 _____   The courtiers swore fidelity to their queen, promising to protect her at all times. 4 _____   The warrior exhibited cowardly fidelity by deserting during the battle. 9 _____   Volunteers were selected from those who had shown complete fidelity to the cause. 8 _____   The patient would have died but for the skill and fidelity of the doctors and nurses. 2 _____   **Fidelity: 1** vigor   **2** faithfulness   **3** disloyalty   **4** dance movement   1 _____

YOUR SENTENCE: _____

_____

[1:2   2:r   3:r   4:r   5:w   6:r   7:w   8:r   9:w]

---

liaison

(lē′ā·zon′, li·ā′zon, or lē′ə·zon)   A close bond or connection.   There was excellent *liaison* between the school and the community.

> In military contexts, *liaison* refers to intercommunication between parts of an army or between allied armies to ensure cooperation and unity of action. A *liaison officer* is one whose duty it is to ensure such coordination.

The table was set afire by a liaison ray. 3 _____   He received instructions to form a liaison with the newly elected government. 4 _____   Activities must cease until liaison is established between the two groups. 5 _____   Ask Dr. Roy for a salve for that liaison. 6 _____   His argument was full of tricky liaisons that were meant to fool his audience. 8 _____   When the delegates stalked out of the conference room, all hopes of a liaison were shattered. 1 _____   The cold war hindered liaison between communist countries and the Western world. 9 _____   Betty Weinstein will serve as liaison officer between the Army and the Air Force. 2 _____   **Liaison: 1** connection or bond   **2** scientific ray   **3** injury or wound   **4** deception   7 _____

YOUR SENTENCE: _____

_____

[1:r   2:r   3:w   4:r   5:r   6:w   7:1   8:w   9:r]

palaver

(pə·lav′ər)   A conference, discussion, or conversation.   The union leaders held a *palaver* with management representatives in an attempt to iron out their differences.

> *Palaver* often refers to mere idle chatter or to smooth, flattering talk that tries to persuade or
> deceive.

To decide the tactics for the game, the players held a palaver in the dugout. 4 _____   The senator and
the congresswoman held a palaver about the new clean-air bill. 1 _____   He was a palaverous old
hermit who never spoke to anyone. 7 _____   The two little boys held a palaver to decide how to
spend their money in the bookstore. 5 _____   As the palaver tossed in the churning waters, the
campers lost their balance. 9 _____   The two old friends enjoyed a long palaver over a game of
checkers. 3 _____   Flattering words will not help you palaver yourself out of the trouble you are in.
6 _____   Milton's *Paradise Lost* is a classic example of the palaver. 2 _____   **Palaver: 1** epic
poem **2** discussion **3** silence **4** flat boat 8 _____

YOUR SENTENCE: _____

_____

[1:r   2:w   3:r   4:r   5:r   6:r   7:w   8:2   9:w]

---

accost

(ə·kôst′)   To approach and speak to.   As soon as he left his home, he was *accosted* by an FBI agent.

> *Accost* sometimes means to speak to first or to greet. It can also mean to confront someone in a
> challenging way or to address someone boldly, as in "The police officer *accosted* us and asked what
> we were doing."

They will never accost to such a scheme. 4 _____   Accosting the police officer, she asked for
directions to the city library. 6 _____   He accosted his ex-employer and demanded to know why he
had been dismissed. 5 _____   Three of the ruffians were injured as they accosted in the street.
9 _____   The sentry stepped forward to accost the approaching figure. 8 _____   In order to accost
Dennis, Iris took a job many miles from where he worked. 3 _____   We accosted our guests at the
door and led them into the living room. 7 _____   Dozens of reporters accosted the ambassador as she
stepped off the plane. 1 _____   **Accost: 1** approach or confront **2** concur or agree **3** brawl or
fight **4** avoid or shun 2 _____

YOUR SENTENCE: _____

_____

[1:r   2:1   3:w   4:w   5:r   6:r   7:r   8:r   9:w]

3 REVIEW EXERCISE

In each blank write a form of one of the words listed below. Use each word only once.

accost	concord	credence	palaver
assent	consistent	fidelity	plaudits
attest	covet	liaison	solidarity

Because she always 12 _____ the accomplishments of others, she is never completely satisfied.

A 2 _____ between labor and management should result in a fair and reasonable contract.

The host walked up and 4 _____ the two silent guests.

The massive stone formations at Stonehenge 9 _____ to its ancient function.

Both sides must 7 _____ to the change in the contract.

The two children were separated by the teacher because they could not play together in 11 _____ .

Lorraine Hansberry's play *A Raisin in the Sun* received the enthusiastic 8 _____ of critics and audiences alike.

Give no 6 _____ to rumors.

Since the two sets of records were 10 _____ with each other, we were assured that the data were genuine.

The butler was handsomely rewarded for having served his employer with such 1 _____ .

With complete 3 _____ of interests, the group of protestors marched on City Hall.

In the early 1900's Agnes Nestor often acted as a 5 _____ between the manufacturers and the union members.

1: *fidelity*   2: *palaver*   3: *solidarity*   4: *accosted*   5: *liaison*   6: *credence*   7: *assent*   8: *plaudits*
9: *attest*   10: *consistent*   11: *concord*   12: *covets*

FOR DICTIONARY STUDY

acclaim	eulogize
acclamation	fealty
accordance	hail
affirm	homogeneous
amity	interlocution
authenticate	laud
commend	paean
compatible	panegyric
concur	parley
conform	powwow
congenial	staunch
consolidation	subscribe
consonance	substantiate
constancy	unanimity
crave	validate
depose	vouch

4 Negative Judgments, Complaints

Dissent (to disagree with or differ from) is the opposite of *assent* (to agree), which occurred in the last section. *Repudiate* is an even stronger word meaning to disown, renounce, or reject completely, as in the sentence, "Those who *dissent* from a position strongly enough may be forced eventually to *repudiate* it." A *harangue* is a long, noisy speech, often pompous and scolding. To *chasten* is to correct by punishment or to subdue or restrain from excess. *Malediction* is an old term for a curse or a calling down of evil upon someone or something; it is the opposite of *benediction*. *Imprecation* is a more common term for a curse or expression of anger or a desire for evil to overtake someone or something.

To *taunt* is to mock, ridicule, or jeer at; to *deride* often means the same thing. However, one *derides* anything that one regards as foolish but *taunts* a person with something of which that person is ashamed. A *derogatory* remark is one that is belittling, disdainful, or tending to lessen in value. To *cull* is to separate out as worthless, as in "We *culled* out all the worthless books and sold them as scrap." It can also mean to gather, choose, or collect.

---

dissent, repudiate, harangue, chasten, malediction, imprecation, taunt, deride, derogatory, cull

---

dissent

(di·sent′)   To object, disagree, or differ.   He *dissents* each time we make a new proposal.

> [Latin *dis–*, apart, and *sensus*, feeling.] The opposite of *dissent* is *assent*, which you have encountered in Section 3. *Dissent* is often followed by *from*. A *dissenter* (or *dissentient*) is one who disagrees; a *Dissenter* is an English or Scottish Protestant who refuses to accept the doctrines of the Church of England. The noun form of *dissent* is *dissent* or *dissension;* the adjective form is *dissenting* or *dissentient*.

Although Lynn hated to be the only dissenter, she felt that she had to stand by her principles. 1 _____
The proposed new highway led to dissension among the residents of the area. 6 _____   It takes a long
time to change customs that have been established by common dissent. 2 _____   The dissenting
element in the audience tried to shout the speaker down. 4 _____   Dissenting from the proposal to
return to work, the members left the union meeting. 5 _____   The removal of a familiar landmark
caused dissent in the town. 9 _____   They found some unusual plants and insects on their pleasant
dissent down the mountain. 8 _____   You have the right to dissent, but not before studying the facts.
7 _____   **Dissent:** 1 respectable 2 downward movement 3 agree 4 differ 3 _____

YOUR SENTENCE: _____

_____

[1:r   2:w   3:4   4:r   5:r   6:r   7:r   8:w   9:r]

repudiate

(ri·pū′di·āt)   To disown, renounce, or reject.   She *repudiated* the contract as being invalid.

> *Repudiate* implies disowning or condemning a person, thing, or idea as having no authority, value, truth, etc.

She appeared in public to repudiate the accusations that had been made against her. 6 _____   You
will probably repudiate soon from your illness. 8 _____   Many Victorian traditions have been
repudiated by our generation. 9 _____   Dermatologists recommend repudiation for the treatment of
skin disease. 1 _____   He repudiated our authority, claiming that we had no right to make such a
decision. 4 _____   He finally repudiated his daughter by welcoming her back to his home. 7 _____
Alice soon found that repudiation of debts is bad for one's credit rating. 3 _____   Because his son had
been involved in a scandal, Mr. Bowers repudiated him. 5 _____   **Repudiate:** 1 forgive 2 heal
3 renounce 4 revive 2 _____

YOUR SENTENCE: _____

_____

[1:w   2:3   3:r   4:r   5:r   6:r   7:w   8:w   9:r]

harangue

(hə·rang′) A long, noisy, ranting speech, often pompous and sometimes scolding. He delivered a tiresome *harangue* on the need for promptness.

Members of the club resented the ceaseless harangues that had replaced discussions of the real issues. 1_____ The coach harangued the team members about putting more spirit into their play. 3_____ The child harangued the puppy until the animal began to wag its tail. 4_____ The travelers agreed to meet at the airport near the harangue. 9_____ Please do not harangue them for not completing the project on time. 6_____ Their constant haranguing almost drove us mad. 8_____ A small harangue met to discuss plans for the town's new swimming pool. 2_____ The experienced politician knew how to handle the troublesome haranguer in the crowd. 5_____ **Harangue:** **1** beat **2** long speech **3** council **4** parking lot 7_____

YOUR SENTENCE: _____

_____

[1:r 2:w 3:r 4:w 5:r 6:r 7:2 8:r 9:w]

chasten

(chās′ən) To punish in order to correct; or to subdue or restrain from excess. Time and experience tend to *chasten* us all.

> *Chasten* is very similar in meaning to *chastise;* but *chastise,* the narrower of the two words, implies corporal punishment, both as a penalty and as a correction, whereas *chasten* implies any kind of affliction or trial in order to improve someone. *Chasten* is often used in religious contexts, as in the "Prayer of Thanksgiving": "He *chastens* and hastens His will to make known."

The boat chastened and sank in the whirling waters. 1_____ Chastening them was useless; they continued to misbehave. 4_____ Chastened by my father's sharp words, I went back to my room to reconsider my actions. 3_____ Chastened by his recent flogging, the prisoner no longer tried to escape. 2_____ The elegant carriage, chastened by two fine horses, swept through the park. 9_____ His rashness has been chastened by the memory of his recent accident. 7_____ The mental torture he went through chastened his hard heart. 5_____ Although we all enjoyed the performance, Williams thoroughly chastened it. 8_____ **Chasten:** **1** dislike **2** punish or subdue **3** draw or pull **4** overturn 6_____

YOUR SENTENCE: _____

_____

[1:w 2:r 3:r 4:r 5:r 6:2 7:r 8:w 9:w]

37

malediction

(mal′ə·dik′shən) A curse or a calling down of evil upon someone; or evil talk or slander. The witches sought to destroy their enemy by uttering *maledictions* against him.

[Latin *male*, badly, ill, and *dictus*, said.] The same prefix appears in *malicious;* the same root appears in *diction, predict, verdict,* and *indicate.* The opposite of *malediction* is *benediction,* a blessing.

Angry at his unexpected defeat, he shouted maledictions at his opponent. 2 _____ Continued use of that drug may lead to malediction. 9 _____ Issuing maledictions against others will not help you achieve your aims. 3 _____ When George uttered his maledictions, we all left the room in disgust. 6 _____ His maledictory remarks were not in good taste. 7 _____ Because of a malediction in his left leg, Simon walked with a slight limp. 5 _____ The treatment was maledictory, and the patient's condition improved. 8 _____ Janet Kline, the school's best student, delivered the maledictory address at graduation. 1 _____ **Malediction:** 1 speech 2 curse 3 error in structure 4 strong habit 4 _____

YOUR SENTENCE: _____

_____

[1:w 2:r 3:r 4:2 5:w 6:r 7:r 8:w 9:w]

imprecation

(im′prə·kā′shən) A curse or a plea or prayer for evil or misfortune. One of the men who had missed the train muttered *imprecations* under his breath.

[Latin *precari*, to pray, demand.] Although *imprecation* can occasionally mean a prayer for something good, this meaning is rather archaic, and the word usually means a curse or a prayer for evil.

The campers imprecated their clothes with an insecticide. 6 _____ Perhaps it is more useful to seek change than to issue imprecations. 3 _____ When he saw the flat tire, he uttered an imprecation. 8 _____ Liz pretended not to hear the imprecatory remark. 2 _____ He imprecated the foul weather that had prevented the picnic. 7 _____ We were happy to hear her imprecate our accomplishments in such glowing terms. 1 _____ Ignoring the imprecations of the team, the coach refused to resign. 5 _____ He tried to imprecate us in his dishonest business deal. 9 _____ **Imprecation:** 1 praise 2 curse 3 spray 4 involve 4 _____

YOUR SENTENCE: _____

_____

[1:w 2:r 3:r 4:2 5:r 6:w 7:r 8:r 9:w]

taunt

(tônt) To mock, ridicule, jeer at, or reproach scornfully. Although the opposing team *taunted* her, she calmly ignored them.

> *Taunt* implies ridiculing someone in an insulting manner and calling attention to a humiliating fact about that person.

They taunted him about his cowardice. 2 _____   After a week of hard work, they taunted to the seashore with carefree spirits. 1 _____   He answered tauntingly just to hurt her feelings. 4 _____ They taunted the boy so often that he finally ran away from home. 6 _____   The taunts of the crowd drove the speaker from the platform. 7 _____   The campers fixed their tent by pulling the ropes taunt. 5 _____   Reprimands to children should be firm but never taunting. 9 _____   After her serious illness her face looked tired and taunt. 8 _____   **Taunt: 1** travel **2** ridicule **3** tightly stretched **4** haggard 3 _____

YOUR SENTENCE: _____

_____

[1:w   2:r   3:2   4:r   5:w   6:r   7:r   8:w   9:r]

deride

(di·rīd′) To mock, ridicule, or laugh at with contempt. Nothing hurts me as much as being *derided* in front of my friends.

> [Latin *de*, down, and *ridere*, to laugh.] The same root appears in *ridiculous*. *Deride* and *taunt* are often used interchangeably; but one *derides* anything one regards as foolish, whereas one *taunts* a person with something of which that person might be ashamed.

All sick sheep must be carefully derided from the rest of the flock. 8 _____   We sensed a tone of contempt in his derisive laughter. 3 _____   After winning a derisive victory in the important race, she was cheered by the crowd. 6 _____   Those who are jealous of the success of others often speak derisively of them. 9 _____   The acting was weak; it was derided by many critics. 5 _____   My aim was to expose and deride the mistakes of my opponent. 1 _____   The fog settling in the valley almost completely derided the village. 7 _____   In the family of humankind, no one should be thought of with derision. 2 _____   **Deride: 1** conceal **2** ridicule **3** separate **4** be obvious 4 _____

YOUR SENTENCE: _____

_____

[1:r   2:r   3:r   4:2   5:r   6:w   7:w   8:w   9:r]

derogatory

(di·rog′ə·tô′ri) Belittling, disdainful, or tending to lessen in value. She tried to belittle the speaker by making *derogatory* remarks about his appearance.

> [Latin *derogatus*, annulling, disparaging, from *de*, down, and *rogare*, to question.] The same root appears in *interrogation*. To *derogate* is to lower in esteem or to detract from; a *derogation* is a decline or a lessening or weakening of power, authority, etc.

By speaking derogatorily of their efforts, Al aroused the anger of the committee. 8_____ The new bill was intended as a derogation of the powers of the president. 6_____ He was so derogatory that he could talk for hours without tiring. 9_____ Although hurt by the derogatory remarks, Luisa remained confident. 3_____ A new derogate was chosen to be sent to the United Nations. 7_____ The speech was an attempt to derogate from her influence and prestige. 5_____ We were thrilled by his derogatory remarks about our plan. 2_____ Although he expected praise for his action, he was met only with derogatory comments. 1_____ **Derogatory:** **1** long-winded **2** belittling or degrading **3** representative **4** flattering 4_____

YOUR SENTENCE: _____

_____

[1:r   2:w   3:r   4:2   5:r   6:r   7:w   8:r   9:w]

---

cull

(kul) To separate out as worthless; or to gather, choose, or collect. The farmer *culled* the diseased plants from the healthy ones.

> [Latin *colligere*, to gather together.] The past participle of this root gives us the word *collect*.

Culling the imperfect gems from the pile, the thief thrust the remainder into a bag and escaped. 2_____ When the new dictionary was being prepared, examples of different senses of each word were carefully culled. 6_____ As soon as he saw the police, he speedily culled from the scene. 3_____ Even after culling over the problem for hours, she was not close to a solution. 1_____ The bank teller culled the forgeries from the package of bank notes. 5_____ Before he made the jam, Charles culled the rotten berries from the basket. 4_____ When I arrived, she was in the garden culling flowers for a bouquet. 9_____ A bird culls its feathers by taking a dust bath. 8_____ **Cull:** **1** run away **2** think or ponder **3** outer shell **4** separate or gather 7_____

YOUR SENTENCE: _____

_____

[1:w   2:r   3:w   4:r   5:r   6:r   7:4   8:w   9:r]

40

4 REVIEW EXERCISE

In each blank write a form of one of the words listed below. Use each word only once.

chasten	deride	dissent	imprecation	repudiate
cull	derogatory	harangue	malediction	taunt

We spent the day 4_____ the nonlaying hens from the brood.

Let's not be late or the director will go into a 9_____ on the values of punctuality.

Don't mind her not agreeing; she usually 3_____ from the majority opinion.

1_____ by the punishment I had endured, I vowed to become a better person.

The foolish statement he issued to the press served only to 2_____ from his own prestige.

Their ridiculous behavior was greeted by 6_____ laughter.

Members of the opposing team 10_____ him about his clumsiness.

He angrily 8_____ all the statements that had been made against him.

In abusive language he 7_____ the man who had caused him so much hardship.

We expected his blessing, but all he uttered were 5_____ against us.

1: *chastened*   2: *derogate*   3: *dissents*   4: *culling*   5: *maledictions*   6: *derisive, taunting*
7: *imprecated*   8: *repudiated*   9: *harangue*   10: *taunted, derided*

FOR DICTIONARY STUDY

anathema

animosity

castigate

cavil

censure

chide

contention

demean

denounce

depreciate

discord

disdain

enmity

execration

fulminate

invective

jeer

objurgate

obloquy

opprobrious

rally

scoff

score

sneer

spurn

variance

vituperation

winnow

5 Influence, Force

The first five words in this section are most clearly related to the idea of force: *omnipotent* (all-powerful), which at the highest level refers only to God; *arbitrary* (dictatorial, or based on a personal decision rather than on a rule); *vanquish* (to conquer); *override* (to prevail over or disregard, as in "The legislature *overrode* the governor's veto by a two-thirds vote"); and *constrain* (to force or restrain).

The next five words all have the notion of influencing or bringing about some result: *provocation* (something that excites or irritates); *militate* (to have weight or effect—usually in preventing something); *embroil* (to involve in a quarrel); *contrive* (to bring about); and *conduce* (to contribute toward).

The next five have the idea of influencing in a favorable or soothing way: *ingratiate* (to gain favor with someone); *incantation* (a magic spell); *conciliate* (to soothe the anger of someone); *mollify* (to soften or reduce in intensity); and *assuage* (to calm, satisfy, or make less severe).

Sufferance in one sense means toleration or noninterference; in another sense it means patient endurance. The last two words have the idea of yielding to influence or force: *succumb* (to yield or give way to some force, or to die); and *susceptible* (easily influenced, or subject, prone, or sensitive to something).

---

omnipotent, arbitrary, vanquish, override, constrain,
provocation, militate, embroil, contrive, conduce,
ingratiate, incantation, conciliate, mollify, assuage,
sufferance, succumb, susceptible

---

omnipotent

(om·nip′ə·tənt)   All-powerful or having unlimited power or influence.   Young children may think of their parents as *omnipotent.*

[Latin *omni–*, all, and *potens*, powerful.] *The Omnipotent* refers to God.

Since I am not omnipotent, I cannot grant you everything you wish. 6 _____   In an ideal government, no leader would be considered omnipotent. 4 _____   He was sent up to his room for his omnipotence. 2 _____   Buses and subways are an omnipotent form of transportation. 1 _____   The pilgrims to the shrine lifted up their thoughts to the Omnipotent. 7 _____   Because the dictator had such great powers, he began to consider himself omnipotent. 8 _____   The omnipotent connects the stomach to the colon. 3 _____   Elena does not share the popular belief in the omnipotence of money. 5 _____   **Omnipotent: 1** misbehaving **2** having unlimited power **3** convenient **4** part of the digestive tract 9 _____

YOUR SENTENCE: _____

_____

[1:w   2:w   3:w   4:r   5:r   6:r   7:r   8:r   9:2]

arbitrary

(är′bə·trer′i)   (1) Dictatorial or characterized by absolute power or authority.   The *arbitrary* king would listen to no one's opinion.   (2) Selected at random; or based on one's whims or notions rather than on rule or law.   He made an *arbitrary* division of his studies into six major categories.

[Latin *arbiter*, judge.] In the first sense given above, *arbitrary* may refer to people (an *arbitrary* ruler) or to ideas, decisions, governments, etc. (an *arbitrary* rule).

Her arbitrary decision left no room for argument. 3 _____   The room had no unity and was decorated with such arbitrary items as travel posters, masks, and driftwood. 7 _____   Vines grew over the latticework of the arbitrary, forming a delightfully shady bower. 9 _____   The ruler made an arbitrary decision in appointing the consul. 4 _____   Because the password had been chosen arbitrarily, it did not make much sense. 5 _____   At the sight of the police officer, the boy felt too arbitrary to utter a sound. 2 _____   The fines were decided arbitrarily. 1 _____   Acts of willfulness and tyranny are signs of an arbitrary government. 6 _____   **Arbitrary** (choose two): **1** tyrannical **2** random or by choice **3** refuge or shelter **4** group of trees **5** frightened or timid 8 _____

YOUR SENTENCE: _____

_____

[1:r   2:w   3:r   4:r   5:r   6:r   7:r   8:1,2   9:w]

vanquish

(vang'kwish) To conquer, overpower, or defeat completely; or to gain mastery or control over. The rebels were finally *vanquished* by Caesar.

> [Latin *vincere*, to overcome in battle.] *Vanquish*, a stronger word than *conquer*, can refer to overcoming someone in battle or in any conflict; or it can refer to overcoming an emotion or condition, as in "He finally managed to *vanquish* his terror."

We could no longer see the Matterhorn, which had vanquished in a misty veil. 3_____   The traitor was vanquished from the country and spent the rest of his life in exile. 4_____   "Macbeth shall never vanquish'd be until/Great Birnam wood to high Dunsinane hill/Shall come against him." 6_____   The weakened troops vanquished to the superior strength of the opposing forces. 2_____   The governor vanquished the opposition with her powerful speech. 5_____   Helen Keller, by her determination, vanquished great obstacles. 1_____   Alexander the Great was able to vanquish every army he fought. 8_____   Morale was low among the members of the vanquished team. 7_____

Vanquish: **1** become misty **2** surrender or yield **3** banish **4** conquer or subdue 9_____

YOUR SENTENCE: _____

_____

[1:r 2:w 3:w 4:w 5:r 6:r 7:r 8:r 9:4]

---

override

(ō'vər·rīd') To dominate, suppress, or prevail over; or to disregard or annul. Our desires at times *override* the laws of justice.

When the bomb exploded, panic overrode all other emotions. 5_____   Many people are unaware of the overriding importance of good diet. 9_____   The club's overriding concern was to preserve the wilderness from developers. 3_____   After the downpour, the riverbanks overrode into the valley. 8_____   The president overrode the committee members by allowing them to do as they wished. 7_____   In some parts of the world, the rights of individuals are frequently overridden. 1_____ The lawyer finally thought of a further, and overriding, reason for the decision. 4_____   The rebellious legislators plan to override the governor's veto. 2_____   **Override:** **1** dominate **2** yield to **3** speed up **4** stabilize 6_____

YOUR SENTENCE: _____

_____

[1:r 2:r 3:r 4:r 5:r 6:1 7:w 8:w 9:r]

45

constrain

(kən·strān′) To force or compel; or to restrain, confine, or stifle. Fear of punishment often *constrains* us to act honestly and justly.

> *Constrain* can also mean to imprison or to restrict the movement of. Another meaning is to force in an unnatural way, as in "His only response to the joke was a *constrained* smile."

Instead of clearing up the issue, all those details merely constrained us, and we were as bewildered as ever. 5_____ They always resented the constraining influence of their elders. 9_____ Constrain the two juices together with a mixer before adding them to the salad dressing. 7_____ The prisoner was constrained in chains in a dungeon. 2_____ Wendy tried to constrain her brother to stay in the house. 4_____ Tensions caused by a difference of opinion about politics constrained their friendship. 8_____ Mr. Trent chafed at the constraint and monotony of his narrow life. 3_____ No matter how hard he constrained, he could not lift the rock. 1_____ **Constrain:** **1** blend **2** confuse **3** restrain or force **4** try or attempt 6_____

YOUR SENTENCE: _____

[1:w   2:r   3:r   4:r   5:w   6:3   7:w   8:r   9:r]

provocation

(prov′ə·kā′shən) Something that irritates, incites, angers, or excites. On the slightest *provocation* Alex was ready to resort to blows.

> [Latin *pro*, forth, and *vocatus*, called.] The same root appears in *vocal, voice, revoke,* and *advocate.*
> The verb form of *provocation* is provoke (prə·vōk′). The adjective *provocative* (prə·vok′ə·tiv) can mean irritating, or it can mean agreeably stimulating or exciting.

The speaker's attack on his opponent served as a provocation to get us involved in the political debate. 9_____ Her constant criticism can be most provoking. 4_____ Until Ellen had decided on a profession, the guidance counselor recommended a provocation course. 8_____ His every movement was a provocation to a fight. 3_____ The critics consider this one of the most provocative novels of our time. 7_____ The provocation assembled to discuss foreign affairs. 1_____ The dull, provocative voice of the speaker lulled her to sleep. 2_____ The congresswoman's report provoked a storm of controversy. 5_____ **Provocation:** **1** incitement or irritation **2** calming influence **3** formal meeting **4** means of livelihood 6_____

YOUR SENTENCE: _____

[1:w   2:w   3:r   4:r   5:r   6:1   7:r   8:w   9:r]

militate

(mil′ə·tāt) To have weight or effect, or to operate against or in favor of something. The facts of the case *militate* against his opinion.

> [Latin *militare*, to serve as a soldier, from *miles*, soldier.] The same root appears in *military* and *militia*. Although *militate* occasionally means to fight or operate *for* something, it far more often means to fight or operate *against* something.

Susan Anthony's actions militated against the notion that a woman belongs only in the home. 4_____

The election of the new mayor militated in favor of reform. 2_____ All of the recent events seemed to militate against the unfortunate king. 3_____ The smile that accompanied the lecture militated it markedly. 8_____ Our inability to decide on a plan militated against our taking action. 9_____ After his many unkind acts, his conscience is so militated that he scarcely knows right from wrong. 1_____ Days of thought and private militation had gone into the decision. 5_____ The evidence supplied by eyewitnesses militated against the defendant. 6_____ **Militate: 1** think deeply **2** have weight or effect **3** corrupt or weaken morally **4** make milder 7_____

YOUR SENTENCE: _____

_____

[1:w 2:r 3:r 4:r 5:w 6:r 7:2 8:w 9:r]

embroil

(em·broil′) To involve in a quarrel, conflict, or problem, or to throw into confusion. The small country wished to stay neutral rather than to become *embroiled* in the international conflict.

They eagerly embroiled themselves of all the pleasures the city offered. 3_____ Their plans for the expedition were embroiled by political complications. 1_____ On the outskirts of the city they became embroiled in a traffic tie-up. 5_____ The sunbathers embroiled themselves in the warm, penetrating rays of the sun. 2_____ The rancher's brand was clearly embroiled on the calf. 4_____ Anna was constantly embroiled in fighting for one cause or another. 8_____ The Secretary of State tried to avoid excessive embroilment in European affairs. 7_____ Those who speak out in favor of change often find themselves embroiled in controversy. 6_____ **Embroil: 1** bask **2** involve or confuse **3** make use of **4** mark or imprint 9_____

YOUR SENTENCE: _____

_____

[1:r 2:w 3:w 4:w 5:r 6:r 7:r 8:r 9:2]

contrive

(kən·trīv′) To scheme or plan, to invent or design, to manage to do, or to bring about. Polonius *contrived* a meeting between Hamlet and Ophelia.

> Although *contrive* most often refers to the devising of ideas and nonmaterial things, it can occasionally refer to the designing of material objects, as in "The inventor *contrived* a new kind of washer." The adjective form *contrived* usually carries the connotation of artificial, forced, unnatural.

The sinner tried to contrive himself of his sins. 8 _____ Through clever arguments he contrived to win support of all the party leaders. 3 _____ Edmund Burke viewed government as a contrivance of human wisdom. 4 _____ His look of defiant contrivance told her that he had no intention of doing as she asked. 2 _____ She contrived to meet us at the ball game. 7 _____ If we were satisfied with what we had, we would cease to contrive new labor-saving devices. 1 _____ The audience became impatient with the contrived simplicity of the dialogue of the play. 6 _____ Scott sought for a contrivable companion to share his evening of fun. 9 _____ **Contrive: 1** plan or design **2** make free from guilt **3** be suitable **4** act stubbornly **5** _____

YOUR SENTENCE: _____

_____

[1:r 2:w 3:r 4:r 5:1 6:r 7:r 8:w 9:w]

---

conduce

(kən·düs′) To contribute toward, further, or promote, or to lead toward a desirable result. The strict, austere atmosphere of their home does not *conduce* to relaxation.

> [Latin *con–*, with, together, and *ducere*, to lead.] The same root appears in *conduct, conductor, abduction, introduction, reproduce,* and *educate.*

In its own way, each circumstance conduces to the final result. 4 _____ She has many qualities that conduce to academic success. 5 _____ Do you agree that regular study habits are conducive to good grades? 3 _____ The promise of a reward is often conducive to obedience. 8 _____ Overeating is conducive to good health. 7 _____ The police had difficulty in capturing the conducive criminal. 2 _____ Such insulting remarks are not at all conducive to goodwill. 9 _____ He correctly conduced that we would be on the first train. 6 _____ **Conduce: 1** reason out **2** avoid or escape **3** contribute toward **4** prevent 1 _____

YOUR SENTENCE: _____

_____

[1:3 2:w 3:r 4:r 5:r 6:w 7:w 8:r 9:r]

ingratiate

(in·grā′shi·āt) To bring oneself into another's favor or good graces. The merchants felt that their good manners would *ingratiate* them with their customers.

> [Latin *in*, into, and *gratia*, favor.] The same root appears in *grace, grateful,* and *congratulate.* Do not confuse *ingratiate* with *ingrate,* an ungrateful person. *Ingratiate* is usually followed by *with.*

The children were scared by his fierce and ingratiating actions. 1 _____ The new rulers tried to ingratiate themselves with the people. 3 _____ The newscaster, who had a pleasant voice, ingratiated herself with her audience. 9 _____ The lawyer presented his case in an ingratiating manner. 4 _____ An ingratiating manner often wins friends. 5 _____ The harsh sound of the motor ingratiated my nerves. 8 _____ His easy smile and praising words show that he is a master of the art of ingratiation. 2 _____ Don't expect thanks from that ingratiate, for he is never grateful for anything. 6 _____ **Ingratiate: 1** frighten **2** ungrateful person **3** irritate **4** win favor 7 _____

YOUR SENTENCE: _____

_____

[1:w 2:r 3:r 4:r 5:r 6:w 7:4 8:w 9:r]

---

incantation

(in′kan·tā′shən) The use of magical words to cast a spell; or magic or sorcery. Perhaps the most famous *incantation* is the one uttered by the three witches in *Macbeth:* "Double, double toil and trouble;/Fire burn and cauldron bubble."

> [Latin *cantus*, chanting, singing.] The same root appears in *cantata, chant,* and *enchant.*

This vinegar is cloudy; please incant it into another bottle. 7 _____ The goddess muttered some incantations to transform the tree into a deer. 8 _____ To prepare for the auction, they made a thorough incantation of the goods in the house. 4 _____ The magician claimed that as soon as he had performed the incantation, a miracle would take place. 6 _____ The incantations of the ancient druids concluded the religious service. 1 _____ After an incantation of twenty years, the released prisoner had difficulty in adjusting to the everyday world. 5 _____ Attracted by their strange incantations, we followed the mysterious figures up the hill. 9 _____ When she writes poetry, Louise uses many mystical words with an incantatory power. 3 _____ **Incantation: 1** itemized list **2** gentle pouring **3** magic **4** confinement 2 _____

YOUR SENTENCE: _____

_____

[1:r 2:3 3:r 4:w 5:w 6:r 7:w 8:r 9:r]

conciliate

(kən·sil'i·āt) To pacify, placate, or soothe the anger of; or to win goodwill by friendly acts. After wrecking the car, he found it hard to *conciliate* his father.

> *Conciliate* often implies the use of persuasion, arbitration, etc. in an attempt to win someone over or to settle a dispute.

He opened the truce meeting with a few conciliatory remarks. 2_____ With good nature and tact, the labor official was able to conciliate the two sides. 1_____ We gazed in awe at the conciliate beauty of the shooting star. 5_____ The two small school districts wished to conciliate into one large unit. 6_____ In order to conciliate the angry mob, the sheriff agreed to release the prisoner. 8_____ As a gesture of conciliation, John gave his sister his favorite record. 7_____ She acted as a conciliator in the argument between the two groups. 3_____ The speaker constantly conciliated from his topic, jumping from one point to another. 4_____ **Conciliate: 1** ultimate **2** ramble **3** pacify **4** join 9_____

YOUR SENTENCE: _____

_____

[1:r 2:r 3:r 4:w 5:w 6:w 7:r 8:r 9:3]

---

mollify

(mol' ə·fī) To soothe, pacify, soften, or reduce in intensity. Their thoughtfulness *mollified* my anger.

> [Latin *mollis*, soft, tender, and *–fy*, to make.] The same root appears in *mollusk*, a soft-bodied animal.

The intensely cold weather caused the rain to mollify as it fell, and soon the entire street was a sheet of ice. 9_____ After all her other attempts at mollification had failed, she tried to soothe her neighbor by paying for the damages. 5_____ Mrs. Richardson was the family mollifer, constantly trying to lessen any tensions between the two generations. 1_____ The senator had to make numerous concessions to the other members of the committee in order to mollify them. 7_____ When it was discovered that one of the parties was underage, the contract was mollified. 4_____ Your apology has mollified my resentment. 3_____ The cookie had a mollifying effect on the baby: as soon as he saw it, he stopped crying. 8_____ His continued misbehavior mollified us, and we finally gave up trying to help him. 6_____ **Mollify: 1** cancel or annul **2** exasperate **3** harden **4** soothe or soften 2_____

YOUR SENTENCE: _____

_____

[1:r 2:4 3:r 4:w 5:r 6:w 7:r 8:r 9:w]

assuage

(ə·swāj′) To pacify, calm, or satisfy, or to make less severe. He *assuaged* his thirst at a brook.

Emergency food supplies were rushed to the besieged village to assuage the hunger of the people. 7_____ He tried to assuage his feeling of guilt by doing good deeds. 8_____ Henry rubbed his knee in order to assuage the severe pain. 6_____ The dancers at the party assuaged to the orchestra's music. 9_____ She did all she could to assuage her husband's sorrow. 5_____ Her fiery speech quickly assuaged the crowd into action; within a few minutes they were marching toward the mayor's office. 2_____ By investing wisely in the stock market, you will be able to assuage your money very rapidly. 1_____ The comforting words of Sally Robinson, the new counselor, helped to assuage their grief. 4_____ **Assuage:** 1 make less severe 2 inflame 3 move slowly 4 make greater 3_____

YOUR SENTENCE: _____

_____

[1:w   2:w   3:1   4:r   5:r   6:r   7:r   8:r   9:w]

sufferance

(suf′ər·əns or suf′rəns) (1) Toleration, or permission implied by failure to interfere. Although their legal rights had expired, the lords kept their estates by royal *sufferance*. (2) Patient endurance, or the ability to bear or endure pain, distress, etc. She remained calm and resolute in the *sufferance* of hardships.

> The expression *on sufferance* means tolerated or permitted but not actually encouraged, as in "He is not really wanted, but he remains in the chorus *on sufferance*."

Jonathan shielded his younger brother from the sufferance of the school bully. 7_____ It was only by sufferance that the shabbily dressed man was allowed to enter the ballroom. 2_____ One way to deal with false accusers is by silence and sufferance. 4_____ The general feels that the chief characteristics of a good soldier are valor and sufferance. 8_____ A sufferance was enacted that prevented the citizens from leaving the country. 1_____ Although the taunts were beyond sufferance, I refused to yield to anger. 3_____ The children were allowed in their parents' study only on sufferance. 9_____ They were permitted to enter the country only by sufferance of the immigration authorities. 6_____ **Sufferance** (choose two): 1 tyranny or domination 2 endurance 3 heartbreak 4 toleration or permission 5 formal proclamation 5_____

YOUR SENTENCE: _____

_____

[1:w   2:r   3:r   4:r   5:2,4   6:r   7:w   8:r   9:r]

succumb

(sə·kum′) To yield or give way to superior force; or to die. Hunger forced the besieged city to *succumb*.

> [Latin *sub*, under, and *–cumbere*, to lie down.] *Succumb* is usually followed by *to*.

Although at first he had seemed to be improving, he finally succumbed to pneumonia. 1_____ She reported that about five hundred small businesses had succumbed during the period. 4_____ Despite contrary evidence he succumbed stubbornly to his own ideas. 7_____ Succumbing to curiosity, the child opened the box. 9_____ The Red Cross succumbed the flood victims in the area. 6_____ The small country was forced to succumb to the invaders. 2_____ Visitors usually succumb to the excitement and drama of foreign cities. 3_____ He fought hard to stay awake, but he finally succumbed to his sleepiness and started to doze. 5_____ **Succumb: 1** help **2** yield or give way **3** improve **4** hold or sustain 8_____

YOUR SENTENCE: _____

_____

[1:r 2:r 3:r 4:r 5:r 6:w 7:w 8:2 9:r]

susceptible

(sə·sep′tə·bəl) Easily influenced or impressionable; or subject to, prone to, or sensitive to. Almost everyone is *susceptible* to flattery.

> [Latin *susceptus*, taken from underneath, undertaken, from *sub*, under, and *–cipere*, to take.] The same root appears in *conception, deception, except,* and *reception. Susceptible* is usually followed by *to* or *of*.

Even the most independent-thinking people are in some way susceptible to public opinion. 5_____ Some metals are more susceptible of corrosion than others. 1_____ Always optimistic, Martha feels that every problem is susceptible of solution. 6_____ Since he had been discovered at the scene of the crime, he was held by the police as a susceptible person. 9_____ His susceptibility allows us to talk him into anything. 3_____ Much to our susceptibility, we could not explain his change of attitude. 8_____ Children are thought to be especially susceptible to television advertising. 7_____ Later in life he became susceptible to diabetes. 4_____ **Susceptible: 1** surprising **2** easily influenced **3** strategic **4** suspected 2_____

YOUR SENTENCE: _____

_____

[1:r 2:2 3:r 4:r 5:r 6:r 7:r 8:w 9:w]

52

5 REVIEW EXERCISE

In each blank write a form of one of the words listed below. Use each word only once.

arbitrary   constrain   ingratiate   override   susceptible
assuage   contrive   militate   provocation   vanquish
conciliate   embroil   mollify   succumb
conduce   incantation   omnipotent   sufferance

By planning carefully, the girls were able to 3_____ a meeting with their favorite singer.

More than half of the voyagers 5_____ to seasickness.

Being totally unprotected, the city was very 17_____ to attack from both the east and the west.

A long, dry summer is 2_____ to forest fires.

The threatening weather 6_____ against the success of the picnic.

Reporters on television interviewed a magician, who recited some of her most popular 12_____

He was not really welcome at their home; he was allowed in on 11_____ only.

When he learned of his victory, his 14_____ emotion was one of intense joy.

Jay found poverty constantly 13_____ his actions.

The great strength of his forces enabled the general to 7_____ the opposing army completely.

Patricia Garciá, the city's progressive new mayor, often finds herself 9_____ in disputes with other officials.

After repeated 16_____ Peter became very angry.

He was resented by his employees because his orders were so 18_____ .

Anita Fernandez acted as a 10_____ in the negotiations between the engineers and the firefighters.

With unswerving politeness and a ready smile, Chuck tried to 8_____ himself with everyone he met.

The ambassador was 4_____ by the new terms of the treaty.

This glass of lemonade should 1_____ your thirst.

Although judges may be powerful, they are by no means 15_____ .

1: *assuage*   2: *conducive*   3: *contrive*   4: *mollified, conciliated*   5: *succumbed*   6: *militates*
7: *vanquish*   8: *ingratiate*   9: *embroiled*   10: *conciliator, mollifier*   11: *sufferance*   12: *incantations*
13: *constraining*   14: *overriding*   15: *omnipotent*   16: *provocation*   17: *susceptible*   18: *arbitrary*

FOR DICTIONARY STUDY

alleviate

almighty

amenable

coercion

compel

docile

dominate

foment

high-handed

impel

imperative

imperious

incite

instigate

magisterial

mitigate

oblige

overbearing

palliate

pique

placate

propitiate

puissance

rout

subdue

tractable

6 Misbehavior, Minor Faults

The first two words refer to behavior that may not be wrong at all but merely odd: *eccentric* (peculiar, unconventional) and *idiosyncrasy* (a personal peculiarity or a characteristic way of acting). Such behavior is sometimes *ludicrous* (laughably absurd) or *frivolous* (silly, trivial, or lacking seriousness or sense).

The next two words refer to verbal kinds of misbehavior: *drivel* (silly or foolish talk) and *glib* (too ready, fluent, or smooth to be sincere). *Pompous* means showy, pretentious, or puffed up by a sense of one's own importance. *Lethargy* is almost the opposite: laziness, great lack of energy, or indifference.

The next two words share the idea of thrusting oneself in where one is not wanted: *encroach* (to trespass, intrude, make inroads upon, or take liberties with) and *interloper* (a meddler or one who intrudes on the rights or affairs of another). An *indignity* is an insult or outrage or something that injures one's dignity or self-respect. The last word, *foolhardy*, means rash, foolishly bold, or recklessly daring.

None of these is necessarily a very serious fault. Worse forms of misbehavior and deception are treated in the next section.

---

eccentric, idiosyncrasy, ludicrous, frivolous, drivel, glib, pompous, lethargy, encroach, interloper, indignity, foolhardy

---

eccentric

(ek·sen′trik) Strange, peculiar, unconventional, or deviating from the normal.   The *eccentric* millionaire cluttered his estate with all sorts of odd statues.

>(Latin *e–*, out of, from, and *centrum*, center; hence, irregular.] *Eccentric* can also mean having a different center (*eccentric* circles) or off-center (an *eccentric* wheel).

After living alone for twenty years, the hermit became eccentric. 3_____   Let's meet at Ann's home; her house is eccentric to everyone. 6_____   His eccentric spelling made his paper hard to read. 2_____   Although he has many eccentricities, he is an intelligent person. 9_____   The doctor gave him an eccentric to steady his nerves. 8_____   The comet moved around the sun in an eccentric ellipse rather than in a perfect circle. 4_____   If you continue to do odd things, you will be branded as an eccentric. 7_____   She was chosen for the job because she is capable, eccentric, and level-headed. 5_____   **Eccentric: 1** ordinary **2** central **3** calming **4** strange 1_____

YOUR SENTENCE: _____

_____

[1:4   2:r   3:r   4:r   5:w   6:w   7:r   8:w   9:r]

---

idiosyncrasy

(id′i·ō·sing′krə·si) A personal peculiarity, or eccentricity.   Because of his numerous *idiosyncrasies*, he was considered the oddest person in the neighborhood.

>[Greek *idios*, one's own, *syn–*, together, and *krasis*, mixing.] The root *idios* appears in *idiot* and *idiom*. *Idiosyncrasy* can also refer to any peculiar characteristic that distinguishes a person or his or her work (artistic *idiosyncrasies*). In medicine, *idiosyncrasy* refers to an individual's oversensitivity to a food, drug, etc., as in "Her severe reaction to aspirin was an *idiosyncrasy*."

The car's new idiosyncratic helped me to shift more easily from one gear to another. 3_____ Marianne Moore's poetry has certain idiosyncrasies that make it easy to identify. 9_____   His only idiosyncrasy was to eat plums with every meal. 6_____   Living alone for many years, he had developed idiosyncratic behavior. 5_____   Johnston's idiosyncratic reaction to sulfa caused him to discontinue use of the drug. 8_____   Digging into the idiosyncrasy, the botanist pulled up the root of a rare plant. 4_____   His most annoying idiosyncrasy is his habit of leaping about when he is excited. 1_____   Instead of the truth, they told us an idiosyncrasy. 7_____   **Idiosyncrasy: 1** falsehood **2** crevice **3** personal peculiarity **4** mechanical part 2_____

YOUR SENTENCE: _____

_____

[1:r   2:3   3:w   4:w   5:r   6:r   7:w   8:r   9:r]

56

ludicrous

(lü′də·krəs) Ridiculous, absurd, or laughable. His suggestion was so *ludicrous* that everyone laughed at him.

[Latin *ludus*, game.] The same root appears in *illusion, delude, interlude,* and *prelude. Ludicrous* implies being so preposterous as to deserve both laughter and scorn.

Politicians sometimes take pleasure in making their opponents seem ludicrous. 8_____   At times the professor was ludicrously absentminded. 2_____   Dr. Atkins should be congratulated for his ludicrous study of the effects of radiation on plant life. 6_____   A ludicrous grin gave a comic effect to his facial expression. 7_____   His actions were so ludicrous that we didn't know whether to be angry or to laugh. 9_____   The ludicrous expression on her face told us of her sorrow. 3_____   Mowing lawns was such a ludicrous business that Yolanda was quickly able to double her weekly income. 1_____   Although the others were embroiled in the discussion, Agatha viewed the whole matter as ludicrous. 5_____   **Ludicrous: 1** careful **2** profitable **3** laughable **4** gloomy 4_____

YOUR SENTENCE: _____

_____

[1:w 2:r 3:w 4:3 5:r 6:w 7:r 8:r 9:r]

frivolous

(friv′ə·ləs) Silly, trivial, lacking seriousness or sense, or of little value or importance. Instead of writing a serious letter to her aunt, she wrote one that was *frivolous* in tone.

Although *frivolous* usually has the negative connotation of superficial or unbecomingly light or trivial, it can occasionally mean gay or playful, as in "The decorator improved the appearance of the room by adding a few *frivolous* ornaments."

Such frivolous behavior was unbecoming to someone in that position. 6_____   Because he is so frivolous, he refuses to part with a penny. 8_____   We decorated the tree with paper flowers and other frivolities. 1_____   That argument is frivolous, and I don't think it worth our attention. 9_____   Frivolity and irresponsible behavior are not likely to lead to greatness. 4_____   The mayor's frivolous speech has set the right tone for this solemn occasion. 5_____   Nick spent his money frivolously at the fair. 7_____   Oliver Cromwell condemned the frivolities of English royalty. 2_____   **Frivolous: 1** solemn or serious **2** silly or trivial **3** stingy **4** frightening 3_____

YOUR SENTENCE: _____

_____

[1:r 2:r 3:2 4:r 5:w 6:r 7:r 8:w 9:r]

drivel

(driv′əl) Silly or foolish talk.   We do not have time to listen to such *drivel*.

As a verb *drivel* means to talk in a silly manner. Another meaning is to slobber or to let saliva drip from the mouth.

The audience became impatient with the comedian's drivel. 6_____   Suddenly a drivel of wild geese appeared in the sky. 2_____   The driveling conversation embarrassed the guests. 4_____   I think you are talking more drivel than sense. 9_____   Sitting in the drivel, he could turn in all directions without getting up. 8_____   The once forceful speaker has become a pathetic driveler. 7_____ The lecturer driveled on and on, boring us all beyond endurance. 3_____   Terry works as a driveler in an automobile plant. 1_____   **Drivel: 1** foolish talk **2** mechanic **3** flock or herd **4** revolving chair 5_____

YOUR SENTENCE: _____

_____

[1:w   2:w   3:r   4:r   5:1   6:r   7:r   8:w   9:r]

glib

(glib) Too ready, fluent, or smooth to be sincere or carefully considered.   When it comes to making excuses, Ira has a *glib* tongue.

Glib is related to an old word meaning slippery. It usually implies shallowness, superficiality, or insincerity.

No one should be convinced by glib generalizations. 9_____   With glib steps the police officer carefully made her way through the deserted building. 3_____   I have a glib feeling that I have been here before. 4_____   Amanda spoke glibly about places she had never seen. 8_____   The candles on the mantelpiece were flickering glibly. 2_____   His glib statement is probably wrong. 5_____ How I dislike the glibness of some orators! 7_____   No matter how difficult the question, she was ready with a glib answer. 6_____   **Glib: 1** ready or fluent **2** deliberate **3** strange **4** bashful or shy 1_____

YOUR SENTENCE: _____

_____

[1:1   2:w   3:w   4:w   5:r   6:r   7:r   8:r   9:r]

pompous

(pom′pəs) Showy, pretentious, or overdignified; or acting self-important. We sat there for an hour, listening to a *pompous* official make a dull speech.

> *Pompous* can refer to people, actions, language, art works, and so on. The noun form is *pomposity*. The related noun *pomp* means splendor, magnificence, or a stately display, as in "The queen was crowned with all the *pomp* that befitted her position."

The formal language he used was much too pompous for his trivial subject matter. 9_____   The officers marched by pompously, refusing to speak to anyone in the audience. 6_____   The actors' pomposity made them seem somewhat ludicrous. 5_____   The house is expensive and far too pompous for my simple tastes. 3_____   The mayor was a very pompous man who thought of himself as being more important than he really was. 2_____   Completely exhausted, the bedraggled traveler dropped pompously into a chair. 7_____   Those unfortunate children are too pompous to understand any of their homework assignments. 1_____   Her humble way of life is an indication of her pomposity. 8_____   **Pompous:** 1 poverty-stricken 2 fatigued or exhausted 3 showy or pretentious 4 unintelligent 4_____

YOUR SENTENCE: _____

_____

[1:w   2:r   3:r   4:3   5:r   6:r   7:w   8:w   9:r]

---

lethargy

(leth′ər·ji) Laziness, great lack of energy, sluggishness, or indifference. The hot summer weather spread a feeling of *lethargy* over all of us.

After that huge feast we all moved around lethargically, too tired to participate in the game. 3_____
Despite the teacher's appeal for help, a discouraging lethargy was displayed by the students. 2_____
A lethargy of necessities makes his life difficult. 9_____   The medication she took made her feel too lethargic to do any work that day. 8_____   Overcome by lethargy, Allison sank down onto the sofa.
5_____   Summoning up all his lethargy, he tried to face the danger that awaited him. 6_____
The president's stirring speech was aimed at getting rid of the lethargy of the nation. 1_____   Full of lethargy, Mr. Hilton jumped into the pool and swam ten lengths without stopping. 4_____   **Lethargy:** 1 energy 2 courage 3 laziness 4 lack or scarcity 7_____

YOUR SENTENCE: _____

_____

[1:r   2:r   3:r   4:w   5:r   6:w   7:3   8:r   9:w]

encroach

(en·krōch′) To trespass, intrude, make inroads upon, or take undue liberties with. The nation became alarmed when the army of a neighboring country *encroached* on its territory.

> *Encroach* often implies making inroads by stealth or by gradual advances. It is usually followed by *on* or *upon*.

Expanding cities and suburbs are now encroaching upon rural areas. 9_____ She was curled up in the armchair, encroached in a thrilling detective story. 4_____ In order not to encroach upon his privacy, they closed the door while he was telephoning. 7_____ The landowner encroached upon the rights of the tenant farmers by selling land that they had improved. 8_____ As the superior enemy force attacked, the platoon encroached back to its own lines. 2_____ She sued the city, claiming that the expansion of the park represented an encroachment on her property. 3_____ They marched heavily armed, encroached by their weapons. 5_____ The incoming tide of the sea gradually encroached upon the unwary sunbathers. 1_____ **Encroach:** **1** absorb **2** burden down **3** retreat or return **4** trespass or intrude 6_____

YOUR SENTENCE: _____

_____

[1:r 2:w 3:r 4:w 5:w 6:4 7:r 8:r 9:r]

---

interloper

(in′tər·lōp′ər) A meddler or one who intrudes on the rights or affairs of another. Since he was an *interloper*, we were justified in putting him out of our house.

> [Latin *inter*, between, among, and Dutch *loopen*, to run.]

As an uninvited guest, he was clearly an interloper at the party. 9_____ Weavers interlope the grass strands to produce beautiful rugs. 3_____ The stranger did not realize that he had interloped until he saw the sign "For Club Members Only." 8_____ He regarded his partner's new associate as an interloper. 2_____ When they were forbidden to marry, the young couple interloped. 4_____ The press secretary, Madeline Novick, acted as interloper between the governor and reporters. 1_____ When he was attacked, he insulted his opponent in interloping terms. 7_____ The unauthorized traders were dealt with as interlopers, trespassing on the rights of others. 5_____ **Interloper:** **1** harsh criticism **2** one who runs off **3** intruder **4** weaver 6_____

YOUR SENTENCE: _____

_____

[1:w 2:r 3:w 4:w 5:r 6:3 7:w 8:r 9:r]

indignity

(in·dig′nə·ti) An insult or outrage, or something that offends, humiliates, or injures one's dignity or self-respect. Being totally ignored at the meeting was the worst *indignity* she had to suffer.

[Latin *in*–, not, and *dignus*, fitting, worthy.] The same root appears in *indignation*, anger or scorn that results from injustice, meanness, or *indignities*.

She suffered the indignity of having the chair collapse beneath her. 8_____ He has far too much indignity to admit that he was wrong. 4_____ She refused to submit to the indignity of having to apologize to her cousin. 5_____ The prisoners suffered many indignities at the hands of their captors. 7_____ Since he was now penniless, he thought of himself as an indignity person. 2_____ The indignity of having to undergo the spanking hurt the child more than the physical pain. 3_____ He said not a word, reacting to all our suggestions only with indifference and complete indignity. 1_____ How many more indignities must we put up with before we rebel? 6_____ **Indignity:** **1** excessive pride **2** lack of interest **3** insult or outrage **4** lacking money 9_____

YOUR SENTENCE: _____

_____

[1:w 2:w 3:r 4:w 5:r 6:r 7:r 8:r 9:3]

---

foolhardy

(fül′här′di) Rash, foolishly bold, or recklessly daring. Only the *foolhardy* will take such risks.

[*Fool* and French *hardir*, to make bold.] *Foolhardy* implies taking unnecessary chances when there is almost no hope of success.

His foolhardy dive into shallow water resulted in a severe head injury. 8_____ Instead of being praised for what he thought was bravery, he was condemned for his foolhardiness. 1_____ The senator was not foolhardy enough to introduce his first bill without public support. 9_____ He is too foolhardy to understand even the simplest words. 5_____ Loving adventure and excitement, she foolhardily welcomes all kinds of danger. 2_____ The foolhardy group chattered on about trivial matters. 6_____ Venturing out alone into the desert was a foolhardy thing to do. 7_____ Her witty talk would interest even the most foolhardy of people. 3_____ **Foolhardy:** **1** unintelligent **2** foolishly bold **3** excessively talkative person **4** unsympathetic 4_____

YOUR SENTENCE: _____

_____

[1:r 2:r 3:w 4:2 5:w 6:w 7:r 8:r 9:r]

6 REVIEW EXERCISE

In each blank write a form of one of the words listed below. Use each word only once.

drivel	foolhardy	idiosyncrasy	lethargy
eccentric	frivolous	indignity	ludicrous
encroach	glib	interloper	pompous

She felt too 9_____ to do anything but sit in a chair all day long.

Just when we most wanted privacy, an unwelcome 12_____ appeared and thrust himself into our conversation.

The government was 11_____ upon the property of the people.

No one should have to suffer the 8_____ of being laughed at in front of others.

The child was interested only in games and other 4_____ .

Although he was once eloquent when he spoke, now he merely 7_____ nonsense.

2_____ words and phrases can turn an effective speech into a boring one.

Despite his efforts to sound convincing, his 6_____ talk deceived nobody.

It is foolish to endanger your life by taking such 3_____ actions.

Everyone laughed at the 1_____ suggestion.

5_____ behavior often makes a person the butt of many jokes.

His chief 10_____ is his insistence on absolute silence whenever he eats.

1: *ludicrous*   2: *pompous*   3: *foolhardy*   4: *frivolities*   5: *eccentric, idiosyncratic*   6: *glib*   7: *drivels*
8: *indignity*   9: lethargic   10: *idiosyncrasy, eccentricity*   11: *encroaching*   12: *interloper*

FOR DICTIONARY STUDY

aberration

affront

antic

bizarre

brash

brazen

erratic

facile

fatuous

garrulous

high-flown

impetuous

impudent

inane

indolent

inertia

infringe

loquacious

oddity

ostentatious

outlandish

precipitate

pretentious

singularity

sluggish

transgress

unctuous

voluble

7 Evil, Offense, Deception

The first seven words in this section can be remembered from the following sentence: "The *diabolic iniquity* (fiendish wickedness) commited by the *wanton malefactor* (deliberately cruel evildoer) was *insidious, flagrant,* and *repugnant* (underhanded, outrageous, and repulsive)." More meaning is added if you know something of the history of these words. *Diabolic* comes from the Latin word for devil; *iniquity* from the Latin word for injustice; *wanton* from two Middle English words meaning undisciplined. *Malefactor* is an actual Latin word (unchanged in spelling) meaning evildoer. *Insidious* comes from a Latin word for a snare or trap; *flagrant* from a Latin word for flaming; and *repugnant* from a Latin word meaning opposed or fighting back.

Eerie simply means strange, mysterious, or weird. The last three words have some connection with the idea of false appearance and deception: *bogus* (counterfeit, not genuine); *feign* (to pretend, imitate, or make a false show of); and *hoodwink* (to deceive).

---

diabolic, iniquity, wanton, malefactor, insidious, flagrant, repugnant, eerie, bogus, feign, hoodwink

---

diabolic

(dī'ə·bol'ik) Fiendish, wicked, or having to do with the Devil. In my nightmare a creature of *diabolic* cruelty tortured me mercilessly.

A variant form of *diabolic* is *diabolical*.

The first prize went to Rita Nils, who played the viola diabolically. 3_____   It was a stormy night, and all his talk about diabolic creatures made our flesh crawl. 8_____   A diabolical look crossed his face as he hit upon his fiendish scheme. 5_____   The guards were diabolically cruel to the prisoners of war. 2_____   In the legend the Devil sheds his diabolic shape and assumes the form of a human in order to fool his victim. 6_____   The evil prince was diabolically clever and calculating. 4_____ In order to disinfect the equipment, we rinsed it in diabolic acid. 7_____   We were all impressed by his sweet, diabolical disposition. 9_____   **Diabolic:** **1** easily molded **2** sharp and biting **3** devilish or fiendish **4** skillful or proficient 1_____

YOUR SENTENCE: _____

_____

[1:3   2:r   3:w   4:r   5:r   6:r   7:w   8:r   9:w]

iniquity

(in·ik'wə·ti) Wickedness, sin, or injustice. The *iniquity* of bribery was not offensive to them.

[Latin *iniquus*, unequal, unfair, from *in–*, not, and *aequus*, equal, just.]

Now that they had bought a house, they would start accumulating iniquity. 6_____   In our prayers we asked that all our iniquities be forgiven. 8_____   He conducted his business in a manner that many called iniquitous. 4_____   Good citizenship is reflected in iniquitous behavior. 3_____   The rebel leader spoke against the oppressions and iniquities of the government. 5_____   The prisoner claimed that the verdict handed down against him was iniquitous. 7_____   They hoped that they would be spared the iniquities of war. 2_____   The sudden bad news threw us into a state of depressed iniquity that prevented us from taking any action. 9_____   **Iniquity:** **1** misery **2** righteousness **3** wickedness **4** capital 1_____

YOUR SENTENCE: _____

_____

[1:3   2:r   3:w   4:r   5:r   6:w   7:r   8:r   9:w]

wanton

(won'tən) Senseless, unjustified, unprovoked, or deliberately cruel or malicious. We greatly resented his *wanton* attacks against us.

> [Middle English *wan–*, lacking, and *towen*, disciplined.] *Wanton* can also mean unrestrained (*wanton* enjoyment or *wanton* plant growth) or extravagant or wasteful (*wanton* spending).

She spent a lifetime protecting animals against the wanton cruelty of humans. 5_____ Being wanton with his money, he had built up a healthy savings account. 1_____ Wanton vegetation choked the jungle trails. 7_____ The cruel captors exercised their powers wantonly. 8_____ The newly polished floor had a wanton finish. 4_____ The wantonness of that spiteful remark cannot be forgiven. 3_____ Rather than driving without any wanton, why don't you check the road map? 2_____ In the writer's statement we sensed a wanton prejudice. 6_____ **Wanton:** 1 unjustified or unprovoked 2 direction 3 shiny 4 cautious or thrifty 9_____

YOUR SENTENCE: _____

_____

[1:w 2:w 3:r 4:w 5:r 6:r 7:r 8:r 9:1]

malefactor

(mal'ə·fak'tər) A criminal, an evildoer, or one who commits a serious offense. The *malefactor* showed no remorse for the crime.

> [Latin *malefactor*, evildoer, from *male*, ill, badly, and *facere*, to do.] The feminine form of *malefactor* is *malefactress*. An evil deed is a *malefaction*. The opposite of *malefactor* is *benefactor*.

We thank all our malefactors, who worked so hard to make the convention a success. 4_____ Malefactors had damaged the statue and vandalized the garden. 1_____ A malefactor broke into her home and escaped with her camera equipment. 3_____ The malefaction is not serious; the patient will recover. 8_____ When a malefactor of one of the engines was discovered, the flight was canceled. 2_____ The malefactor entered the house by means of an open window in the basement. 9_____ History will record the leader as a malefactor who abused power and public support. 7_____ In the space of one year, the town endured two malefactors—a flood and an earthquake. 6_____ **Malefactor:** 1 evildoer 2 defect 3 one who helps 4 disaster or catastrophe 5_____

YOUR SENTENCE: _____

[1:r 2:w 3:r 4:w 5:1 6:w 7:r 8:w 9:r]

insidious

(in·sid'i·əs) Sly, crafty, underhanded, or treacherous. Unfortunately, we were all taken in by the *insidious* scheme.

> [Latin *insidiae*, snare, trap, ambush.] *Insidious* implies a watching for an opportunity to entrap, or a carefully masked underhandedness. A related meaning is to operate in a slow, subtle manner or to be more dangerous than is evident, as in "The *insidious* disease caused the patient to waste away slowly."

Guy Fawkes took part in an insidious plot to blow up Parliament. 9_____ Are you too insidious to realize what is happening? 3_____ The insidious pressures of modern life can wear us down. 7_____ I was not aware of the danger of the insidious drug until I felt its harmful effects. 5_____ The audience was deafened by the speaker's insidious voice. 8_____ When summer came, our swimming team no longer had to use the insidious pool. 1_____ The disease developed insidiously, until it was too late to seek a cure. 6_____ Someone who has a reputation for insidiousness cannot be trusted. 2_____ **Insidious:** 1 noisy 2 unaware 3 useless 4 sly 4_____

YOUR SENTENCE: _____

_____

[1:w 2:r 3:w 4:4 5:r 6:r 7:r 8:w 9:r]

flagrant

(flā'grənt) Scandalous, outrageous, or glaringly bad. His *flagrant* crime must not go unpunished.

> [Latin *flagrans*, flaming, burning.] Something that is *flagrant* is so obviously wrong as to be notorious.

The compound contained flagrances of carbon. 4_____ How can you believe that flagrant lie? 9_____ The flagrancy of their vicious conduct shocked the townspeople. 1_____ Merry elves, pixies, and other flagrant creatures danced joyfully in the forest. 5_____ Because the hobo had no visible means of support, he was arrested for flagrancy. 2_____ The minister referred to the act as a flagrant violation of religious beliefs. 8_____ Slums side-by-side with luxurious modern apartments showed the flagrant extremes of poverty and wealth that existed in the community. 3_____ The builder flagrantly violated the building code of the city. 6_____ **Flagrant:** 1 unreal 2 wandering about idly 3 odorous 4 outrageous 7_____

YOUR SENTENCE: _____

_____

[1:r 2:w 3:r 4:w 5:w 6:r 7:4 8:r 9:r]

repugnant

(ri·pug′nənt) Repulsive, loathsome, offensive, or very distasteful. Because the plan was *repugnant* to her, she refused to take part in it.

[Latin *re–*, back, and *pugnans*, striking, fighting.] *Repugnant* can also mean contradictory to or inconsistent with, as in "The new law is *repugnant* to the Constitution."

The repugnance of their greeting made us feel most welcome. 4_____ The very nature of the disease may be repugnant to sensitive people. 2_____ Because the doctor thought my repugnance was endangering my health, he put me on a strict diet. 5_____ Violent displays of emotion were repugnant to Cecilia. 1_____ The crude manner in which he eats his food is repugnant. 3_____ She expressed a repugnance toward the political tactics of fascist nations. 7_____ She was overcome by a feeling of repugnancy as a worm slithered across her path. 6_____ As the two repugnants entered the ring for the rematch, the crowd began to cheer wildly. 9_____ **Repugnant: 1** fighter or boxer **2** enthusiastic **3** overweight **4** repulsive 8_____

YOUR SENTENCE: _____

_____

[1:r 2:r 3:r 4:w 5:w 6:r 7:r 8:4 9:w]

eerie

(ēr′i) Weird, frightening, strange, or mysterious. Wandering through the ancient graveyard at midnight was an *eerie* experience.

Something that is *eerie* usually causes a vague or mysterious feeling of uneasiness or dread.

The trees seemed to moan eerily, as if they sensed the approaching storm. 9_____ The mysterious traveler told eerie tales about strange lands and strange people. 1_____ The weird case of the tiger footprints remains one of the eeriest mysteries in police records. 6_____ The staff complained that their daily routines were dull, eerie, and uneventful. 2_____ The eeriness of the hound's howling on the distant moors made us all shudder. 7_____ For lunch we had eerie cheese, fresh vegetables, fruitcake, and milk. 5_____ Marjory was very eerie of the treasurer's plan. 8_____ We watched their silhouettes moving eerily in the moonlight. 4_____ **Eerie: 1** commonplace **2** weird **3** nutritious **4** cautious or suspicious 3_____

YOUR SENTENCE: _____

_____

[1:r 2:w 3:2 4:r 5:w 6:r 7:r 8:w 9:r]

69

bogus

(bō′gəs) Counterfeit or not genuine.   We quickly realized that they had given us *bogus* money.

> *Bogus*, an informal synonym of *counterfeit* and an equivalent of the slang word *phony*, implies imitating with intent to deceive or defraud. It can also refer to pretending to possess qualities not actually possessed, as in "Her writing style has a *bogus* elegance."

The record books proved to contain very little except bogus transactions. 4_____   I rooted a cutting of a bogus, and it is blossoming on the windowsill. 9_____   A slash with his bogus cut the pineapple in two. 1_____   The border guards immediately spotted the bogus passport. 3_____   The bogus masterpiece had been on display for a week before the museum director discovered the fraud. 8_____   Wearing a bogus ermine robe, John came to the masquerade party as a king. 2_____ Only an expert would realize that the document was bogus. 5_____   We could tell by the bogus look in his eyes that he was not in a mood to be contradicted. 6_____   **Bogus: 1** sharp tool **2** not genuine **3** kind of plant **4** frightening 7_____

YOUR SENTENCE: _____

_____

[1:w   2:r   3:r   4:r   5:r   6:w   7:2   8:r   9:w]

---

feign

(fān) To pretend, imitate, or invent falsely, or to make a false show of.   A number of animals *feign* death when they think they are in danger.

> [Latin *fingere*, to form, imagine, pretend.] The past participle *fictus* is the root of *fiction*.

When confronted by his teacher, he feigned an excuse that was totally unbelievable. 8_____ Recklessly feigning all the dangers, the soldier went unarmed behind the enemy lines. 6_____   Her look of feigned innocence fooled no one. 5_____   In an attempt to win our sympathy, he feigned illness. 1_____   Despite our request to discuss the matter with him, he repeatedly feigned to see us. 3_____   Although she was terribly upset, she feigned calmness. 4_____   In order to get what he wants, he feigns everybody who gets in his way. 9_____   We were unable to say whether we were hearing a true or a feigned account of what had actually happened. 2_____   **Feign: 1** treat poorly **2** pretend **3** refuse **4** ignore 7_____

YOUR SENTENCE: _____

_____

[1:r   2:r   3:w   4:r   5:r   6:w   7:2   8:r   9:w]

70

hoodwink

(hud′wingk) To deceive, or to prevent from seeing the truth. He was so naïve that anyone could *hoodwink* him.

> *Hoodwink* originally meant to blindfold. It now means to fool another person or to conceal the truth. It can occasionally refer to self-deception that arises from an inability to distinguish the false from the true.

His clever talking enabled him to hoodwink the seller into accepting a low price. 8 _____   It was an obvious trick, but many were hoodwinked by it. 1 _____   After the death of his sister, he felt completely hoodwinked and forlorn. 7 _____   Attractive packaging often hoodwinks purchasers into buying worthless products. 9 _____   Although you've hoodwinked my friend, you can't fool me. 6 _____   By spending carelessly, he managed to hoodwink his money and is now penniless. 5 _____   Because you want to believe that story, you are hoodwinking yourself into accepting it as true. 4 _____   Hoodwinking over the landscape, the rider was filled with a sense of exhilaration. 2 _____   **Hoodwink:** **1** waste **2** deceive **3** move swiftly **4** sorrow or mourn 3 _____

YOUR SENTENCE: _____

_____

[1:r   2:w   3:2   4:r   5:w   6:r   7:w   8:r   9:r]

71

7 REVIEW EXERCISE

In each blank write a form of one of the words listed below. Use each word only once.

bogus	feign	iniquity	repugnant
diabolic	flagrant	insidious	wanton
eerie	hoodwink	malefactor	

My excuse was not 4_____; I could not attend the meeting because I was sick.

She refused to be 10_____ by the manufacturer's false claims for the product.

It wasn't until much later that he realized that he had been given a 8_____ twenty-dollar bill.

When he was caught, the 6_____ confessed to the crime.

He was guilty of theft, murder, and other 7_____.

You may have a feeling of 3_____ when you see my room; it is badly in need of cleaning.

The strange, 9_____ stillness that settled over the camp made us all feel somewhat uneasy.

The 2_____ poison had a more serious effect than was at first apparent.

The speaker talked about Satan and his 5_____ characteristics.

His lie was so 11_____ that everyone was aware of it.

The 1_____ cruelty of the invaders shocked the world.

1: *wanton*   2: *insidious*   3: *repugnance*   4: *feigned*   5 *diabolic*   6: *malefactor*   7: *iniquities*
8: *bogus*   9: *eerie*   10: *hoodwinked*   11: *flagrant*

FOR DICTIONARY STUDY

abhorrent

abominable

arrant

bamboozle

baneful

barbarous

barefaced

beguile

chicanery

delude

demoniac

dissemble

egregious

feint

flagitious

hoax

imposture

infamous

infernal

knavery

loathsome

malignant

Mephistophelian

nefarious

perfidious

pseudo

reprehensible

ruse

satanic

sham

sinister

surreptitious

uncanny

unearthly

wayward

8 Measurement, Quantity

The words in this section deal with quantity, degree, scope, and other kinds of measures or amounts. The first two words are contrasted with the next three. *Consummate* means perfect, supreme, or in the highest degree; *ultimate* means final, greatest possible, or that beyond which it is impossible to go. On the other hand, *finite* means having limits or bounds; *inconsiderable* means trivial or unimportant; and *parochial* means narrow-minded or restricted in range or scope. *Parochial* originally meant belonging to a parish of a church; *parochial* school still has this meaning. The more general meaning comes from the fact that those who never leave their own parishes—or their own communities or groups—are likely to have narrow views.

Integral has several meanings, the most central of which is whole, complete, and lacking nothing that is essential. Something that is an *integral* part of something else is essential to it and sometimes formed with it as a single unit. This is opposed to *piecemeal* (made piece by piece) and to *sundry* (various, several, miscellaneous).

The next four words share the meaning of abundance: *teem* (to abound, swarm, or be filled to overflowing); *prevalent* (widespread or generally accepted); *copious* (plentiful or abundant); and *exorbitant* (excessive, extravagant, or immoderate).

The final word, *tally,* has an interesting history (given in the headnote) that explains how the four meanings of *tally* are all related to cutting notches in a stick—an ancient way of recording an amount to be paid.

---

consummate, ultimate, finite, inconsiderable,
parochial, integral, piecemeal, sundry, teem,
prevalent, copious, exorbitant, tally

---

consummate

(kən·sum′it) Perfect, extreme, supreme, or in the highest degree. He was a *consummate* actor, both on and off the stage.

> As a verb *consummate* (kon′sə·māt) means to finish or to bring to completion or fulfillment, as in "Her ambition was *consummated* when she graduated from medical school." The noun *consummation* (kon′sə·mā′shən) means completion or an end or conclusion, as in "A mutually agreeable contract was the *consummation* of their lengthy discussions."

His answers proved that he was a consummate liar. 4_____   With one nation holding back, it was impossible to consummate the military alliance. 2_____   Although the skin had not been broken, a painful consummation started where he had been hit. 7_____   The pianist's performance was executed with consummate skill. 1_____   After a sailor dies, they consummate the body and scatter the ashes at sea. 9_____   With her consummate wisdom she will easily find a solution to our problem. 8_____   Both signatures were required before the contract could be consummated. 6_____ When she lost her passport in France, she reported it to the American consummate there. 3_____ **Consummate:** **1** extreme **2** government official **3** swelling **4** burn 5_____

YOUR SENTENCE: _____

_____

[1:r   2:r   3:w   4:r   5:1   6:r   7:w   8:r   9:w]

ultimate

(ul′tə·mit) Final, furthest, greatest possible, or beyond which it is impossible to go. Eleanor Roosevelt believed that everyone's *ultimate* wish was for a lasting world peace.

He believes that the string quartet is the ultimate vehicle for deep musical expression. 2_____   Dean desired an automobile that was the ultimate in speed. 3_____   A public-interest law firm will ultimate these offices when they are vacated next month. 8_____   Ultimate fireflies filled the air at dusk. 7_____   Iris Kim ultimated that she would run for the office if nominated. 1_____   Our ultimate destiny is still a mystery. 6_____   Ultimately the only solution will be for him to resign. 9_____   The ultimate outcome of the investigation was not known for weeks. 4_____ **Ultimate:** **1** inhabit **2** very numerous **3** hint or imply **4** final 5_____

YOUR SENTENCE: _____

_____

[1:w   2:r   3:r   4:r   5:4   6:r   7:w   8:w   9:r]

finite

(fī′nīt) Having measurable or definable limits or bounds. Anything that can be counted is *finite*.

[Latin *finis*, limit, boundary.] The same root appears in *final, finish, confine, define,* and *refine.* As an extension of the meaning above, *finite* can also mean mortal, limited in power, or having imperfections, as in "Humans are *finite* beings." The opposite of *finite* is *infinite* (in′fə·nit), endless.

Because his strength was finite, Superman could do anything he wished. 6_____ Even the greatest scientists must remember that their power is finite. 9_____ Using a finite, the surveyor was able to determine the slope of the terrain. 8_____ No matter how large a circle may be, it is finite. 4_____ The more we learned, the more we realized the finiteness of our knowledge. 1_____ Such a tiny house cannot possibly hold those finite pieces of furniture. 2_____ On clear nights the stars in the sky seem infinite in number. 7_____ It is hard for a finite mind to grasp the extent of the universe. 5_____ **Finite: 1** measuring instrument **2** great in number **3** endless **4** limited 3_____

YOUR SENTENCE: _____

_____

[1:r 2:w 3:4 4:r 5:r 6:w 7:r 8:w 9:r]

inconsiderable

(in′kən·sid′ər·ə·bəl) Trivial, petty, unimportant, or not worth consideration. Since his duties were *inconsiderable,* he was not paid a high salary.

Because it was inconsiderable, the small boy took very good care of his new wristwatch. 4_____ He is an inconsiderable fellow; we have never heard of him. 7_____ The computer that processed the club's mailing list functioned inconsiderably well. 9_____ As a result of the drought, the harvest was inconsiderable. 6_____ Dick was becoming a very self-centered boy, inconsiderable of everyone else. 2_____ Millicent grew up in an inconsiderable village fifty miles from the nearest town. 5_____ The fact that her savings were inconsiderable did not stop her from attending law school. 3_____ The liquid lost through evaporation was so inconsiderable as to make no difference. 8_____ **Inconsiderable: 1** exceptional **2** insignificant **3** too great to be counted **4** thoughtless 1_____

YOUR SENTENCE: _____

_____

[1:2 2:w 3:r 4:w 5:r 6:r 7:r 8:r 9:w]

77

parochial

(pə·rō′ki·əl) Narrow, provincial, restricted, or limited in range or scope. She disagreed with the *parochial* attitudes of her small-town neighbors.

You are probably already familiar with another meaning of *parochial:* relating to a church parish, as in "They sent their children to a *parochial* school."

The speaker, parochially Canadian in his views, could not understand the aims of other nations. 3_____ Only a parochial person could know and understand so much. 7_____ One role of international organizations is to overcome parochialism among individual nations. 9_____ He attacked the parochial mentality of the townspeople who shunned anyone and anything that was different. 6_____ The parochiality of her point of view suggested that she needed more experiences to broaden her horizons. 5_____ He was so parochial with his money that he was soon penniless. 4_____ Although he lived in cosmopolitan New York City, he was parochial in his outlook. 8_____ He worked late into the night and fortunately was able to accomplish a parochial amount of work. 1_____ **Parochial: 1** narrow **2** enormous **3** wasteful **4** broad 2_____

YOUR SENTENCE: _____

_____

[1:w   2:1   3:r   4:w   5:r   6:r   7:w   8:r   9:r]

integral

(in′tə·grəl) Essential to completeness, organically linked, or formed as a unit; or complete or lacking nothing essential. Music has become an *integral* part of her life.

[Latin *integer*, whole, untouched.] The same root appears in *integrate* and *integrity.*

Their ideas are too integral to be taken seriously. 2_____ Computers have become such an integral part of our culture that we would be lost without them. 5_____ In most good novels character and plot are integral with each other. 4_____ The School of Education and the experimental elementary school form an integral group. 7_____ Because the principal was so integral, no one questioned his uprightness. 1_____ The detective's discovery of the forgery was integral to the story's plot. 8_____ They worked integrally, each one at odds with the others. 3_____ The family was an integral unit in thought and action. 9_____ **Integral: 1** unimportant **2** essential or linked together **3** separate or apart **4** morally sound 6_____

YOUR SENTENCE: _____

_____

[1:w   2:w   3:w   4:r   5:r   6:2   7:r   8:r   9:r]

78

piecemeal

(pēs'mēl') Made or accomplished gradually or piece by piece. That book was written *piecemeal*, whenever the author had free time.

Piecemeal may be used as an adjective (*piecemeal* progress) or as an adverb (working *piecemeal*).

Piecemeal by nature, Mrs. Anderson would never get involved in a quarrel. 6_____ Because timber was scarce, he finished his cabin piecemeal. 2_____ She was against piecemeal reform; instead, she wanted complete and immediate change. 5_____ In order to keep from becoming bored by it, I did the research piecemeal. 7_____ Once he starts his piecemeal chattering, there is no stopping him. 8_____ The chickens thrived on the new brand of piecemeal. 4_____ The towering smokestack was torn down piecemeal. 3_____ The information was hard to locate and had to be assembled piecemeal. 9_____ **Piecemeal:** 1 continuous 2 animal food 3 harmonious 4 gradually 1_____

YOUR SENTENCE: _____

_____

[1:4 2:r 3:r 4:w 5:r 6:w 7:r 8:w 9:r]

sundry

(sun'dri) Various, several, or miscellaneous. He learned from *sundry* hints that he was to be promoted.

As a noun *sundries* (always used in the plural) refers to miscellaneous small articles or odds and ends, as in "The auctioneer sold all the *sundries* to a junk dealer." *All and sundry* means everyone collectively and individually.

Sundry persons have contributed a total of five thousand dollars. 7_____ Gale always chose the sundry pony if it was available. 5_____ Before he decided to specialize in chemistry, he took courses in sundry fields. 8_____ Her business had branched out into sundry operations. 1_____ Your paper is too vague; try to be more sundry in making your point. 9_____ He gave advice to all and sundry. 3_____ The little boy emptied his pockets of two marbles, a nail, chewing gum, a worm, and other sundries. 4_____ The day was hot and sundry. 2_____ **Sundry:** 1 specific 2 several 3 moist or damp 4 of many colors 6_____

YOUR SENTENCE: _____

_____

[1:r 2:w 3:r 4:r 5:w 6:2 7:r 8:r 9:w]

teem

(tēm) To abound, swarm, or be filled to overflowing. The lakes in our area *teem* with trout at this time of the year.

A related meaning of *teem* is to rain in torrents.

The teeming streets of Jerusalem fascinated him, for he had never seen so many people. 3 _____ He teemed it advisable to insure his house against theft as well as against fire. 5 _____ Paris teems with interesting things to see and do. 6 _____ By the time she left the meeting, many new ideas were teeming in her mind. 4 _____ The orchards teemed with rich, ripe fruit. 1 _____ Teemed together, they were sure that they could win the race. 9 _____ Because of the teeming rain, they were forced to remain indoors all day. 7 _____ Do you know the line by the poet Emma Lazarus: "The wretched refuse of your teeming shore"? 8 _____ **Teem: 1** think or believe **2** group together **3** overflow **4** confine 2 _____

YOUR SENTENCE: _____

_____

[1:r 2:3 3:r 4:r 5:w 6:r 7:r 8:r 9:w]

---

prevalent

(prev′ə·lənt) Widespread, or generally occurring, practiced, or accepted. That drafts cause colds is a *prevalent* belief but an inaccurate one.

[Latin *pre–*, before, above others, and *valens*, having power.] The same root appears in *value, evaluate,* and *invalid.* The closely related word *prevailing* shares the meanings of *prevalent* but can also mean being superior in strength or influence, as in "The *prevailing* power during the Middle Ages was that of the Church."

In her poetry she resisted the temptation to use phrases prevalent among other writers. 2 _____ The facts were not prevalent to the topic under discussion. 1 _____ Poverty is prevalent in many parts of the world. 6 _____ The prevalence of rumors at the outset of the war worried the government. 4 _____ Hindered by a prevalence of funds, they could not make plans for an expensive trip. 9 _____ The tourists tried to keep away from areas where yellow fever was prevalent. 5 _____ As a gesture of prevalence, they knelt before their queen. 7 _____ This custom is similar to customs that are prevalent in other parts of Europe. 3 _____ **Prevalent: 1** widespread **2** respectful **3** appropriate **4** scarce 8 _____

YOUR SENTENCE: _____

_____

[1:w 2:r 3:r 4:r 5:r 6:r 7:w 8:1 9:w]

copious

(kō′pi·əs) Plentiful or abundant. The farmers were overjoyed to discover a *copious* supply of water near their fields.

[Latin *copia*, abundant supply.]

We had difficulty in following the copious instructions that accompanied the pattern. 1_____
Wrapped in the copious folds of her cloak, she stepped out into the cold night air. 5_____ The term paper contained copious footnotes. 7_____ The copiousness of the contents of the picnic hamper put a sparkle in his eye. 4_____ I made a photostat of the document on the copious machine in the office.
6_____ Because food was in short supply, only copious rations could be distributed. 2_____
Rachel's copious vocabulary and thorough grasp of the English language enabled her to express herself perfectly. 3_____ The ballerina's execution of the dance step was absolutely copious. 9_____
Copious: **1** duplicating **2** meager **3** plentiful **4** faultless 8_____

YOUR SENTENCE: _____

_____

[1:r 2:w 3:r 4:r 5:r 6:w 7:r 8:3 9:w]

---

exorbitant

(eg·zôr′bə·tənt) Excessive, extravagant, or immoderate. Some airplanes use an *exorbitant* quantity of fuel during takeoffs.

[Latin *ex*, out of, and *orbita*, course, track; hence, departing from what is reasonable, proper, or normal.]

Outraged farmers protested against the exorbitance of the freight charges. 7_____ We were exorbitant over the success of our team. 1_____ Driven by exorbitant greed, the man was willing to steal. 2_____ The children's exorbitant demands angered their relatives. 9_____ The price of food has risen exorbitantly this year. 3_____ Instead of ranting and raving, try to exhibit exorbitant behavior. 8_____ They expressed their exorbitance for the performance by cheering and clapping.
6_____ If he continues to spend an exorbitant amount of time watching television, he will never get anything accomplished. 5_____ **Exorbitant:** **1** excessive **2** joyful **3** appreciative **4** reasonable 4_____

YOUR SENTENCE: _____

_____

[1:w 2:r 3:r 4:1 5:r 6:w 7:r 8:w 9:r]

tally

(tal'i) To count and record; the amount recorded; the record itself; or to agree or correspond.   Each judge will *tally* the points independently and hand his or her *tally* to the referee; if the scores *tally*, the *tally* for each player will be announced.

> These four meanings can be remembered from the origin of *tally*: a stick with notches cut on one side of it to record an amount to be paid. The stick was split lengthwise across the notches so that the buyer could keep one side, the seller the other side. If any question arose, the two sides could be fitted together so that the notches *tallied*. Hence *tally* meant (1) to cut the notches (to record the amount); (2) the amount indicated by the notches (the score); (3) either side of the stick, considered as a record; and (4) to agree or correspond (like the notches when the two sides were fitted together).

Do not tally after the movie; I want you home in time for dinner. 4 _____   Because they rarely make mistakes, their accounts never tally. 8 _____   This is the first time my checkbook does not tally with the bank statement. 6 _____   His story tallied with Arnold's. 3 _____   Please tally your expenses for the day. 5 _____   This instrument tallies the number of automobiles that use the road each day. 9 _____   Only a tally of students appeared at the football game. 2 _____   Denise made a tally of 180 for 36 holes of golf. 1 _____   **Tally:** **1** be in error **2** linger or delay **3** small number **4** record or agree 7 _____

YOUR SENTENCE: _____

_____

[1:r 2:w 3:r 4:w 5:r 6:r 7:4 8:w 9:r]

8 REVIEW EXERCISE

In each blank write a form of one of the words listed below. Use each word only once.

consummate	inconsiderable	piecemeal	tally
copious	integral	prevalent	teem
exorbitant	parochial	sundry	ultimate
finite			

Since the rental price was 3_____ , the young couple did not lease the apartment.

"Rome was not built in a day" means that important things are often accomplished 13_____ rather than all at once.

The game warden 6_____ the number of trout taken from the stream.

Before Alfred Chiang and Geraldo Kilsung 11 _____ their contract, they held several meetings with their lawyers.

Keep away from the swamp, for it 9_____ with mosquitoes.

We may never learn the 7_____ result of the foolish action.

The number of grains of sand on this beach is very large but nevertheless 1_____ .

All the youngsters helped themselves to apples, leaving an 5_____ amount of fruit in the barrel.

With that 8_____ supply of food, nobody at the banquet will go hungry.

Colds are 2_____ during the winter months.

We need people with broad rather than 4_____ viewpoints.

They looked forward to the 10_____ pleasures that awaited them at the county fair.

The use of large expanses of glass is an 12_____ part of modern architecture.

1: *finite*   2: *prevalent*   3: *exorbitant*   4: *parochial*   5: *inconsiderable*   6: *tallies*   7: *ultimate*
8: *copious*   9: *teems*   10: *sundry*   11: *consummated*   12: *integral*   13: *piecemeal*

FOR DICTIONARY STUDY

abound	multiplicity
amplitude	multitudinous
catholic	paltry
cosmopolitan	paucity
current	plenary
enumerate	plenitude
exhaustive	plethora
exiguous	prodigious
fractional	rife
fragmentary	scant
inappreciable	sparing
incalculable	sparse
infinitesimal	supererogatory
inordinate	supernumerary
intact	tell
lavish	thoroughgoing
lush	titanic
magnitude	ultra
manifold	voluminous
multifarious	

9 Shape, Position, Movement

A *labyrinth* is an intricate maze or a perplexing situation. A *facet* is a small, polished surface of a cut gem or any aspect of a many-sided object or person. A *pinnacle* is a high peak or the highest point in the development of anything. Note that each of these three words has a meaning that refers to an object and also an extended meaning that bears some resemblance to the object on which it is based.

A *protuberance* is a bulge or swelling. A *cleft* is a crack or crevice; something that is *cleft asunder* is split apart or into separate pieces. *Taut* means tightly drawn or firm. *Proximity* means nearness or closeness. *Incumbent* means resting upon a person as a duty or obligation; as a noun it means an officeholder. To *immure* is to imprison or confine or to seclude or isolate oneself. Its Latin root means to wall in.

To *gesticulate* is to express by gestures, such as waving the arms. To *palpitate* is to throb, quiver, or beat rapidly and strongly. To *plummet* is to drop sharply or fall straight downward.

The last three words share the idea of quick, easy movement: *dexterity* means expertness or skill; *agile* means nimble or spry; and *lithe* means nimbly graceful or bending easily.

---

labyrinth, facet, pinnacle, protuberance, cleft,
asunder, taut, proximity, incumbent, immure,
gesticulate, palpitate, plummet, dexterity, agile, lithe

---

labyrinth

(lab′ə·rinth) An intricate maze, or a complicated and perplexing situation.   Minos, a legendary king of Crete, had a *labyrinth* constructed in order to confine the Minotaur, a monster.

> A *labyrinth* is a structure with intricate passageways that make it difficult for one to find one's way; often it is a maze in a garden or park formed by confusing paths that are separated by high hedges. In a broader sense *labyrinth* can refer to something bewilderingly involved or complex.

He led his companions through the confusing labyrinths of the subway system. 7_____   The statue had been mounted on a short marble labyrinth. 4_____   Amy was lost in the labyrinthine plot of the novel. 2_____   She wandered for days through a labyrinth of uncertainty. 6_____   His rock collection contained many fine specimens of labyrinth. 9_____   Katherine made handcrafted jewelry of labyrinth and sterling silver. 8_____   The tourists made their way through the small labyrinth in the amusement park. 1_____   The park at Hampton Court is famous for its labyrinth, but the most complex in the world is at Versailles. 5_____   **Labyrinth: 1** ornament **2** many-colored rock **3** maze **4** base or pedestal 3_____

YOUR SENTENCE: _____

_____

[1:r   2:r   3:3   4:w   5:r   6:r   7:r   8:w   9:w]

---

facet

(fas′it) A small, polished surface of a cut gem; or any phase or aspect of a many-sided object or person. The best-liked *facet* of Jan's leadership was her eagerness to hear all points of view.

> [Latin *facies*, form, shape.] The same root appears in *face, facial,* and *superficial.*

Every facet of the newspaper business was known by the old editor. 9_____   The more facets a diamond has, the more it will sparkle. 3_____   This was one facet of the problem he had never dealt with before. 8_____   By facet agreement the women decided to meet in Florida. 7_____   People find him fascinating because of his many-faceted personality. 2_____   We admired the skill with which the jeweler faceted the gem. 6_____   In order to build a fire, the campers had brought along a facet. 4_____   The funny facets told by the comedian threw the group into gales of laughter. 1_____   **Facet: 1** bundle of sticks **2** phase or aspect **3** joke **4** silent or unspoken 5_____

YOUR SENTENCE: _____

_____

[1:w   2:r   3:r   4:w   5:2   6:r   7:w   8:r   9:r]

pinnacle

(pin'ə·kəl) A high peak, or the highest point in development. He stood in the desert and stared at three *pinnacles* of rock on the horizon.

In architecture, *pinnacle* refers to a small turret or spire.

The captain used a mechanical pinnacle to check the compass reading. 9_____ They looked in wonder at the pure white pinnacle of the Weisshorn Mountain. 1_____ The disappointing results of the examination plunged Nancy into the pinnacle of her school career. 8_____ They read about the men and women who had reached the pinnacles of their professions. 6_____ Receiving the Nobel Prize for peace represented the pinnacle of Ralphe Bunche's success. 7_____ Until they reach the pinnacle of the steep cliff, the mountain climbers will not be satisfied. 4_____ Passengers were carried from the liner to the shore in a pinnacle. 5_____ Even in summer the pinnacle of the mountain was covered with snow. 3_____ **Pinnacle:** 1 small boat 2 scientific instrument 3 lowest point 4 highest point 2_____

YOUR SENTENCE: _____

_____

[1:r 2:4 3:r 4:r 5:w 6:r 7:r 8:w 9:w]

protuberance

(prō·tü'bər·əns) A bulge or swelling, or something that protrudes or bulges. The *protuberance* on his leg was painful as well as unsightly.

[Latin *pro*, forward, and *tuber*, swelling.]

We could tell by the protuberance in the draperies that someone was lurking behind them. 7_____ Her coat was pulled out of shape by the protuberant package in her pocket. 6_____ Corporations are hiring many highly trained, protuberant men and women. 8_____ Continued medical treatments were required to reduce the protuberance on his neck. 9_____ The many protuberances that jutted out from the roof ruined the appearance of the house. 5_____ The astronomers studied the protuberances on the surface of the moon. 2_____ Cyrano de Bergerac is famous for his protuberant nose. 1_____ The judge was protuberant in her praise for the quality of the exhibits. 3_____ **Protuberance:** 1 bulge 2 lavish 3 intelligence 4 division 4_____

YOUR SENTENCE: _____

[1:r 2:r 3:w 4:1 5:r 6:r 7:r 8:w 9:r]

cleft

(kleft)   A crack, opening, or split.   A few blades of grass grew through a *cleft* in the rock.

Cleft may be used as a noun, adjective, or verb. As a verb it is a past tense or past participle of *cleave*, to split. A *cleft palate* is a *cleft* that runs from front to back along the middle of the roof of the mouth.

The veterinarian studied the cleft in the horse's hoof. 2 _____   The bitter argument left a permanent cleft in their relationship. 6 _____   Paula's extremely cleft movements made her a good tennis player. 3 _____   "O Hamlet! thou hast cleft my heart in twain." 4 _____   Finding the water contaminated left the travelers cleft of all hope. 8 _____   She placed a G cleft at the beginning of the musical staff. 5 _____   The cleft in my chin resembles a dimple. 9 _____   The bolt of lightning cleft the oak tree down the middle. 7 _____   **Cleft:**   **1** split   **2** deprived   **3** musical sign   **4** swift   1 _____

YOUR SENTENCE: _____

_____

[1:1   2:r   3:w   4:r   5:w   6:r   7:r   8:w   9:r]

asunder

(ə·sun′dər)   Into different parts or pieces; or apart or separate.   The lawyer felt that if his recommendations were ignored, the legal system of the state would be torn *asunder*.

Asunder may be used as an adjective or as an adverb.

Asunder to our home was a babbling brook in which we waded each afternoon. 8 _____   Taxation and representation are inseparably united; no parliament can put them asunder. 6 _____   With arms linked, the two friends walked asunder down the street. 9 _____   The new committee cast asunder all that we had worked to build. 7 _____   In his anger he tore his cloak asunder. 1 _____   The asundering applause rang through the auditorium. 4 _____   A mob, when taken asunder, may seem made of reasonable people, but when confused together, they become one great beast. 3 _____   Although the two candidates are of the same age and background, their political ideas are poles asunder. 5 _____   **Asunder:**   **1** bordering on   **2** apart   **3** together   **4** appreciative   2 _____

YOUR SENTENCE: _____

_____

[1:r   2:2   3:r   4:w   5:r   6:r   7:r   8:w   9:w]

taut

(tôt)   Tightly drawn or firm; tense; or neat or trim.   Are the sails *taut* enough?

> *Taut* usually refers to that which has been stretched and pulled out to the limit so that no slackness or looseness remains. It can also mean strict, severe, or well disciplined, as in "The captain ran a *taut* ship." The verb form of *taut* is *tauten.*

A wooden frame kept the yarn taut as the weavers worked. 4_____   The sailor tautened the ropes that braced the mast. 3_____   That frightening experience put an added strain upon our already taut nerves. 2_____   The president of the health club gave a taut lecture on nutrition. 8_____   The skin on her face seemed to be drawn back tautly. 5_____   Wandering about the field, the soldier fell into a taut hole full of debris. 1_____   Before the tennis game she checked the tautness of her racket strings. 7_____   They mocked and tauted the child until she cried. 9_____   **Taut: 1** academic **2** open or gaping **3** tightly drawn **4** ridicule 6_____

YOUR SENTENCE: _____

_____

[1:w 2:r 3:r 4:r 5:r 6:3 7:r 8:w 9:w]

proximity

(proks·im′ə·ti)   Nearness or closeness.   The professor's research was made easier by the *proximity* of her home to a good library.

> [Latin *proximus,* nearest.] The same root appears in *approximate,* coming near. Although *proximity* usually refers to nearness in space, it can occasionally refer to nearness in time.

The doctor gave the patient an antidote to cut down the effects of the proximity. 5_____   A deciding factor in their selection of the house was its proximity to good schools. 6_____   The proximity of the two events does not necessarily mean that one caused the other. 1_____   A proximity of rainfall caused numerous crop failures that year. 2_____   Because of its proximity to the sea, the town enjoys relatively mild summers. 9_____   Since he loved to see plays, Mr. Gonzalez insisted on proximity of his home to the theater district. 4_____   Because she could not attend the meeting, she was allowed to vote by proximity. 8_____   We are all delighted about the proximity of our town to a state park. 3_____   **Proximity: 1** poison **2** substitution **3** nearness **4** scarcity 7_____

YOUR SENTENCE: _____

_____

[1:r 2:w 3:r 4:r 5:w 6:r 7:3 8:w 9:r]

incumbent

(in·kum′bənt) Resting or falling upon a person as a duty or obligation. The guide felt it *incumbent* upon him to warn the travelers of the dangers of the trip.

> [Latin *in*, in, upon, and *–cumbens*, lying.] You have seen the same root in *succumb* (Section 5). *Incumbent*, which is followed by *in* or *upon*, occasionally means lying or pressing down on something in a physical sense. As a noun *incumbent* means a holder of office, as in "George Washington was the first *incumbent* of the United States Presidency."

He defeated the incumbent mayor in the election. 4_____   It is incumbent upon those in positions of responsibility to make wise decisions. 6_____   The Ecology Society will hold an incumbent debate on farming. 3_____   Can you name the incumbents in the Senate? 7_____   Incumbent in bed, I turned off the radio and went to sleep. 5_____   The boxes are incumbent, but we can lift them anyway. 2_____   Congresswoman Barbara Jordan felt it was incumbent upon her to express her views. 1_____   She doesn't feel any incumbency and is eager to address the meeting. 9_____

Incumbent: 1 shy 2 resting or falling upon 3 important 4 heavy 8_____

YOUR SENTENCE: _____

_____

[1:r 2:w 3:w 4:r 5:r 6:r 7:r 8:2 9:w]

immure

(i·mūr′) To imprison or confine, or to seclude or isolate oneself. The troops *immured* themselves in an isolated outpost.

> [Latin *im–*, in, and *murus*, wall.] The same root appears in *mural* and *intramural*. *Immure* can be used in the sense of confining someone within walls; or it can be used in the sense of shutting up as though within walls, as in "He *immured* himself in his books."

Students often have to immure themselves in the library on Saturday afternoons. 2_____   We saw in the paper that many packaged foods are immure. 5_____   The number of letters arriving daily was immure. 7_____   In the movie, the scientist was immured in a laboratory until she found the source of vitamin Z. 1_____   The jury was immured in a hotel until it reached a verdict. 8_____   We were immure and happy when we went dancing. 9_____   The prisoner had been immured for thirty years. 6_____   Don't immure yourself in your room; try to go out more. 3_____   **Immure:** 1 poison 2 imprison 3 fill with joy 4 overwhelm 4_____

YOUR SENTENCE: _____

_____

[1:r 2:r 3:r 4:2 5:w 6:r 7:w 8:r 9:w]

gesticulate

(jes·tik′ū·lāt) To use gestures, often while speaking; or to express by gestures.   When he is excited, he cannot talk without *gesticulating*.

> [Latin *gestus*, gesture.]

We often express ourselves more by gesticulations than by words. 7_____   Blockage prevented the water from gesticulating around the pipes. 5_____   The invalid was on a diet of poached eggs and fish because they are easy to gesticulate. 8_____   Some languages customarily involve more gesticulations than others. 9_____   Because Robert was hoarse, he could not gesticulate well that day. 2_____   Although he was gagged, he communicated his plight by gesticulating. 1_____   Angela gesticulated to the waiter for the bill. 6_____   Skilled gesticulators can communicate complicated ideas without speaking. 4_____   **Gesticulate: 1** absorb easily **2** express clearly **3** move freely **4** express by gestures 3_____

YOUR SENTENCE: _____

_____

[1:r 2:w 3:4 4:r 5:w 6:r 7:r 8:w 9:r]

---

palpitate

(pal′pə·tāt) To throb or quiver; or to beat rapidly and strongly.   Her heart *palpitates* whenever she is frightened.

> [Latin *palpitare*, to flutter.] Although *palpitate* is used especially to refer to an abnormally rapid heartbeat, it can also refer to other throbbing or quivering movements.

The program palpitated in the presentation of awards. 5_____   The sights and sounds of the huge foreign city made her palpitate with excitement. 3_____   The dancers moved furiously to the palpitating rhythm of the bongo drums. 2_____   Becoming alarmed, she consulted a physician about her frequent heart palpitations. 7_____   When he saw the enemy, his body palpitated with terror. 8_____   His excuses did little to palpitate his faults. 6_____   The painting provided palpitating evidence of her artistic skill. 4_____   A sudden palpitation proved that the wounded man was still alive. 9_____   **Palpitate: 1** come to an end **2** throb **3** hide **4** be obvious 1_____

YOUR SENTENCE: _____

_____

[1:2 2:r 3:r 4:w 5:w 6:w 7:r 8:r 9:r]

91

plummet

(plum′it) To drop sharply and abruptly or to fall straight downward. Shortly after the explosion the plane *plummeted* to the ground.

> As a noun *plummet* usually refers to a weight (commonly called a *plumb bob*) that is attached to a line and that is used to determine the depth of water or the straightness of a wall.

As it sat perched on a tree branch, the owl ruffled its plummets. 5 _____   News of the president's illness caused the stock market to plummet. 1 _____   It is better to let your pride plummet than to let your temper rise. 4 _____   The boy was as proud as a peacock as he plummeted around the neighborhood in his new cowboy outfit. 2 _____   Giving no warning at all, huge hailstones suddenly plummeted down. 3 _____   Mr. Roy plummeted on the door until we opened it. 7 _____   The pebble I dropped went plummeting down the mountain. 9 _____   Within a few years the actor's career plummeted from success to failure. 6 _____   **Plummet:** **1** feather **2** strut or swagger **3** drop sharply **4** rap or knock 8 _____

YOUR SENTENCE: _____

_____

[1:r   2:w   3:r   4:r   5:w   6:r   7:w   8:3   9:r]

dexterity

(deks·ter′ə·ti) Expertness or skill in using one's hands or one's mind. Her *dexterity* as a factory worker led to a rapid promotion.

> [Latin *dexter,* of or situated on the right.] The adjective form of *dexterity* is *dexterous* or *dextrous.* *Ambidextrous* means equally skilled with both hands.

Performing dexterously, she completed the operation in an hour. 5 _____   Because of her dexterity in debating, no one is a match for her. 2 _____   By showing extreme dexterity toward her responsibilities, she failed the entire group. 7 _____   Since my dexterity is not very keen, I would rather not handle the fragile glassware. 3 _____   He suddenly sank into a dexterous, melancholy mood. 6 _____   With a dexterous turn of the wrist, she threw her attacker onto the ground. 1 _____   His mental dexterity enables him to come up with many witty statements. 4 _____   Karl Czerny wrote a series of piano exercises designed to improve finger dexterity. 9 _____   **Dexterity:** **1** skill **2** despondence **3** carelessness **4** awkwardness 8 _____

YOUR SENTENCE: _____

_____

[1:r   2:r   3:r   4:r   5:r   6:w   7:w   8:1   9:r]

agile

(aj′əl) Nimble, spry, or quick and easy in movement or thought.   Leaping about the fields, Rina seemed as *agile* as a gazelle.

[Latin *agilis*, nimble.]

Staggering agilely and slowly to his feet, the boxer dragged himself to his corner. 5_____   The children bounded from tree to tree with agility. 4_____   The sun setting over the still waters left an impression of peace and agility. 3_____   With his agile mind, he had no trouble at all in solving the difficult set of puzzles. 1_____   In childhood both mind and body are nimble; they can frisk about with wonderful agility. 6_____   Her quick response pointed to the agility of her mind. 8_____   Thomas is too agile to participate in athletics. 2_____   Agilely skipping from rock to rock, Teresa made her way across the stream. 7_____   **Agile: 1** nimble or quick   **2** clumsy or awkward   **3** lazy   **4** serene 9_____

YOUR SENTENCE: _____

_____

[1:r   2:w   3:w   4:r   5:w   6:r   7:r   8:r   9:1]

lithe

(līᵷH) Agile, nimbly graceful, or bending easily.   No one in the audience failed to appreciate the grace of the *lithe* ballerina.

Moving quickly, the cat jumped lithely across the room. 4_____   The lithe motion of the swimmer made diving look simple. 1_____   The lithe trapeze artist swung easily from one bar to another. 6_____   Compared with the lithe motions of the professional ballplayer, the movements of the amateur seemed very clumsy. 9_____   After the heavy rainstorm the ground was too lithe for cars to pass over it easily. 3_____   For many years she has paid an annual lithe to her church. 8_____   A palette knife is a slim blade of lithe metal. 5_____   If you want something lithe to eat, try cottage cheese and fruit. 2_____   **Lithe: 1** tax or payment   **2** nourishing   **3** soggy   **4** graceful 7_____

YOUR SENTENCE: _____

_____

[1:r   2:w   3:w   4:r   5:r   6:r   7:4   8:w   9:r]

9 REVIEW EXERCISE

In each blank write a form of one of the words listed below. Use each word only once.

agile	facet	labyrinth	plummet
asunder	gesticulate	lithe	protuberance
cleft	immure	palpitate	proximity
dexterity	incumbent	pinnacle	taut

At the time of the French Revolution, only seven prisoners were 2 _____ in the French prison, the Bastille.

Mona watched the diamond cutter polish the 5 _____ of the gem to increase its beauty.

Their long journey took them through a confusing 8 _____ of swamps and bogs.

Over millions of years, the wind had cut a deep 11 _____ into the mountain.

Their beliefs were as wide 1 _____ as the North and South Poles.

Elizabeth Agassiz reached the 4 _____ of her career as president of Radcliffe College.

As Muriel talked excitedly, she 12 _____ with her hands.

The 7 _____ of their homes made it easy for the two friends to see each other frequently.

During the period of depression, prices of consumer goods 13 _____ sharply.

The sails were 15 _____ before we began our trip, but now they are loose.

Violent exercise may produce abnormally fast 9 _____ of the heart.

After the accident Judy had a very noticeable 16 _____ on her forehead.

She felt it 14 _____ upon her to respond to the critical review.

We saw her coming down the slope like some wild, 6 _____ creature with a sure sense for moving correctly.

Their 10 _____ bodies moved gracefully to the sound of the music.

Magicians rely on the 3 _____ of their hands to fool their audiences.

1: *asunder*   2: *immured*   3: *dexterity*   4: *pinnacle*   5: *facets*   6: *agile, lithe*   7: *proximity*
8: *labyrinth*   9: *palpitations*   10: *lithe, agile*   11: *cleft*   12: *gesticulated*   13: *plummeted*
14: *incumbent*   15: *taut*   16: *protuberance*

FOR DICTIONARY STUDY

abyss	juxtaposed
acme	lissome
adjacent	malleable
adroit	nadir
apex	oscillate
chasm	pantomime
circuitous	phase
circumscribe	pliable
concave	projection
conterminous	propinquity
convex	protrusion
deft	pulsate
ductile	resilient
excrescence	sinuous
fissure	spry
hiatus	superimpose
impound	supple
incarcerate	tortuous
intern	tremor
intricate	vertex
involution	zenith

10 Start, Stop

Only the first two words in this section share the idea of starting; the remainder are all connected in one way or another with stopping. The *genesis* of anything is its beginning, and a *novice* is a beginner.

The next three words are alike in that they involve stopping oneself; the others all involve stopping something or someone else. To *abstain* is to avoid doing something (such as smoking). *Abnegation* is the giving up of a right, belief, or idea. To *recant* is to declare publicly that one no longer holds a belief or policy that one has formerly expressed: in other words, to take back something one has said.

A *breach* is the breaking of a law, promise, or obligation (such as a *breach* of contract) or the breaking of friendly relations. To *obviate* is to make unnecessary or to prevent; the root sense is to clear out of the way.

Deter and *debar* share the meaning of keeping others from doing something. To *deter* is to prevent by fear of unpleasant consequences; to *debar* is to prevent by some sort of barrier, such as a rule or requirement.

To *rescind* is to cancel, repeal, or make void (as in *rescinding* a contract or a license). To *raze* is to destroy some physical object completely, often to level it to the ground. A *cessation* of anything is a stopping or discontinuance. *Oblivion* is forgetfulness or the condition of being entirely forgotten.

---

genesis, novice, abstain, abnegation, recant,
breach, obviate, deter, debar, rescind, raze,
cessation, oblivion

---

genesis

(jen'ə·sis)   The origin, creation, or beginning of something.   English had its *genesis* in ancient Indo-European roots.

> [Greek and Latin *gen–*, to give birth, produce.] When *Genesis* is capitalized, it refers to the first book of the Old Testament, the account of the Creation. The plural form is *geneses.*

Anthropologists often study the genesis of the traditions of various cultures. 1 _____   To greet the parishioners, the minister paused in the genesis of the church. 7 _____   The battery ran down because the genesis was not working. 8 _____   His troubles had their genesis in the mistake he made years ago. 5 _____   Under her microscope the scientist studied the genesis of bacterial growth. 9 _____   A genesis of applause greeted the actor. 3 _____   Henry Ford's simple workshop was the genesis of a whole new industry. 4 _____   The genesis of our concepts of democracy can be traced to the ancient Greeks. 2 _____   **Genesis:** **1** entry hall **2** origin **3** abundance **4** machine 6 _____

YOUR SENTENCE: _____

_____

[1:r   2:r   3:w   4:r   5:r   6:2   7:w   8:w   9:r]

---

novice

(nov'is)   A beginner or one who has no training or experience in a specific field.   The troops were *novices* at guerrilla warfare.

> [Latin *novus,* new.] The same root appears in *novel, novelty, innovate,* and *renovate. Novice* also refers to a person on probation in a religious order before taking final vows or to a recent convert (especially to Christianity). The related word *novitiate* refers either to the state of being a *novice* or to the period of probation of a religious *novice.*

It is often difficult to distinguish between the novice in crime and the confirmed criminal. 8 _____ Since he was a novice, he knew all there was to know about the company. 1 _____   His mother's objections put a novice to his plans. 7 _____   Because she was a novice at fishing, her first day's catch was not very large. 2 _____   Although Lena was still a novice at her trade, her work was skillful. 4 _____   Are you a novice at writing, or have you had your work published? 5 _____   With a graceful movement the mountain goat leaped over the deep novice in the cliff. 3 _____   The eerie sounds coming from his trombone labeled John as a novice in music. 6 _____   **Novice:** **1** beginner **2** split or opening **3** end **4** old-timer 9 _____

YOUR SENTENCE: _____

_____

[1:w   2:r   3:w   4:r   5:r   6:r   7:w   8:r   9:1]

abstain

(ab·stān′) To refrain from or to withhold oneself from participation in.   Vegetarians *abstain* from eating meat.

> [Latin *abstinere*, to withhold, from *abs–*, from, and *tenere*, to hold.] *Abstain* implies a deliberate self-denial or nonparticipation. The adjective form is *abstinent*, the noun form *abstinence* or *abstention*. *Abstainer* usually refers to one who refrains from drinking alcoholic beverages.

I decided to abstain from watching television for a week. 5 _____   You are abstinent if you do not agree with us. 9 _____   Abstinence is the opposite of overindulgence. 3 _____   Bernard abstained from expressing an opinion. 6 _____   To abstain your strength, you must eat more protein. 8 _____   While they were in training, the athletes had to abstain from smoking. 7 _____   There were five votes for the measure, three against it, and two abstentions. 1 _____   They abstained with the money and disappeared. 2 _____   **Abstain: 1** make greater **2** refrain from **3** run off **4** be stubborn 4 _____

YOUR SENTENCE: _____

_____

[1:r   2:w   3:r   4:2   5:r   6:r   7:r   8:w   9:w]

abnegation

(ab′nə·gā′shən) A renunciation or surrender of a right, belief, idea, pleasure, etc.   The old couple resigned themselves to *abnegation* of almost all social activities.

> [Latin *ab*, from, and *negatus*, refused, denied.] The same root appears in *negative* and *deny*. *Abnegation* very often refers to self-denial, as in "The monk lived a life of *abnegation*."

Vegetarians abnegate the custom of eating meat for both moral and health reasons. 4 _____   How can a man or a woman abnegate the possibility of success by not trying? 6 _____   She was totally unmoved by all the jeering abnegations shouted at her. 2 _____   When she entered politics, she abnegated her right to a private life. 8 _____   The author abnegated his latest book to his mother. 9 _____   Berkowitz lived a life of luxury and self-abnegation. 3 _____   The committee members were critized for their abnegation of the doctrines of the organization. 1 _____   The hermit abnegated wordly pleasures. 5 _____   **Abnegation: 1** denial or surrender **2** dedication **3** enjoyment or pleasure **4** criticism 7 _____

YOUR SENTENCE: _____

_____

[1:r   2:w   3:w   4:r   5:r   6:r   7:1   8:r   9:w]

recant

(ri·kant′) To withdraw or renounce publicly a statement or belief one has formerly held. Sometimes candidates are forced by political pressure to *recant* some of their statements.

> [Latin *re–*, back, and *cantus*, chanting, singing; hence, to take back one's words.] You have seen this root in *incantation* (Section 5).

Galileo was forced to recant his belief that the earth revolves around the sun. 9 _____ Some people will recant their opinions whenever it is convenient. 5 _____ The newscaster gave a recanting of the day's events. 2 _____ Under pressure from environmentalists, some of the nominees for governor recanted their earlier views. 6 _____ Because of a busy schedule, she had to recant the invitation to speak. 3 _____ The public demanded a recantation by the executives of statements they had made. 1 _____ The ambassador said she had been recanted to Paris for talks. 7 _____ Did the witnesses recant what they had said in court yesterday? 8 _____ **Recant:** 1 send back 2 renounce or withdraw 3 refuse 4 recount 4 _____

YOUR SENTENCE: _____

_____

[1:r 2:w 3:w 4:2 5:r 6:r 7:w 8:r 9:r]

breach

(brēch) A breaking or violating of a law, promise, or duty; or a breaking of friendly relations. The public announcement of our confidential statements represents a *breach* of trust.

> You are probably familiar with the phrase *breach of contract,* a legal term. *Breach* can also refer to an actual gap or opening that is made by breaking something, as in "The blow caused a *breach* of the skin." Do not confuse *breach* with *breech,* the under or back part of something.

A trivial argument can often cause a breach between friends. 5 _____ Their crossing the border constituted a breach of the treaty. 1 _____ Medieval physicians used live breaches to bleed patients. 8 _____ His kind gesture helped to heal the breach that had existed between the two families. 7 _____ The sailors breached the ship's bottom of shells and seaweed. 2 _____ If the builder does not complete the work on time, Diane will sue for breach of contract. 6 _____ It was not breach of duty that kept me home; it was illness. 9 _____ Nothing but a breach could remove the stain once it had set. 3 _____ **Breach:** 1 break 2 bloodsucker 3 get rid of 4 chemical 4 _____

YOUR SENTENCE: _____

_____

[1:r 2:w 3:w 4:1 5:r 6:r 7:r 8:w 9:r]

obviate

(ob′vi·āt) To make unnecessary or to prevent by effective measures. The arrival of the letter *obviated* the need for a visit.

Careful planning now may obviate mistakes later on. 6_____ The attorneys came to an out-of-court settlement, obviating a trial. 1_____ I obviated the crystal until it shone. 7_____ Can you obviate the reason why the judge announced her decision today? 2_____ Boxing Day is obviated in England and Wales on December 26. 4_____ The quick reaction of the pilot and the copilot obviated disaster. 8_____ A single agency might do much to obviate confusion in government policy. 3_____ Fresh fruit should be washed or peeled to obviate any health hazard. 5_____ **Obviate:** **1** polish **2** prevent **3** understand **4** celebrate 9_____

YOUR SENTENCE: _____

_____

[1:r 2:w 3:r 4:w 5:r 6:r 7:w 8:r 9:2]

deter

(di·ter′) To discourage or prevent someone from action through fear or other unpleasant circumstances or consequences. Because they feared the consequences, they were *deterred* from taking action.

[Latin *de*, from, and *terrere*, to frighten badly.] The same root appears in *terror, terrify,* and *terrible.*

It is not easy for a liar to escape deterrent by his friends. 9_____ The heavy undercurrent deterred them from swimming too far from shore. 8_____ Are we to deter from that remark that you do not care to join us? 4_____ Threatening weather deterred us from going on a camping trip. 3_____ His severity had a deterring effect: no one dared to oppose him. 1_____ Fear of punishment often acts as a deterrent to crime. 5_____ Until permanent provisions could be made, the displaced persons were deterred in a temporary camp. 6_____ The householder hoped that her wolfhound would deter intruders. 2_____ **Deter:** **1** figure out **2** confine **3** discourage **4** discover 7_____

YOUR SENTENCE: _____

_____

[1:r 2:r 3:r 4:w 5:r 6:w 7:3 8:r 9:w]

debar

(di·bär′) To exclude, deprive, or prohibit; or to prevent an action. Government contractors are *debarred* from holding public offices through which they might obtain contracts.

> [Latin *de*, from, and French *barre*, piece of wood that serves to obstruct.] The same root appears in *barrier*, *barricade*, and *embargo*. Although *debar* can occasionally mean to obstruct with a physical object (like a bar), as in "A gate *debarred* the passage to the first-class quarters," it more often means to exclude by a rule, requirement, etc.

The passengers prepared to debar from the plane. 2_____   Rigid qualifications for membership in the club debar most applicants. 1_____   A shortage of funds debars him from many social activities. 5_____   She deeply resented her debarment from amateur sports. 3_____   The state senator debarred the rumor that she would run for Congress. 9_____   After his dismissal he was debarred from the factory grounds. 4_____   Its unfair employment policy debarred the company from receiving government contracts. 7_____   He felt weak and feeble as a result of the debarring effect of the drug. 8_____   **Debar: 1** exclude or prevent **2** deny or reject **3** leave **4** weaken 6_____

YOUR SENTENCE: _____

_____

[1:r   2:w   3:r   4:r   5:r   6:1   7:r   8:w   9:w]

rescind

(ri·sind′) To annul, cancel, repeal, or make void. After continued pressure the State Senate *rescinded* the unpopular law.

> [Latin *re–*, back, and *scindere*, to tear, cut.] *Rescind* usually refers to the abolishing of laws, orders, permits, contracts, etc.

She indicated her rescindment of his action by refusing to talk to him. 7_____   The rescindment of the statute was to become effective at the beginning of the new year. 2_____   After he had committed numerous traffic violations, his driver's license was rescinded. 3_____   In his weakness the parolee rescinded by stealing once more. 6_____   Heavy rain made it necessary to rescind the driveway. 4_____   Either the seller or the buyer can rescind the contract within thirty days. 1_____   Since the law no longer applied, it was rescinded by the town council. 9_____   Because Ms. Schelling suspected fraud, she rescinded her order. 5_____   **Rescind: 1** start again **2** fall back **3** show displeasure **4** annul or repeal 8_____

YOUR SENTENCE: _____

_____

[1:r   2:r   3:r   4:w   5:r   6:w   7:w   8:4   9:r]

raze

(rāz) To destroy, demolish, or tear down completely.   Many houses had to be *razed* to make room for the new highway.

> [French *raser*, to shave, scrape.] The same root appears in *razor*. *Raze* usually implies leveling a structure to the ground, either by sudden destruction or by an orderly wrecking process. It is applied only to material objects, not to people or ideas.

The hurricane razed many homes along the New England coast. 4＿＿＿＿   Using bitter language, he mercilessly razed his former friend. 7＿＿＿＿   The vandals had planned to raze the sanctuary. 8＿＿＿＿   Enemy gunfire razed the upper decks of the warship. 3＿＿＿＿   Thoroughly razed by the delightful play, we watched it in enthralled silence. 2＿＿＿＿   The soldiers razed the Norman castle. 1＿＿＿＿   The governor planned to raze the old state prison and to erect a new one in its place. 5＿＿＿＿   Before the duke could attack, he needed to raze a larger army. 9＿＿＿＿   **Raze:** **1** move emotionally **2** gather **3** destroy **4** insult 6＿＿＿＿

YOUR SENTENCE: ＿＿＿＿＿＿＿＿＿＿＿＿＿＿＿＿＿＿＿＿＿＿＿＿＿＿＿＿＿＿＿＿＿＿＿＿＿＿

＿＿

[1:r 2:w 3:r 4:r 5:r 6:3 7:w 8:r 9:w]

cessation

(se·sā'shən) A stopping, pausing, or discontinuance.   The citizens looked forward to the *cessation* of hostilities between the warring groups.

> [Latin *cessatus*, ceased.] The same root appears in *cease* and *incessant*. *Cessation* can refer to either a final or a temporary stopping.

Boxing gloves have replaced the cessations worn by Roman boxers. 8＿＿＿＿   Labor Day marks the cessation of the summer holiday. 5＿＿＿＿   The truce called for a temporary cessation of fighting. 3＿＿＿＿   The cessation of eleven states from the Union preceded the War Between the States. 4＿＿＿＿   A serious accident led to a cessation of traffic for two hours. 1＿＿＿＿   Some people believe that the cessation of the earth's rotation would send us all into space. 2＿＿＿＿   When one has worked for fifty years, it may be difficult to adjust to a cessation of activity. 9＿＿＿＿   When he took off the tight bandage, he felt a tingling cessation in his arm. 6＿＿＿＿   **Cessation:** **1** stop **2** feeling **3** breaking away **4** protective glove 7＿＿＿＿

YOUR SENTENCE: ＿＿＿＿＿＿＿＿＿＿＿＿＿＿＿＿＿＿＿＿＿＿＿＿＿＿＿＿＿＿＿＿＿＿＿＿＿＿

＿＿

[1:r 2:r 3:r 4:w 5:r 6:w 7:1 8:w 9:r]

oblivion

(əb·liv′i·ən) Forgetfulness or unawareness; or the condition of being entirely forgotten. The tired traveler longed for the *oblivion* brought by sleep.

The adjective form *oblivious*, forgetful or unaware, is followed by *of* or *to*.

Wilson stood dazed in the middle of Times Square, oblivious to the crowds that surrounded him. 3_____ We tried to bury our unhappy memories in oblivion. 5_____ The wrecking crew estimated that it would take two weeks to make the building oblivious. 4_____ The priest was grateful for our generous oblivion to the church. 1_____ The professor was frequently oblivious of what was going on around her. 7_____ White marble pillars graced the oblivion of the main building. 6_____ In his state of oblivion, he could no longer remember all the events that had led to the catastrophe. 9_____ The defeated candidate refused to accept political oblivion. 8_____

Oblivion: **1** entrance **2** offering **3** forgetfulness **4** removal 2_____

YOUR SENTENCE: _____

_____

[1:w 2:3 3:r 4:w 5:r 6:w 7:r 8:r 9:r]

10 REVIEW EXERCISE

In each blank write a form of one of the words listed below. Use each word only once.

abnegation	debar	novice	raze
abstain	deter	oblivion	recant
breach	genesis	obviate	rescind
cessation			

The 3 _____ in cooking had never prepared a complete meal on her own.

Ten years ago she was an internationally famous star, but now no one remembers her and she has sunk into 7 _____ .

The doctor was 10 _____ from practicing medicine when the investigating medical board found him incompetent.

A great part of the city was 2 _____ by a single earthquake.

By studying for an hour each day, Susan 9 _____ the need for cramming the night before the examination.

None of your threats can 13 _____ us from doing what we think is right.

Several million people 12 _____ from voting in the last presidential election.

Daisy felt quite relieved after the 5 _____ of pain.

A team of medical specialists studied the 1 _____ of the disease.

When he married Wallis Warfield Simpson, the Duke of Windsor 6 _____ his right to the British throne.

If you break your promise, you will be accused of a 4 _____ of faith.

Although he was tortured, he refused to 8 _____ his religious beliefs.

The colonel was unwilling to 11 _____ his harsh order.

1: *genesis* 2: *razed* 3: *novice* 4: *breach* 5: *cessation* 6: *abnegated* 7: *oblivion* 8: *recant*
9: *obviates* 10: *debarred* 11: *rescind* 12: *abstained* 13: *deter*

FOR DICTIONARY STUDY

abdicate

abjure

annihilate

avert

commence

countermand

delete

demolition

devastate

disbar

disclaim

dissolution

efface

enjoin

eradicate

exordium

extinction

extinguish

extirpate

forbear

forswear

inaugurate

inception

incipience

inhibit

initiate

injunction

neophyte

nullify

obliterate

relinquish

renounce

repeal

retract

revoke

suspend

terminate

tyro

veto

11 Develop, Spread, Change

The root sense of *ramification* is branching out: something (like the topic for an essay) that first appears to be one thing turns out to have many parts, subdivisions, consequences, or extensions. To *reverberate* is to resound or re-echo. To *garner* is to collect, accumulate, or gather up and store. To *assimilate* is to absorb or digest (food, ideas, etc.).

The next three words share the idea of spreading: to *infuse* means to pour into or to inspire; to *permeate* is to penetrate and spread throughout; to *satiate* is to fill up with more than enough so as to weary or disgust.

To *supplant* is to take the place of or to replace with something else. To *detract* is to take away from or to diminish in importance or value. To *enhance* is almost the opposite: it means to heighten, increase, or intensify.

To *rejuvenate* is to make young or vigorous again, whereas to *regress* is to grow worse, decline, or move backward. To *adulterate* is to make something impure or inferior by putting something of little value into it or by cutting down or taking out some valuable ingredient. To *partition* is to divide into parts; a *partition* is something (such as a wall) that divides another thing (such as a room) into separate parts.

---

ramification, reverberate, garner, assimilate, infuse,
permeate, satiate, supplant, detract, enhance,
rejuvenate, regress, adulterate, partition

---

ramification

(ram'ə·fə·kā'shən) An outgrowth, subdivision, consequence, or branching out. His mind brooded on all the *ramifications* of the philosopher's remark.

> [Latin *ramificare*, to branch out, from *ramus*, branch, and *facere*, to make.] In biology, *ramification* refers to an actual branch or offshoot from a main stock, as in "The charts showed the *ramifications* of the artery." *Ramification,* however, is now chiefly used to mean an extension of a basically simple idea or problem.

An inquiry into the field of modern art ramifies in many directions. 6_____ Let us stick to the main point and ignore all the ramifications for the time being. 8_____ The ramification of the crowd was music to her ears. 1_____ Swerving away from the ramification, the car went into a spin. 9_____ The cold war between East and West was a ramification of World War II. 4_____ It is evident that the committee must ramify itself to discussing only one issue at each meeting. 5_____ The plan has many far-reaching ramifications. 2_____ It is impossible to foresee now what all the ramifications of space travel will be. 3_____ **Ramification:** **1** boundary wall **2** outgrowth or consequence **3** praise or applause **4** limit 7_____

YOUR SENTENCE: _____

_____

[1:w 2:r 3:r 4:r 5:w 6:r 7:2 8:r 9:w]

---

reverberate

(ri·vėr'bər·āt) To resound or re-echo; or to reflect light or heat. The sound of the cannons *reverberated* throughout the countryside.

> Although *reverberate* is most often used of sounds, it can also be used of light, heat, etc.

The signpost indicated that they would have to reverberate and go in the opposite direction. 5_____ As they walked through the tunnel, they heard the sound of their voices reverberating. 6_____ The light was reverberated in the mirror. 2_____ They reverberated the night away in a festive, riotous manner. 3_____ The reverberant drums of the band could be heard in the hall. 9_____ Edgar's arm was less painful as a result of the reverberating effect of the medication. 4_____ The reverberation of their voices kept her awake all night. 8_____ The room was so reverberatory that we could not concentrate on our work. 7_____ **Reverberate:** **1** heal **2** waste **3** turn or reverse **4** resound or reflect 1_____

YOUR SENTENCE: _____

_____

[1:4 2:r 3:w 4:w 5:w 6:r 7:r 8:r 9:r]

garner

(gär′nər) To collect, accumulate, or gather up and store. I *garnered* information for my study from many sources.

> [Latin *granum,* seed.] The original meaning of *garner* was to gather and deposit seeds in a granary; *garner* still retains this meaning but by extension can also refer to any accumulating or storing away.

The chef garnered the fish with parsley. 3_____   In his nervousness he gave a garnered report that no one could understand. 1_____   Going from house to house, the candidate tried to garner votes from every possible source. 8_____   Whenever the movie star appears in public, his primary interest is in garnering publicity for himself. 7_____   The farmer had not yet garnered the crops. 5_____   The children filled an entire bucket with the garnerings of their trip to the seashore. 2_____   Buddy tried to garner his toad for two marbles and a peashooter. 6_____   She had garnered precious memories in her heart. 4_____   **Garner:** **1** exchange **2** decorate **3** mutilate **4** gather 9_____

YOUR SENTENCE: _____

_____

[1:w   2:r   3:w   4:r   5:r   6:w   7:r   8:r   9:4]

assimilate

(ə·sim′ə·lāt) To take up and make part of itself, or to absorb and incorporate. The body *assimilates* food.

> [Latin *assimilatus,* made similar, from *ad,* to, and *similis,* similar.] *Assimilate* can also mean to make something resemble something else, as in "The poor reader keeps from *assimilating* (absorbing) a new idea by *assimilating* it to (thinking it is the same as) an idea the reader already has."

The United States has assimilated people of many different nationalities. 5_____   The deranged youth attempted to assimilate the king. 7_____   In the process of assimilation they grew to love their new country. 3_____   The speaker presented more material than the students could assimilate. 2_____   Plants assimilate carbon dioxide for growth. 9_____   The president offered the earthquake victims assimilation in the form of surplus food. 1_____   We will have to assimilate the proposal, since it is too impractical. 4_____   The young woman assimilated a great deal of knowledge during her travels. 8_____   **Assimilate:** **1** reject **2** aid **3** put an end to **4** absorb 6_____

YOUR SENTENCE: _____

_____

[1:w   2:r   3:r   4:w   5:r   6:4   7:w   8:r   9:r]

infuse

(in·fūz') To pour into or fill; or to introduce, instill, or inspire. The success of the project can be attributed to the fact that the leader *infused* inspiration into the workers.

> [Latin *in*, into, and *fusus*, poured.] The same root appears in *fuse, confuse, refuse,* and *transfusion*. *Infuse* usually implies introducing one thing into another in order to give it new life, vigor, or significance. *Infuse* can also mean to soak something in a liquid so as to extract certain qualities, as in "To make tea, *infuse* the tea leaves in boiling water."

The principal infused over the problem for days before he came to a decision. 7_____ After new courage had been infused into them, the soldiers fought tirelessly. 4_____ Going to the concerts infused a passion for classical music into her. 3_____ He infused the spirit of his time into his poetry. 2_____ Within a few weeks Lila had infused quite a lot of money. 1_____ Before he selected the one he wanted, he infused through many library books. 8_____ The minister was able to bring an infusion of hope to the congregation. 9_____ They became infused with the feeling that they were at the mercy of blind economic forces. 5_____ **Infuse: 1** fill or inspire **2** add to **3** glance over **4** ponder or consider 6_____

YOUR SENTENCE: _____

_____

[1:w 2:r 3:r 4:r 5:r 6:1 7:w 8:w 9:r]

---

permeate

(pèr'mi·āt) To penetrate or spread throughout. A feeling of joy *permeated* the entire group.

> [Latin *per*, through, and *meare*, to pass, go.]

The monument was designed to permeate the memory of those killed in action. 7_____ A pleasant fragrance of roses permeated her living room. 1_____ Shall we permeate our subscription after this issue? 6_____ Dante's *Divine Comedy* is permeated with the spirit of courtly love. 5_____ Although the manufacturer claimed that the fabric was impermeable by water, the rain soaked through it within a few minutes. 8_____ Jessica Peixotto's goal was the permeation of ideas of reform throughout the country. 2_____ It was clear to everyone that Allen had permeated the act of kindness. 9_____ An atmosphere of trust and goodwill permeated the organization. 4_____ **Permeate: 1** spread throughout **2** cancel **3** commit **4** keep from forgetting 3_____

YOUR SENTENCE: _____

_____

[1:r 2:r 3:1 4:r 5:r 6:w 7:w 8:r 9:w]

satiate

(sā′shi·āt) To satisfy with more than enough so as to weary or disgust. She so loved sweet things that no amount of candy could *satiate* her.

> [Latin *satis*, enough.] The same root appears in *satisfy*. *Satiate* originally meant to satisfy fully or gratify completely. It still retains this meaning occasionally but more often refers to overindulging to the point where all pleasure or desire is lost. The noun form is either *satiation* or *satiety* (sə·tī′ə·ti).

The child was given so many toys that he grew satiated and had no interest in any of them. 3_____
When questioned by the police, he satiated all knowledge of the incident. 7_____ She hoped her mother would not satiate which record she could buy. 2_____ He monopolized the conversation until people, satiated with his views, began to drift away. 6_____ Although she loved Haydn, six continuous hours of his music satiated her. 9_____ The more she learned, the more she wanted to know; she was insatiable. 4_____ The defeated army satiated to the enemy. 8_____ Our hosts plied us with food to a point of satiety. 5_____ **Satiate: 1** surrender or yield **2** be ignorant of **3** spell out **4** provide with too much 1_____

YOUR SENTENCE: _____

_____

[1:4 2:w 3:r 4:r 5:r 6:r 7:w 8:w 9:r]

supplant

(sə·plant′) To take the place of; or to remove in order to replace with something else. Linda was unhappy because the new baby seemed to have *supplanted* her in her mother's affection.

> *Supplant* sometimes carries the connotation of displacing someone through the use of force, fraud, or treachery; at other times it suggests replacing with something better, newer, or more effective.

The true prince had been supplanted by an imposter. 6_____ Modern machinery has supplanted hand labor in many factories. 5_____ The judge refused to listen to him as he supplanted for mercy. 9_____ Through trickery Jacob obtained his brother Esau's birthright and supplanted him. 4_____ Supplanting herself in the doorway, she refused to let anyone pass. 1_____ The reformer tried to supplant the outmoded notions with progressive ideas. 3_____ While Jan was ill, Joy was chosen to supplant her as lead runner on the track team. 8_____ He hoped to supplant his pocket money by delivering newspapers. 7_____ **Supplant: 1** beg **2** add to **3** replace **4** install 2_____

YOUR SENTENCE: _____

_____

[1:w 2:3 3:r 4:r 5:r 6:r 7:w 8:r 9:w]

detract

(di·trakt') To take away from; or to diminish in importance or value. Do not let these side issues *detract* from the importance of what really happened.

> [Latin *de*, from, and *tractus*, drawn, pulled.] The same root appears in *tractor, subtract, attract,* and *contract.* As an extension of the meaning given above, *detract* can also mean to belittle or to harm (*detract* from) someone's reputation. One who does this is known as a *detractor;* the act is known as *detraction.*

Although he is popular, he has some detractors who speak ill of him. 8 _____ Claudius' foolish acts detracted from his kingly dignity. 5 _____ The political campaign was marred by slander and detraction. 3 _____ Many English words are detracted from Latin. 7 _____ As they detracted from the plane, the passengers took out their passports. 4 _____ In envy and anger they spoke detractively of their rivals. 1 _____ Although he had detracted a clever device, no one was interested in purchasing it. 6 _____ The rumors of a shaky economy detracted from the volume of foreign investment. 2 _____ **Detract:** 1 leave 2 come from 3 take away from 4 create or build 9 _____

YOUR SENTENCE: _____

_____

[1:r 2:r 3:r 4:w 5:r 6:w 7:w 8:r 9:3]

---

enhance

(en·hans') To heighten, increase, or itensify. He did all he could to *enhance* our enjoyment.

> *Enhance* implies an addition that serves to make something greater in cost, value, beauty, etc.

The movie *The Sting* was enhanced by the music of Scott Joplin. 4 _____ Having enhanced itself comfortably in a chair near the fire, the kitten soon dropped off to sleep. 6 _____ Rather than enhancing the loveliness of the room, those gaudy ornaments tend to detract from it. 5 _____ They enhanced cautiously, watching for snipers in the war-torn buildings. 2 _____ The hurricane enhanced as it moved up the coast and soon lost all of its force. 8 _____ She felt that traveling around the country would enhance her understanding of politics. 9 _____ Her knowledge of several languages enhances her usefulness to her employer. 3 _____ Pleasant weather enhanced their delightful holiday. 7 _____ **Enhance:** 1 diminish 2 increase 3 move slowly 4 settle securely 1 _____

YOUR SENTENCE: _____

_____

[1:2 2:w 3:r 4:r 5:r 6:w 7:r 8:w 9:r]

rejuvenate

(ri·jü′və·nāt) To make young or vigorous again, or to renew. The speaker *rejuvenated* their mental outlook by his cheerful attitude.

[Latin *re*–, back, and *juvenis*, young.] The same root appears in *juvenile* and *junior*.

If we are to attract new people, the social life of our community will have to be reorganized and rejuvenated. 3_____ With no plan at all, he haphazardly rejuvenated from one thing to another. 7_____ When it was exposed to the air, the mummy rejuvenated and crumbled. 4_____ "Use of vitamin Z will rejuvenate your spirit," the advertisement claimed. 1_____ If she cannot rejuvenate her case, the lawyer will file an appeal. 2_____ The professor spoke of plans for rejuvenation of the drama. 8_____ Millions of dollars are being poured into the rejuvenation of run-down cities. 9_____ After a dip in the ocean, I felt rejuvenated. 6_____ **Rejuvenate:** 1 fall apart 2 win 3 change course 4 renew 5_____

YOUR SENTENCE: _____

_____

[1:r 2:w 3:r 4:w 5:4 6:r 7:w 8:r 9:r]

regress

(ri·gres′) To grow worse or move backward. Just as we thought he was getting better, he began to *regress*.

[Latin *re*–, back, and *–gressus*, stepped.] *Regression* may also refer to the progressive lessening of the symptoms of an illness.

Regression sometimes causes us to forget recent incidents and to remember those that happened long ago. 2_____ Radiation had a regressive effect on the tumor; it grew smaller. 4_____ The hypnotist brought about a state of psychological regression in which the patient thought she was only three years old. 9_____ Although his actual speech was dull, his regressions about his travels were fascinating. 3_____ By offering financial assistance, she tried to regress the wrong she had done. 1_____ It will not help you to regress over your mistake. 7_____ I regressed a smile, since I did not want to hurt his feelings. 8_____ Under stress, adults may regress to the behavior patterns of a child. 5_____ **Regress:** 1 compensate 2 move backward 3 smother 4 turn aside from 6_____

YOUR SENTENCE: _____

_____

[1:w 2:r 3:w 4:r 5:r 6:2 7:w 8:w 9:r]

113

adulterate

(ə·dul′tər·āt) To make impure or inferior by the addition of a substance of less value or by the removal of a valuable ingredient. The government closed down the company that had *adulterated* frankfurters with horsemeat.

Adulterate sometimes refers to artificially concealing the defects of something.

Most feel that additives adulterate the value of our food. 8_____ The bartender adulterated the champagne with a cheaper wine. 3_____ An adulterant was added to the medicine to conceal its bitter taste. 7_____ The adulteration told us to return home. 1_____ Pablo eagerly tried to adulterate as much knowledge as he could. 4_____ The adulteration of the food was not discovered until someone became ill. 5_____ The judge adulterated the case in favor of the defendant. 9_____ A sudden adulteration of events led to her entering law school 2_____ **Adulterate:** 1 decide 2 link together 3 absorb 4 make impure 6_____

YOUR SENTENCE: _____

_____

[1:w   2:w   3:r   4:w   5:r   6:4   7:r   8:r   9:w]

---

partition

(pär·tish′ən) A division, separation, or distribution into parts; or to divide into parts. A conference was called to decide the *partition* of power among the various members of the ruling council.

[Latin *pars*, part, or *partitus*, divided.] The same root appears in *partial, particular, participate, apartment,* and *compartment. Partition* can also refer to an interior wall that divides one room from another. Consult your dictionary for technical meanings of *partition* in law, logic, etc.

The historian conceived of a permanent partition of the continent in terms of natural boundaries. 2_____ John Dryden once wrote: "Great wits are sure to madness near alli'd,/And thin partitions do their bounds divide." 8_____ They considered his rude answer to be a partition. 9_____ His money gradually partitioned, and by the time he was forty he was a millionaire. 5_____ The traitor was found guilty of partition with the enemy. 1_____ The huge office space was subdivided by light, movable partitions. 6_____ Foreign powers partitioned the whole country. 3_____ The estate was partitioned among the children. 7_____ **Partition:** 1 division 2 impertinence 3 betrayal 4 increase 4_____

YOUR SENTENCE: _____

_____

[1:w   2:r   3:r   4:1   5:w   6:r   7:r   8:r   9:w]

11 REVIEW EXERCISE

In each blank write a form of one of the words listed below. Use each word only once.

adulterate	garner	ramification	satiate
assimilate	infuse	regress	supplant
detract	partition	rejuvenate	
enhance	permeate	reverberate	

The dairy distributor was accused of 8_____ milk by removing the cream and adding water.

One section of the office was 13_____ off to accommodate the new printing equipment.

Under hypnosis the patient 11_____ to her childhood behavior.

His tattered sweater 1_____ from his otherwise dignified appearance.

As fall approached, the woodland creatures 3_____ their supply of food for the winter.

The beauty of the estate was 5_____ by the care given to the gardens.

We hoped to 2_____ the tired-looking armchairs by sewing new slipcovers for them.

The rebels tried to 9_____ the democratic form of government by a dictatorship.

Strolling through the cave, they could hear their voices 14_____.

The development of nuclear weapons is one of the many far-reaching 4_____ of Einstein's theory of relativity.

All the rich foods served at the Thanksgiving dinner 7_____ the guests.

His teacher's praise 12_____ a new feeling of confidence into him.

During her apprenticeship she 10_____ a wide range of knowledge about law.

Japanese color prints demonstrate how deeply a sense of beauty has 6_____ the whole nation.

1: *detracts*   2: *rejuvenate*   3: *garnered*   4: *ramifications*   5: *enhanced*   6: *permeated*   7: *satiated*
8: *adulterating*   9: *supplant*   10: *assimilated*   11: regressed   12: *infused*   13: *partitioned*
14: *reverberate*

FOR DICTIONARY STUDY

accretion

admixture

alloy

amalgam

bifurcate

cloy

decrement

dichotomy

diffuse

disperse

glean

glut

imbue

implant

increment

inculcate

infiltrate

ingrain

recession

redouble

refurbish

renovate

repercussion

resound

retrograde

retrogression

reversion

sate

saturate

suffuse

surfeit

12 Order, Time

The first four words deal with order, the last six with time. The first two are concerned with order of importance: *momentous* means very important, having serious or far-reaching consequences; *accessory* means additional, extra, or contributing in a secondary or less important way. The next two words deal with the order in which things come: *prefatory* means introductory or preliminary; *terminal* means final or concluding.

The next two words come from the same Latin root meaning time: *extempore* means offhand, impromptu, or without preparation; *temporal* means temporary, lasting only for a time, or relating to time; it can also mean worldly, civil, or nonreligious.

An *epoch* can refer either to a period of time or to an event that marks the beginning of such a period. An *interim* is the period of time between two events; as an adjective it means temporary or for the time being.

Something that is *belated* is delayed or too late. *Nocturnal* means nightly, relating to night, or occurring or active during the night. The same root appears in *nocturne*, a dreamy and romantic painting or musical composition thought to be appropriate to night.

---

momentous, accessory, prefatory, terminal,
extempore, temporal, epoch, interim,
belated, nocturnal

---

momentous

(mō·men'təs)   Very important.   He made the *momentous* decision to leave school.

Do not confuse *momentous* with *momentary*, lasting for only a moment.

Every President of the United States has been faced with momentous problems. 2_____   Her illness caused a momentous change in her personality. 1_____   Henry knew that his determination to break from family tradition was a momentous decision. 5_____   The astronaut was proud to be a part of such a momentous venture. 4_____   The coaches were not impressed by the momentous size of the opponents. 9_____   In spring, the days become longer and the weather momentous. 3_____   The momentousness of what she was saying impressed us deeply. 6_____   We all yawned as the speaker hesitated, momentously at a loss for words. 7_____   **Momentous: 1** very important **2** huge **3** boring **4** pleasant 8_____

YOUR SENTENCE: _____

_____

[1:r   2:r   3:w   4:r   5:r   6:r   7:w   8:1   9:w]

---

accessory

(ak·ses'ə·ri)   Additional, extra, or aiding or contributing in a secondary or less important way.   An *accessory* function of the tongue is to aid in digestion.

As a noun *accessory* refers to an object of secondary importance; to an object that is nonessential but that adds to the beauty or convenience of something else; or to a person who, although absent when a crime is committed, helps another person to break or escape from the law. A variant spelling of *accessory* is *accessary*.

We shopped for such household accessories as vases and lamps. 5_____   The lawyer's brief was an absolute accessory: he could not conduct the case without it. 2_____   He was indicted as an accessory after the fact for withholding information about the thief. 7_____   An accessory contract was designed to ensure fulfillment of the original contract. 4_____   She felt that character development was essential in a novel and that plot was merely accessory. 8_____   The chief architect planned the basic structure of the house and left the accessory details to her assistant. 1_____   A muddy footpath was the only means of accessory to the castle. 6_____   The price of the suit was too accessory for his limited budget. 3_____   **Accessory: 1** excessive **2** approach or entrance **3** of utmost importance **4** additional or contributing 9_____

YOUR SENTENCE: _____

_____

[1:r   2:w   3:w   4:r   5:r   6:w   7:r   8:r   9:4]

118

prefatory

(pref′ə·tô′ri) Introductory or preliminary. The author's purpose is given in his *prefatory* statement.

> [Latin *pre–*, before, and *fari*, to speak.] *Prefatory* simply means like or serving as a *preface*, an introductory statement in a book or speech.

He opened his speech with a few prefatory anecdotes. 1 _____   The prefatory exercises set the tone of the whole ceremony. 5 _____   The book contained rambling prefatory remarks by the author's friend. 2 _____   Smith is so prefatory about his work that he is sure to succeed. 9 _____   She dismissed the subject with a prefatory shake of her head. 6 _____   In his prefatory statements he explained the purpose of the course. 4 _____   She found herself writing prefatory comments when she should have been working on the speech itself. 3 _____   To close the meeting, the leader added some prefatory remarks. 7 _____   **Prefatory:** 1 eager 2 concluding 3 introductory 4 strong 8 _____

YOUR SENTENCE: _____

_____

[1:r 2:r 3:r 4:r 5:r 6:w 7:w 8:3 9:w]

---

terminal

(tėr′mə·nəl) Final or concluding; or an end, end part, or limit. Only a small station was built at the *terminal* point of the railroad.

> [Latin *terminus*, boundary, end.] The same root appears in *determine, exterminate,* and *term.* You are already familiar with *terminal* in the sense of either end of a transportation line. When *terminal* is applied to a disease, it means occurring at or contributing to the end of life.

The terminal volume—the fourth and last one—in the series has been published. 1 _____   A terminal of two years passed before he returned home. 5 _____   A terminal manner will win you many friends. 8 _____   The terminal disease was diagnosed as pneumonia. 2 _____   Susan spent weeks preparing for the terminal examination in her biology course. 9 _____   Throngs of vacationers milled about in the bus terminal. 4 _____   Because the license is only a terminal one, it will have to be renewed in one month. 3 _____   As soon as I had made the terminal payment on my auto, I started to think about buying a new car. 6 _____   **Terminal:** 1 temporary 2 period of time 3 final 4 abrupt 7 _____

YOUR SENTENCE: _____

_____

[1:r 2:r 3:w 4:r 5:w 6:r 7:3 8:w 9:r]

extempore

(eks·tem′pə·ri) Offhand, impromptu, without preparation, or on the spur of the moment.   Many of our actions are *extempore;* that is, they are not planned in advance.

> [Latin *ex*, out of, and *tempus,* time.] *Extempore* may be used either as an adjective or as an adverb. *Extemporaneous, extemporary* (adjectives), and *extemporaneously* (adverb) are variant forms of *extempore.* Something done on the spur of the moment is an *extemporization.*

Only a few of Sophocles' plays are now extempore. 8 _____   Since I had not prepared a talk, I had to extemporize. 7 _____   The fact that he spoke extemporaneously gave his speech a fresh and sincere quality. 9 _____   For weeks the police planned extempore precautions to ensure the president's safety. 3 _____   Mark Twain was one of the most gifted extemporaneous wits of his time. 1 _____ As they sang, we realized that this was an extempore rather than a planned performance. 5 _____ Marlowe and Shakespeare were extemporary to each other. 4 _____   He made an extempore translation of the Greek passage into English. 6 _____   **Extempore:** **1** without preparation **2** in existence **3** of the same period **4** of wide extent 2 _____

YOUR SENTENCE: _____

_____

[1:r   2:1   3:w   4:w   5:r   6:r   7:r   8:w   9:r]

---

temporal

(tem′pə·rəl or tem′prəl) (1) Temporary, lasting only for a time, or relating to time.   *Temporal* relationships refer to time; spatial matters refer to space.   (2) Worldly, civil, or nonreligious.   The duke was the *temporal* leader of his people.

> When *temporal* means temporary, its opposite is *eternal;* when it means worldly, its opposite is *spiritual;* when it means civil, its opposite is *ecclesiastical* (relating to the church).

The king's scepter was the symbol of temporal power. 9 _____   The court was more concerned with temporal aims than with religious aims. 4 _____   Events that occur at the same time are said to coincide temporally. 8 _____   The universal character of Shakespeare's plays makes them temporal. 5 _____   Temporal in her habits, she refused the wine. 6 _____   Ignore temporal issues of passing importance. 2 _____   She made a temporal decision and followed her chosen course. 1 _____ Temporal matters relate to life on earth. 3 _____   **Temporal** (choose two): **1** final **2** moderate **3** temporary **4** lasting **5** nonreligious 7 _____

YOUR SENTENCE: _____

_____

[1:w   2:r   3:r   4:r   5:w   6:w   7:3,5   8:r   9:r]

epoch

(ep'ək)   A period of time; or the starting point of an important period of time.   The feudal *epoch* was followed by the Renaissance.

> *Epoch* most often refers to a period of time considered in terms of noteworthy events (the revolutionary *epoch*). It can also refer to a time or event that marks the beginning of a new period or development (a new *epoch* in automation) or to a turning point (an *epoch* in one's life).

He was satisfied with reading only an epoch of the report. 4_____   The nation had two epochs of civil discord. 6_____   The invention of the steam engine marked an epoch in transportation. 2_____ For the immigrants who arrived in the early part of this century, the journey was an epochal event. 9_____   Reading that book marked an epoch in my life, one of the turning points of my career. 8_____   Let us tackle the important problems first and leave the epochal ones for later. 7_____ His years in the army were a happy epoch in his life. 5_____   A moving epoch had been carved on the monument. 3_____   **Epoch:**   1 unimportant thing   2 summary   3 period of time   4 inscription 1_____

YOUR SENTENCE: _____

_____

[1:3   2:r   3:w   4:w   5:r   6:r   7:w   8:r   9:r]

interim

(in'tər·im)   Meantime, an interval of time, or the period of time between; or temporary or for the time being.   The *interim* government was dissolved when a new cabinet was formed.

[Latin *interim,* meanwhile, from *inter,* between.]

After medical school she served as an interim in the new hospital. 8_____   Interim report cards were issued to students who were in danger of failing. 9_____   The king issued an interim that prohibited petition or assembly. 7_____   In the interim between battles, the soldier fell asleep. 3_____ Until a new contract could be drawn up, the interim lease served as a pledge. 6_____   During the interim it had grown dark. 5_____   There was a brief interim between the lighting of the fuse and the explosion. 2_____   She invited only her most interim friends to her engagement party. 1_____ **Interim:**   1 new physician   2 meantine   3 decree or order   4 important 4_____

YOUR SENTENCE: _____

_____

[1:w   2:r   3:r   4:2   5:r   6:r   7:w   8:w   9:r]

belated

(bi·lāt′id) Delayed or too late. His *belated* message arrived after we had left.

> *Belated* differs from *late* in that *belated* suggests an undesirable or blamable delay. *Belated* can occasionally mean out-of-date (*belated* ideas) or existing or appearing beyond the normal time or season (a *belated* robin in December).

He offered a belated apology for his improper conduct. 8_____   He felt belated to the other members for supporting his motion. 7_____   The belated warning reached the island only seconds before the tidal wave struck. 4_____   She appeared belatedly, just as the party was about to end. 5_____   We could tell by the belated pupils of her eyes that she had just come from a darkened room. 2_____   Because he had been belated in arriving at the conference, he missed the most important discussion. 9_____   Other belated nations agreed to send financial assistance. 3_____   The belatedness of his reply to her invitation angered the hostess. 1_____   **Belated: 1** obligated **2** delayed **3** allied **4** enlarged 6_____

YOUR SENTENCE: _____

_____

[1:r   2:w   3:w   4:r   5:r   6:2   7:w   8:w   9:r]

---

nocturnal

(nok·tėr′nəl) Of or relating to night, or occurring or active at night. *Nocturnal* animals sleep during the day and are active at night.

> [Latin *nocturnus*, nightly, from *nox*, night.] The opposite of *nocturnal* is *diurnal*, daily, relating to daytime.

The villagers were suspicious of his nocturnal wanderings. 6_____   The stars in the sky are among the most beautiful of nocturnal sights. 1_____   The building was to be nocturnal in shape. 3_____   Some plants produce flowers that close during the daytime and open nocturnally. 8_____   Some people who have trouble sleeping listen to nocturnal radio programs. 5_____   The nocturnal rays of the sun awakened him each morning. 9_____   As the train sped through the night, the passengers admired the striking beauty of the nocturnal landscapes. 7_____   Fearing that the snake venom might be nocturnal, the doctor rushed the victim to a hospital. 2_____   **Nocturnal: 1** very powerful **2** relating to dawn **3** having eight sides **4** relating to night 4_____

YOUR SENTENCE: _____

_____

[1:r   2:w   3:w   4:4   5:r   6:r   7:r   8:r   9:w]

12 REVIEW EXERCISE

In each blank write a form of one of the words listed below. Use each word only once.

accessory	epoch	interim	nocturnal	temporal
belated	extempore	momentous	prefatory	terminal

Cats are said to have good 3＿＿＿＿＿＿ vision but relatively poor daylight vision.

Because he had helped the criminal plan the robbery, he was arrested for being an 5＿＿＿＿＿＿ to the crime.

The patient died shortly after his illness had been diagnosed as 9＿＿＿＿＿＿ cancer.

Even though his speech was 7＿＿＿＿＿＿, it was as good as the carefully prepared ones given by the other speakers.

During the Middle Ages the king was the 10＿＿＿＿＿＿ authority and the Pope the spiritual authority.

Until a permanent committee could be set up, an 8＿＿＿＿＿＿ committee ruled.

In April she sent her friend a 2＿＿＿＿＿＿ thank-you note for the Christmas gift.

The invention of the radio marked a new 1＿＿＿＿＿＿ in communications.

We felt weighed down by all the 4＿＿＿＿＿＿ decisions we had to make.

The 6＿＿＿＿＿＿ note in the front of the book is very enlightening.

1: *epoch*   2: *belated*   3: *nocturnal*   4: *momentous*   5: *accessory*   6: *prefatory*   7: *extempore*
8: *interim*   9: *terminal*   10: *temporal*

FOR DICTIONARY STUDY

adjuvant

ancillary

antecedent

anterior

appurtenance

auxiliary

cardinal

consequential

contributory

dilatory

eon

ephemeral

era

evanescent

eventide

foreword

fugitive

gloaming

impromptu

improvisation

instantaneous

interlude

matutinal

millennium

minutiae

paramount

posthumous

preamble

precedence

prelude

primacy

proem

prologue

spontaneous

transient

transitory

unpremeditated

vesper

13 Literature, Music, Art

To *depict* is to represent, portray, or describe. In poetry this is often done through *imagery:* the descriptions, figures of speech, and the like that present images to the mind of the reader. If these are excessively flowery or showy, the passage may be called *florid.* At the opposite extreme, a dull, commonplace, unoriginal remark or idea is called a *platitude.*

Alliteration is the repetition of the same sound at the beginning of words or syllables. An *epigram* is a short, witty poem or saying. Quite the opposite is a *dissertation,* a formal, lengthy, and often scholarly treatment of a subject in writing. *Missive* is a rather formal word for a letter or message.

The next two words deal with forms of humor: a *farce* is an exaggerated form of comedy, full of improbable situations and ridiculous characters; a *parody* is a funny imitation, usually of a literary or musical work.

Sounds that are deep, rich, and impressive are described as *sonorous;* sounds or combinations of sounds of words that are pleasing to the ear are said to have *euphony.* *Lilt* refers to a light, graceful, swingy rhythm.

The last two words refer to forms of music: an *aria* is a melody for a solo voice with instrumental accompaniment; a *sonata* is a long musical composition, usually in three or four movements, for a solo instrument.

---

depict, imagery, florid, platitude, alliteration,
epigram, dissertation, missive, farce, parody,
sonorous, euphony, lilt, aria, sonata

---

depict

(di·pikt′) To represent, portray, or describe. Mr. Armstrong bought five paintings that *depict* some of the major battles of the Revolutionary War.

[Latin *pictus,* painted.] The same root appears in *picture.*

Monet's paintings depict the countryside in soft, muted colors. 4_____ Beethoven's deafness was a terrible depiction. 9_____ Before the operation the patient's hair was depicted from his head. 8_____ His poem depicts the history of immigrants in America. 5_____ No words can adequately depict the chaos that follows an aerial attack. 1_____ The floats in the parade depicted the origin and development of college football. 3_____ In order not to depict hardship on the family, the landlord gave them more time to pay the rent. 2_____ Photographer Dorothea Lange was highly praised for her depictions of the mood of the Depression. 6_____ **Depict:** 1 portray 2 remove 3 cause suffering 4 impose 7_____

YOUR SENTENCE: _____

_____

[1:r 2:w 3:r 4:r 5:r 6:r 7:1 8:w 9:w]

imagery

(im′ij·ri) Descriptions and figures of speech. Poetry is often very rich in *imagery.*

Imagery can also refer to images in general (especially statues) or to mental images produced by memory or imagination, as in "His nightmare was full of terrifying *imagery.*"

The weird imagery in the story made it apparent that Poe was the author. 8_____ Pamela bears a striking imagery to her grandmother. 2_____ The imagery in the poem created a mood of blissful tranquillity. 7_____ According to Keats, imagery in poetry should rise and progress in a very natural manner. 9_____ We watched anxiously for the diver's imagery from the pool. 6_____ Shakespeare's plays abound in imagery appropriate to the mood he wanted to create. 3_____ The concert program consisted of two long symphonies and one short imagery. 5_____ To preserve the mood of directness and simplicity, Lucille Clifton avoided using elaborate imagery in her poem "The 1st." 1_____ **Imagery:** 1 figures of speech 2 close resemblance 3 appearance 4 musical composition 4_____

YOUR SENTENCE: _____

_____

[1:r 2:w 3:r 4:1 5:w 6:w 7:r 8:r 9:r]

florid

(flôr′id) Very ornamental and showy, often excessively so. The elaborate screen was made of gilt Spanish leather that was stamped with a *florid* pattern.

> [Latin *floridus*, flowery, from *flor–*, flower.] The State of *Florida* was so named because it was discovered on Easter (*Pascua Florida*, the Feast of Flowers), 1513, by Ponce de León.

Florid wallpaper suited the elaborate furniture of the house. 4_____ The room seemed to shake as the pianist pounded out the chords in the florid passage of the concerto. 3_____ Would you consider the writing style of that author to be simple or florid? 6_____ We enjoyed the story's plot but disliked the floridity of the writing style. 2_____ It was florid on the porch—hot, humid, and airless. 5_____ Because she is against excessive ornamentation, she wears only florid clothes. 8_____ The public genuinely admired the florid forms of Victorian art. 1_____ Admission to the theater was two florids. 9_____ **Florid: 1** European coin **2** scorching **3** simple or plain **4** elaborately ornamented 7_____

YOUR SENTENCE: _____

_____

[1:r 2:r 3:r 4:r 5:w 6:r 7:4 8:w 9:w]

platitude

(plat′ə·tüd) A commonplace, dull, or trite remark; or dullness or staleness of ideas or language. Ned's favorite *platitude* was "You can't win them all."

> [Greek *platus*, flat, plus the suffix *–tude*, state of being.] *Platitude* refers especially to a dull statement or idea uttered as though it were original or important. An informal synonym of *platitude* is *bromide*.

Most platitudes have animals as characters and all attempt to teach moral lessons in an interesting manner. 2_____ A dull speaker substitutes platitudes for substance. 5_____ Tired of the mayor's empty platitudes, the council demanded action. 7_____ After a long climb they finally reached the platitude. 1_____ What we need are original ideas, not mere platitudes. 6_____ The statement that all fat men are jolly is not only platitudinous but incorrect. 4_____ Both the platitude and the content were fine, and everyone applauded when Eva finished her remarks. 8_____ Teachers who value creativity are not satisfied by students who platitudinize. 3_____ **Platitude: 1** fable **2** level part **3** speech **4** commonplace remark 9_____

YOUR SENTENCE: _____

_____

[1:w 2:w 3:r 4:r 5:r 6:r 7:r 8:w 9:4]

127

alliteration

(ə·lit'ər·ā'shən)   The repetition of the same first sound in two or more neighboring words or syllables. "Tiny turnips teem in Tennessee" is an example of *alliteration*.

> Although *alliteration* usually involves the repetition of first sounds in two or more words, the repeated sounds occasionally fall in the middle of words (a*f*ter li*f*e's *f*it*f*ul *f*ever).

The bomb resulted in the alliteration of the factory. 4 _____   Langston Hughes's line "A bright bowl of brass is beautiful to the Lord" is alliterative. 3 _____   The stresses fell on the alliterated syllables in the verse. 5 _____   The alliteration in "Peter Piper picked a peck of pickled peppers" appeals to children. 8 _____   Plants do well in Manuel's kitchen because the alliteration is just right. 7 _____ To emphasize a point or achieve an effect, Ann occasionally wrote alliteratively. 6 _____   If a line of poetry is too alliterative, it may be difficult to read aloud. 2 _____   We were dismayed by the alliteration of the picnic grounds by papers, boxes, and bottles. 9 _____   **Alliteration: 1** untidiness or disorder **2** repetition of the same sound **3** complete destruction **4** sunlight 1 _____

YOUR SENTENCE: _____

_____

[1:2   2:r   3:r   4:w   5:r   6:r   7:w   8:r   9:w]

---

epigram

(ep'ə·gram)   A short and witty poem or saying.   Whenever we talked too much, our father cited the *epigram*, "Speech is silver, but silence is golden."

> An *epigram* is always brief, witty, and pointed and often achieves its effect by containing a seeming contradiction, as in "All general statements are false, including this one."

Our teacher asked us to sum up our favorite idea in an epigram. 2 _____   His conversation was full of amusing epigrams. 9 _____   Most fables are marked by epigrammatic simplicity. 1 _____ Homer's epigram, the *Iliad*, is a long tale of the war between the Greeks and the Trojans. 3 _____   A true philosopher must write more than a series of epigrams. 6 _____   Almanacs are epigrams of useful information. 5 _____   "Tact is after all a kind of mind-reading" is an epigram by Sarah Jewett. 4 _____   She initialed the contract with her epigram, "SJC." 7 _____   **Epigram: 1** long poem **2** interwoven initials **3** collection **4** witty saying 8 _____

YOUR SENTENCE: _____

_____

[1:r   2:r   3:w   4:r   5:w   6:r   7:w   8:4   9:r]

dissertation

(dis'ər·tā'shən) A treatise or a formal and lengthy discussion of a subject, usually in writing. Kemp's *dissertation* discussed the influences of vocabulary study upon student writing.

> *Dissertation* often refers to a long paper submitted to the faculty of a university by a candidate for an advanced degree; it is based on independent research and is designed to show the student's mastery of his own field and of scholarly method.

Before she wrote her dissertation, she had to conduct a series of experiments. 1_____ Each chapter begins with a short dissertation that outlines its contents. 2_____ His dissertation on nutrition is the best treatise of its kind. 6_____ Her dissertation dealt with Amy Lowell's influence on modern poetry. 5_____ Although he did not mean to be unkind, dissertation came naturally to him. 9_____ A dissertation would be rejected by the faculty if it were not based on reliable sources. 3_____ We warned him against dissertating his energies at all-night parties. 7_____ He presented his dissertational study to the faculty committee. 4_____ **Dissertation:** 1 criticism 2 brief summary 3 waste 4 long, formal report 8_____

YOUR SENTENCE: _____

_____

[1:r 2:w 3:r 4:r 5:r 6:r 7:w 8:4 9:w]

missive

(mis'iv) A letter or other form of written communication, often formal or official. The queen sent an angry *missive* to her prime minister.

> [Latin *missus*, sent.] The same root appears in *missile, commission, dismiss, intermission,* and *transmit. Missive,* a formal word for *letter* or *message,* is not ordinarily used in everyday conversation.

Caring for the sick and needy was his missive in life. 6_____ The official missive she received requested her presence before the committee. 4_____ The duke received a missive stamped with the king's seal. 8_____ The club sponsored a missive clean-up campaign in the parks. 7_____ He was part of the missive sent to negotiate for peace. 9_____ Under the cover of night, the secret messenger delivered the missive. 1_____ After receiving the missive, Mary, Queen of Scots, began to plan her escape. 5_____ The seal on the missive indicated the importance of the contents. 2_____ **Missive:** 1 written message 2 large 3 goal 4 organization 3_____

YOUR SENTENCE: _____

_____

[1:r 2:r 3:1 4:r 5:r 6:w 7:w 8:r 9:w]

farce

(färs) An exaggerated comedy based on broadly humorous situations; or ridiculous mockery or empty show.   The *farce* was about the complicated relationships among a small group of people.

> A *farce* usually contains highly improbable situations and highly exaggerated characters. *Farce* can refer to the play itself, to the class of comedy containing such plays, to the kind of broad humor that goes into such plays, or to any passage that contains this kind of comic element. It can also refer to absurd mockery or pretense, as in "The trial was so unfair as to be a *farce*."

After a strict farce that lasted for ten days, he was weak and thin. 6＿＿＿＿   The audience roared with laughter as the funny situation in the farce got more and more confused. 8＿＿＿＿   His farcical actions emphasized his clownish side. 1＿＿＿＿   The mourners chanted a melancholy farce as they moved slowly and sadly through the streets. 9＿＿＿＿   It is a farce to pretend that he has any authority around here. 3＿＿＿＿   The speech she delivers in the movie is a complete farce. 2＿＿＿＿   That law has now become a mere farce. 5＿＿＿＿   Shakespeare's *Comedy of Errors* contains many farcical elements. 4＿＿＿＿   **Farce: 1** abstinence   **2** broad comedy   **3** song of mourning   **4** block 7＿＿＿＿

YOUR SENTENCE: ＿＿＿＿＿＿＿＿＿＿＿＿＿＿＿＿＿＿＿＿＿＿＿＿＿＿＿＿＿＿＿＿＿＿＿＿＿＿

＿＿

[1:r   2:r   3:r   4:r   5:r   6:w   7:2   8:r   9:w]

---

parody

(par'ə·di)   A musical or literary work that imitates the style of another work or author for comic effect; or a poor imitation.   The poem was a *parody* of nineteenth-century romantic verse.

> A *parody* ridicules an author or a serious work by imitating the style closely in order to point up its peculiarities or by distorting the content nonsensically and making it absurd. *Parody* can also refer to any feeble imitation, as in "The fuzz on his upper lip was but a *parody* of a moustache."

Some works of literature lend themselves to parody better than others. 5＿＿＿＿   There was little parody between her income and her expenses. 4＿＿＿＿   The song parodied the sentimental nature of popular love songs. 9＿＿＿＿   He set himself up as a parody for his children to follow. 6＿＿＿＿   The doctor feared that the parody might be fatal. 3＿＿＿＿   He was a good parodist but was unable to write serious literature. 7＿＿＿＿   The wilted flowers were but a parody of a bouquet. 2＿＿＿＿   The humor magazine contains a story that parodies Hemingway's style. 8＿＿＿＿   **Parody: 1** good example   **2** sickness   **3** equality   **4** humorous imitation 1＿＿＿＿

YOUR SENTENCE: ＿＿＿＿＿＿＿＿＿＿＿＿＿＿＿＿＿＿＿＿＿＿＿＿＿＿＿＿＿＿＿＿＿＿＿＿＿＿

＿＿

[1:4   2:r   3:w   4:w   5:r   6:w   7:r   8:r   9:r]

sonorous

(sə·nô′rəs) Producing or having a deep, rich, or impressive sound. The child was fascinated by the *sonorous* tones of the organ.

[Latin *sonus*, sound.] When *sonorous* is applied to speeches or writing, it often suggests an imposing or excessively high-flown quality, as in "The essay is full of *sonorous* phrases."

The actress was selected because she had a sonorous voice. 8 _____   Speaking sonorously, he rambled on about his own accomplishments. 5 _____   John Milton's poetry is enhanced by the richness and sonority of his language. 6 _____   It was a sonorous time to plant the seedlings. 2 _____   As soon as the sonorous effects of the anesthetic wore off, the patient awakened. 9 _____   From afar I heard the sonorous baying of hounds. 7 _____   The announcer's sonorous voice impressed us. 3 _____   He thinks he is sonorous, but he is really narrow-minded. 4 _____   **Sonorous: 1** producing sleep **2** cultivated **3** full sounding **4** ideal 1 _____

YOUR SENTENCE: _____

_____

[1:3   2:w   3:r   4:w   5:r   6:r   7:r   8:r   9:w]

euphony

(ū′fə·ni) Sweetness of sounds or combinations of sounds, especially in speech. Words should be chosen and put together with some regard to *euphony*.

[Greek *eu*, well, sweetly, and *phone*, sound.] The same root appears in *telephone, phonograph,* and *phonetics* (the science of speech sounds). The opposite of *euphony* is *cacophony*, harshness of sound. *Euphony* sometimes refers to ease of pronunciation that accounts for changes in the final letter of prefixes when combined with roots with which they are hard to pronounce: *illegal* for *inlegal, announce* for *adnounce,* etc.

Poets usually pay more attention than prose writers to euphony. 6 _____   She covered her ears to shut out the harsh euphony of the street noises. 1 _____   The class wrote a brief euphony on *The Red Badge of Courage.* 7 _____   Drugs to calm the nerves were first called *ataraxics,* later *tranquilizers,* probably because the latter is more euphonious. 9 _____   The melodious poems of Edgar Allan Poe are noted for their euphony. 8 _____   Mrs. Gomez delivered the euphony at her friend's funeral. 3 _____   He changed several words in his speech to make it more euphonious. 5 _____   Writers sometimes sacrifice euphony to give an effect of violence. 4 _____   **Euphony: 1** pleasing sound **2** harsh sound **3** speech of praise **4** critical essay 2 _____

YOUR SENTENCE: _____

_____

[1:w   2:1   3:w   4:r   5:r   6:r   7:w   8:r   9:r]

lilt

(lilt)   To sing, play, or speak with a light and graceful swing or rhythm; or a gay tune or swingy rhythm. To enliven the group, she *lilted* a gay tune.

Lilt can also mean a springy movement, to move in a lively and springy way, or to sway slightly from side to side.

The sound and meter of her poem had a pleasant lilt. 3_____   The fiddler lilted a country tune for the square dance. 5_____   The medieval dagger had a lavishly carved lilt. 6_____   The lilt of her step was what he remembered now. 8_____   The picture frame was obviously nothing but lilt. 2_____   Delighted by the lovely weather, he walked down the street with a lively, lilting stride. 9_____   Sean tried to remember the name of the rollicking lilt he had heard on the radio. 4_____   Lilt and cotton are examples of natural fibers. 1_____   **Lilt: 1** natural substance **2** sword handle **3** gold surfacing **4** sing gracefully 7_____

YOUR SENTENCE: _____

_____

[1:w   2:w   3:r   4:r   5:r   6:w   7:4   8:r   9:r]

aria

(ä′ri·ə)   A melody or tune.   The soprano sang a beautiful *aria* from *Carmen*.

More specifically *aria* refers to an extended or elaborate melody in an opera, cantata, or oratorio, sung by a solo voice with musical accompaniment.

The Roman arias were places of bloodshed and death. 7_____   The theme of the aria was repeated in the second scene of the opera's last act. 4_____   Opera singers are judged principally by their renditions of arias. 6_____   She loved to escape to the aria in which she grew up. 1_____   His heart beat fast each time he heard that particular aria. 8_____   Taking her painting materials with her, Mrs. Cummings planned to sketch an aria of the countryside. 5_____   The arias in older operas are quite different from simple songs. 9_____   The arias from *La Boheme* are especially moving. 3_____   **Aria: 1** painting **2** melody **3** place **4** amphitheater 2_____

YOUR SENTENCE: _____

_____

[1:w   : 2:2   3:r   4:r   5:w   6:r   7:w   8:r   9:r]

sonata

(sə·nä′tə)   An extended musical composition, usually written for the piano or other solo instrument. Early eighteenth-century *sonatas* consisted chiefly of dance movements.

> [Latin *sonus,* sound.] A *sonata* usually consists of three or four movements that are similar in subject and style but that differ in tempo, rhythm, and melody. A short or simplified *sonata* is called a *sonatina.*

The flute sounded particularly lovely in the rondo movement of the sonata. 6_____   In choosing his concert program, the pianist rejected the Mozart sonata in favor of one by Beethoven. 1_____   After a session at a sonata bath, he felt refreshed and invigorated. 5_____   The sonata was one of the few instruments Inés had not learned to play. 2_____   When she composed the sonata, she tried to give it the mood of the countryside at daybreak. 4_____   The second movement of a sonata is generally written in a slower tempo than the first and third movements. 8_____   The audience was impressed by the young musician's rendition of the organ sonata. 3_____   Sonata equipment detected the presence of an underwater mine. 9_____   **Sonata:**   **1** musical composition   **2** steam bath   **3** relating to sound   **4** percussion instrument 7_____

YOUR SENTENCE: _____

_____

[1:r   2:w   3:r   4:r   5:w   6:r   7:1   8:r   9:w]

133

13 REVIEW EXERCISE

In each blank write a form of one of the words listed below. Use each word only once.

alliteration	dissertation	farce	lilt	platitude
aria	epigram	florid	missive	sonata
depict	euphony	imagery	parody	sonorous

"Some people are too foolish to commit follies" is an example of an 5_____ .

They think they are clever and original, but all they utter are dull 1_____ .

His deep, 8_____ voice boomed throughout the large auditorium.

Only in a 10_____ could a character become involved in such confused situations.

The students wrote and produced a play that was a 13_____ of the style of old-fashioned American melodrama.

I used the expression "wild, woolly West" as an example of 6_____ .

The opera director asked her to sing the 12_____ from the beginning.

The sixteenth-century tapestries 4_____ the story of Vulcan.

To convey the spirit of chaos and destruction, the poet used warlike 2_____ .

Sandy listened happily as the children 7_____ a cheerful tune.

He preferred the clean, straight lines of modern furniture to the 3_____ style of the Romantic Period.

She was awarded a Ph.D. in physics shortly after her 15_____ was accepted by the faculty.

That poem is too harsh-sounding; I prefer poetry that is more 9_____ .

Although this 11_____ was originally written for the harpsichord, it is often played on the piano.

The messenger delivered the official 14_____ at the embassy door.

1: *platitudes* 2: *imagery* 3: *florid* 4: *depict* 5: *epigram* 6: *alliteration* 7: *lilted* 8: *sonorous*
9: *euphonious* 10: *farce* 11: *sonata* 12: *aria* 13: *parody* 14: *missive* 15: *dissertation*

FOR DICTIONARY STUDY

adage	maxim
air	mellifluous
aphorism	metaphor
apothegm	oratorio
assonance	ornate
banality	overture
baroque	paraphrase
cantata	rococo
caricature	rondo
conceit	satire
concerto	simile
delineate	spoonerism
epistle	stereotyped
exposition	symphony
extravaganza	thesis
flamboyant	toccata
fugue	tract
hackneyed	truism

14 Reasoning, Clarity, Certainty

In Section 9 a *facet* was defined as a small, polished surface of a cut gem, or as any aspect of a many-sided person or situation. The first is the *literal* (ordinary, plain sense) meaning; the second is the *figurative* (extended, metaphorical) meaning. Statements may also have *literal* and *figurative* meanings, as in "Let sleeping dogs lie."

Subjective means existing only in the mind, as opposed to *objective*, based on observation (see headnote). The core meaning of *subtlety* is the quality of being hard to understand. *Definitive* means decisive, final, or conclusive. *Inexplicable* means unexplainable. To *construe* is to interpret, explain, or make out the meaning of something that is not clear. To *ascribe* something *to* someone is to say that he or she caused it; to *ascribe* a quality *to* someone is to say that he or she possesses that quality.

The *pith* of a statement is its substance or essential meaning. An *epitome* is a condensed representation of anything; it can also mean a summary. To *recapitulate* is to summarize or to repeat briefly or in outline form. *Scrutiny* means a careful look at something. A *semblance* is an outward appearance or likeness. A *guise* is also an outward appearance, but it is usually intended to deceive. Anything that is *provisional* is temporary until certain requirements are met or more permanent arrangements are made. A *tenet* is a principle or doctrine.

---

literal, figurative, subjective, subtlety,
definitive, inexplicable, construe, ascribe,
pith, epitome, recapitulate, scrutiny,
semblance, guise, provisional, tenet

---

literal

(lit′ər·əl)   Actual, real, true to fact, or following the exact words of; or plain or unadorned.   He gave a *literal* translation of the Spanish passage.

> [Latin *littera*, letter.] The same root appears in *literacy, illiterate,* and *alliteration. Literal* usually suggests taking words in their usual and exact meaning, without exaggerating or using the imagination. It can also mean relating to or expressed by letters, as in "The code was *literal*, not numerical."

The literal meaning of a word is often different from the suggestions the word carries. 8_____   He is so literal that he will call an undertaker if you say that you are dying of the heat. 2_____   Bad weather made it literally impossible to climb any farther that day. 4_____   Even the most literal-minded person will grasp what the writer is trying to imply. 3_____   The quarterback's literal pass saved the day for Marks College. 7_____   Her symbolic story was so literal that few of us understood it. 5_____   He lived in literal solitude, refusing to see anyone. 9_____   Her literalism prevented her from reading between the lines and getting the real message. 6_____   **Literal: 1** actual or exact   **2** hard to understand   **3** sideways   **4** educated 1_____

YOUR SENTENCE: _____

_____

[1:1   2:r   3:r   4:r   5:w   6:r   7:w   8:r   9:r]

figurative

(fig′yər·ə·tiv)   Using language in a nonliteral way, or metaphorical or containing figures of speech. "I am dying of curiosity" is a *figurative* expression.

> [Latin *figura*, shape given to something.] *Figurative* is usually viewed as the opposite of *literal. Figurative* can also mean representing by means of a figure or likeness, as in "He lectured on the *figurative* arts of America."

Figurative and literal meanings of the same story are often quite different from each other. 7_____   Figuratively speaking, I would say that life begins at forty. 4_____   Although we realized that it was now figurative, we continued to apply artificial respiration. 9_____   When he called you a healthy horse, he was using the word *horse* figuratively. 1_____   In a figurative sense we can say that all people are the same. 2_____   Figurative language lends color to her writing. 3_____   Her career as a writer was long and figurative. 6_____   A good diet is figurative to health. 8_____   **Figurative: 1** useless   **2** basic   **3** nonliteral   **4** productive 5_____

YOUR SENTENCE: _____

_____

[1:r   2:r   3:r   4:r   5:3   6:w   7:r   8:w   9:w]

subjective

(səb·jek′tiv) Personal, or existing in the mind or arising from the feelings of a person rather than from the object thought of. The prime minister was completely *subjective* in her choice of aides.

> Something *subjective* is personal and peculiar to an individual and to his or her biases and limitations; it has no external reality and is difficult to prove, since it is rarely based on anything that all people can see and verify. The opposite of *subjective* is *objective*.

It was difficult for the critic to judge the subjective poem. 2_____   Subjective judgment rarely reaches the same conclusions as careful reasoning. 9_____   The politician hurled bitter subjectives at his opponent. 3_____   Falling in love is a purely subjective experience. 1_____   His research was too full of subjectivity to be accepted as valid. 6_____   The report should be written on a subjective book rather than on a novel. 8_____   Whenever possible she tried to base her subjective opinions on objective facts. 4_____   The unpopular professor was subjective to much abuse by his students. 7_____   **Subjective: 1** full of content **2** exposed **3** personal **4** verbal attack 5_____

YOUR SENTENCE: _____

_____

[1:r   2:r   3:w   4:r   5:3   6:r   7:w   8:w   9:r]

subtlety

(sut′əl·ti) A fine-drawn and delicate distinction, or the ability or practice of drawing delicate distinctions; or mental acuteness. The *subtlety* of her hints passed by him completely.

> *Subtlety* can also refer to something that is difficult to understand (the *subtlety* of an argument); to something that is delicate or fine (the *subtlety* of an odor); to something that is faint or mysterious (the *subtlety* of a smile); or to an instance of slyness or trickery (the *subtlety* of a scheme).

The difference between what is right and what is wrong is sometimes very subtle. 2_____   All the subtleties of the French language at first escaped him. 9_____   He argued subtly but forcefully and was easily able to convince his audience. 3_____   Everyone admired the subtlety of her mind. 1_____   The subtlety printed beneath the painting identified the artist. 6_____   He came up with endless subtle schemes that were designed to trick the public. 8_____   In time she learned to cope with all the subtleties of diplomacy. 4_____   The bus line was a subtlety of the railroad. 7_____   **Subtlety: 1** company controlled by another company **2** explanatory title **3** complete reversal **4** delicate distinction 5_____

YOUR SENTENCE: _____

_____

[1:r   2:r   3:r   4:r   5:4   6:w   7:w   8:r   9:r]

definitive

(di·fin′ə·tiv) Decisive, final, or conclusive; or most nearly complete, accurate, and reliable.   The troops won a *definitive* victory over the enemy.

> [Latin *definitus*, defined, from *de*, from, and *finis*, boundary, end.] The same root appears in *definite* and *define*. *Definitive* can also mean serving to define, distinguish, or specify exactly (*definitive* names, *definitive* laws, etc.). In biology, *definitive* means fully developed.

The highest court in the land passed down a definitive decision. 9_____   Samuel Johnson worked for years on what he hoped would be a definitive edition of Shakespeare's plays. 3_____   Her definitive nature kept her to herself at the parties. 6_____   The definitive of the verb was irregular. 2_____   A definitive collection of the letters of Virginia Woolf has been published. 5_____   The historian believed there could be no definitive history of the world. 8_____   Until he could prove his worth, he was hired on a definitive basis. 1_____   The committee's decision definitively ended the meeting. 4_____   **Definitive: 1** temporary or conditional **2** verb form **3** having two or more meanings **4** decisive or final 7_____

YOUR SENTENCE: _____

_____

[1:w   2:w   3:r   4:r   5:r   6:w   7:4   8:r   9:r]

---

inexplicable

(in·eks′plə·kə·bəl or in′eks·plik′ə·bəl) Impossible to explain, understand, or account for.   Janet's *inexplicable* anger on the day of the picnic upset us all.

> [Latin *in–*, not, and *explicatus*, explained.] The opposite of *inexplicable* is *explicable;* its verb form, *explicate*, means to make clear or explain, often in a detailed and scholarly way.

Because he was inexplicable, he could not perform the task well. 8_____   An inexplicable silence suddenly came over the dancers. 5_____   After the old man died, the cause of his final illness became more inexplicable than ever. 2_____   Philosophers have always pondered the inexplicability of the true nature of reality. 9_____   Professor Madden was able to clarify what had formerly seemed inexplicable. 4_____   She inexplicably turned down the good job when it was offered to her. 1_____   Unlike food, water, and air, luxuries are inexplicable to life. 3_____   After only an inexplicable amount of time, the clock resumed operation. 7_____   **Inexplicable: 1** very small **2** without skill **3** unnecessary **4** not explainable 6_____

YOUR SENTENCE: _____

_____

[1:r   2:r   3:w   4:r   5:r   6:4   7:w   8:w   9:r]

construe

(kən·strü′) To interpret, explain, or try to find the meaning of. Did you *construe* the passage to mean that the author favors self-discipline?

> [Latin *con–*, together, and *struere*, to arrange; hence, to construct a meaning.] *Construe* often means trying to interpret something whose meaning is not entirely clear; it sometimes suggests interpreting to one's own advantage, as in "He *construed* her answer as he pleased." In grammar, *construe* means to analyze the structure of a sentence. *Misconstrue* means to misinterpret.

They construed his silence as an insult. 7_____   The children watched in fascination as the beavers construed a dam across the river. 8_____   I construed with my lawyer; her advice was helpful. 3_____   Two different judges can construe the same law differently. 4_____   By planning carefully, he construed a sizable amount of interest from his invested money. 6_____   Because they had misconstrued the purpose of your letter, they were offended. 5_____   Some people see things as they want to see them and construe events to fit their own desires. 9_____   The public construed Mona Felina's speech to mean that she was willing to run for the Senate. 1_____   **Construe:** 1 build 2 interpret 3 accumulate 4 consult 2_____

YOUR SENTENCE: _____

_____

[1:r 2:2 3:w 4:r 5:r 6:w 7:r 8:w 9:r]

ascribe

(əs·krīb′) To assign or attribute to a supposed cause or source. He *ascribed* his success to luck.

> [Latin *a–*, to, toward, and *scribere*, to write; hence, to write down as a cause.] *Ascribe* can also mean to regard a quality as belonging to someone or something, as in "Miserliness was *ascribed* to him, but the fact was that he simply had no money."

I refuse to ascribe to such an unethical plan. 8_____   The fire was ascribed to negligence. 4_____ After the disaster all kinds of cruel motives were unfairly ascribed to the leader. 9_____   Many scholars have ascribed Shakespeare's plays to other writers. 5_____   Some computers can record a human voice and then ascribe the words on paper. 1_____   Using a stick, you can ascribe a circle in the sand. 2_____   Such conceit is often ascribable to lack of intelligence. 7_____   The newspapers ascribed the candidate's defeat to the unpopular stand he had taken on the nuclear energy issue. 3_____   **Ascribe:** 1 favor or consent to 2 attribute or assign 3 make a copy of 4 engrave 6_____

YOUR SENTENCE: _____

_____

[1:w 2:w 3:r 4:r 5:r 6:2 7:r 8:w 9:r]

pith

(pith) The core, essence, or essential part of something; or force or meatiness. We feel that freedom of speech is the very *pith* of liberty.

> *Pith* also refers to the soft and spongy tissue found at the center of some plant stems and branches or occasionally to the soft interior of a part of the human body. From this meaning of *pith* is derived the more general meaning given above. The adjective *pithy* means compact and forceful, full of substance and meaning.

His report was brief but pithy. 2_____   Because his speech lacked pith, no one was convinced by what he said. 7_____   It was a pith that we could not attend Miss Francavilla's lecture. 9_____ The eye of a sewing needle is also called the pith. 4_____   Instead of rambling, state your ideas pithily. 6_____   The pithiness of his statements brought the audience to attention. 5_____   The pith of her philosophy is that every creature has dignity. 8_____   This article represents the very pith of my views. 3_____   **Pith: 1** shame **2** fictitious story **3** small hole **4** essential part 1_____

YOUR SENTENCE: _____

[1:4   2:r   3:r   4:w   5:r   6:r   7:r   8:r   9:w]

---

epitome

(i·pit′ə·mi) A condensed representation of something; or anything regarded as a symbol or image of a quality or type.   Ralph Waldo Emerson once wrote: "London is the *epitome* of our times, and the Rome of today."

> *Epitome* can also mean a summary or abridgment, especially one that is extremely accurate and yet represents the briefest possible condensation of a subject. The verb *epitomize* can mean either to summarize or to typify, embody, or symbolize.

The epitome of the cathedral was gilded with pure gold leaf. 1_____   That hardened criminal is the epitome of wickedness. 4_____   She wrote a lengthy epitome to the editor. 3_____   We love to visit him, for he is the epitome of the gracious host. 8_____   The orator epitomized his friend at length and in glowing terms. 5_____   Our community is the epitome of the American small town. 7_____   For centuries King Solomon has epitomized wisdom. 2_____   Since she epitomized the virtues of her profession, she succeeded rapidly. 6_____   **Epitome: 1** letter **2** typical representation **3** speech of praise **4** top part 9_____

YOUR SENTENCE: _____

[1:w   2:r   3:w   4:r   5:w   6:r   7:r   8:r   9:2]

recapitulate

(rē′kə·pich′u̇·lāt) To give a summary of, or to repeat briefly or in outline form. Mill's statement *recapitulated* the entire chain of events that had led to the disaster.

> In biology, *recapitulation theory* is the theory that every organism, in its embryonic stages of development, goes through all the various stages that its ancestral types went through. Do not confuse *recapitulate* with *capitulate*, to surrender.

The secretary recapitulated the events of the last meeting. 1_____   At the end of the lesson the teacher recapitulated the points she had made. 7_____   The new state highway recapitulated their house. 4_____   His essay recapitulates the plot of the novel. 9_____   It took four prison guards to recapitulate the escaped prisoner. 5_____   In his recapitulation of my speech, he forgot to mention that I had withdrawn my support for the candidate. 8_____   The sportscaster recapitulated all the important plays of the football game. 6_____   Even though they suffered heavy losses, they refused to recapitulate to the enemy. 2_____   **Recapitulate:** **1** capture **2** summarize **3** surrender **4** replace 3_____

YOUR SENTENCE: _____

_____

[1:r   2:w   3:2   4:w   5:w   6:r   7:r   8:r   9:r]

scrutiny

(skrü′tə·ni) A careful inspection or close examination. Careful *scrutiny* disclosed several clues.

> [Latin *scruta*, old clothes, or *scrutare*, to search, as an old-clothes dealer would search in a pile of discarded garments.] The same root appears in *inscrutable*, mysterious.

Hoping to determine her true feelings, David made a careful scrutiny of Alexandra's face. 7_____   Bad working conditions on the ship led to a scrutiny by the crew against the captain. 1_____   The senator feels that the scrutiny of our country depends upon an adequate defense program. 4_____   A team of accountants made a thorough scrutiny of the company books. 6_____   She felt very uneasy under her father's scrutinizing stare. 9_____   Since she was a holder of public office, she was under scrutiny by the press. 2_____   Before she bought the record player, she scrutinized the guarantee. 3_____   I unrolled the scrutiny and read it. 5_____   **Scrutiny:** **1** revolt **2** document **3** safety **4** careful inspection 8_____

YOUR SENTENCE: _____

_____

[1:w   2:r   3:r   4:w   5:w   6:r   7:r   8:4   9:r]

semblance

(sem′bləns) The outward form or appearance of something; or a similarity, likeness, or copy. Their confused meeting did not have even the *semblance* of order.

> *Semblance* often implies that the outward appearance differs from the inner reality. Usually no deceit is implied, but *semblance* can refer to a deceptive appearance or to mere empty show.

A large semblance gathered to welcome the celebrity. 9 _____ Only a semblance of his former vigor remained. 3 _____ He barged into the meeting late without offering even the semblance of an apology. 7 _____ When the arm of the semblance is upright, the train may continue to go forward. 1 _____ In order to give his activities the semblance of legality, the gangster rented a respectable office. 8 _____ The ghost was an ashen semblance of Hamlet's father. 2 _____ The conductor gave the signal for the semblance to be played. 4 _____ That lie does not have even the semblance of truth. 6 _____ **Semblance:** 1 musical instrument 2 outward appearance 3 gathering of people 4 signal system 5 _____

YOUR SENTENCE: _____

_____

[1:w 2:r 3:r 4:w 5:2 6:r 7:r 8:r 9:w]

guise

(gīz) An outward appearance, semblance, or manner of dress; or a pretense or false and deceiving appearance. She appeared at the masquerade ball in peasant *guise*.

> When *guise* means a form or style of dress, it refers especially to a manner of dress that is unexpected on or foreign to the wearer. When it means an outward appearance, it is sometimes used as a synonym of *semblance*, but it often implies a deliberately misleading or deceiving appearance.

On Halloween, young people may appear in strange guises. 9 _____ Sometimes improper conduct takes the guise of official action. 6 _____ The Current Affairs Club published a guise of community officeholders. 4 _____ Might someone put on a guise of honesty in order to gain an advantage? 2 _____ Consumers should be more concerned with the worth of a product than with its guise. 5 _____ The singers in the glee club sang a guise at graduation. 7 _____ The leaders, in the guise of helpfulness, were actually improving their own position. 1 _____ We prepared a fruit salad and seasoned it with guises. 3 _____ **Guise:** 1 list 2 choral work 3 outward appearance 4 spice 8 _____

YOUR SENTENCE: _____

_____

[1:r 2:r 3:w 4:w 5:r 6:r 7:w 8:3 9:r]

provisional

(prə·vizh′ən·əl) Conditional, tentative, or temporary. A *provisional* government ruled during the interim between the monarchy and the republic.

> Something that is *provisional* (or *provisory*) is established for the time being and is subject to change. A *proviso* (prə·vī′zō) is a clause that states a condition, qualification, or limitation, as in "He was admitted to college with the *proviso* that he was to take two years of French."

A proviso in the charter prevented the use of funds for social activities. 6＿＿＿＿ The church felt that it could not be without at least a provisional pastor. 1＿＿＿＿ Since a lease had not yet been signed, only provisional arrangements could be considered. 9＿＿＿＿ He was appointed to the military academy provisionally; permanent appointment was dependent upon his first-year grades. 8＿＿＿＿ The company accepted the contract with the provisio that it could reject substandard work. 7＿＿＿＿ She warned her children to be provisional near the lake. 5＿＿＿＿ Until the final contract could be written up, they used the provisional agreement. 2＿＿＿＿ Since she has never left her hometown, her viewpoint tends to be provisional. 4＿＿＿＿ **Provisional:** **1** narrow or limited **2** cautious **3** definitive **4** conditional or temporary 3＿＿＿＿

YOUR SENTENCE: ＿＿

＿＿

[1:r 2:r 3:4 4:w 5:w 6:r 7:r 8:r 9:r]

---

tenet

(ten′it) A belief, principle, or doctrine. What are the *tenets* of your political party?

> [Latin *tenet,* he holds.] *Tenet* refers to any doctrine generally held to be true, especially one held in common by members of an organization, religious group, or profession.

The main tenet of that school of art is that simplicity is better than ornamentation. 1＿＿＿＿ She applied for a special parking tenet from the police department. 9＿＿＿＿ The tenets of modern communism are not always in whole agreement with the doctrines of Karl Marx. 6＿＿＿＿ Two trios and a quartet joined forces to form a tenet. 7＿＿＿＿ Are you familiar with some of the basic tenets of Buddhism? 5＿＿＿＿ Justice for all is one of the tenets of democracy. 3＿＿＿＿ One of the tenets of science is that the world has order. 4＿＿＿＿ You should try to overcome your tenet of interrupting me! 8＿＿＿＿ **Tenet:** **1** group of ten **2** belief **3** permission **4** tendency 2＿＿＿＿

YOUR SENTENCE: ＿＿

＿＿

[1:r 2:2 3:r 4:r 5:r 6:r 7:w 8:w 9:w]

14 REVIEW EXERCISE

In each blank write a form of one of the words listed below. Use each word only once.

ascribe	figurative	pith	semblance
construe	guise	provisional	subjective
definitive	inexplicable	recapitulate	subtlety
epitome	literal	scrutiny	tenet

Getting down to the 7_____ of the matter, they discussed the best way to proceed in the campaign.

The young couple 4_____ the house thoroughly before they decided to buy it.

His statement should not be 2_____ as meaning that he is in agreement with you.

The need to sympathize with and to help unfortunate people is one of the basic 8_____ of many religions.

Their defeat was 11_____ to poor organization and lack of planning.

Until a permanent appointment could be made, Nancy was named 9_____ head of the department.

Louisa thinks of herself as the 12_____ of sophistication, but actually she is quite naïve.

Hoping that no one would recognize him, the famous writer appeared in the 6_____ of a soldier.

Although his strange story at first had the 13_____ of truth, we later learned that it was completely false.

His odd action is completely 14_____; no one can explain why he did it.

Few of us could follow all the delicate 10_____ of her argument.

After the meeting Mrs. Watts was asked to 3_____ the important points that had been made.

He based all of his conclusions on his 15_____ feelings rather than on objective facts.

When she said that time was standing still, she was speaking 5_____.

The 16_____ meaning of the story is quite different from the figurative meaning.

He proudly pointed to his book, a 1_____ study of the Triangle Shirtwaist fire.

1: *definitive*   2: *construed*   3: *recapitulate*   4: *scrutinized*   5: *figuratively*   6: *guise*   7: *pith*   8: *tenets*   9: *provisional*   10: *subtleties*   11: *ascribed*   12: *epitome*   13: *semblance*   14: *inexplicable*   15: *subjective*   16: *literal*

FOR DICTIONARY STUDY

abridgment

ambiguous

aspect

canon

compendium

concise

conclusive

conspectus

contingent

denote

digest

enigmatic

equivocal

essence

facsimile

generality

gist

import

impute

incomprehensible

laconic

occult

précis

quintessence

résumé

sententious

similitude

simulation

stipulation

synopsis

tentative

undecipherable

unfathomable

unintelligible

verbatim

15 Religion

A *pontiff* is a high priest or chief religious figure, especially a bishop or the Pope. A *curate* is a member of the clergy who assists either a vicar or a rector who has charge of a parish. A *vestment* is a ceremonial garment, especially one worn by clerics during religious services. A *cassock* is one of these *vestments:* it is a full-length gown with sleeves, worn by members of the clergy and also by the members of some choirs.

To *consecrate* is to make holy or sacred, to set apart as sacred, or to make someone a bishop or ruler by a religious ceremony. The *Apocalypse* is the Book of Revelation in the New Testament; an *apocalypse* is a revelation of the future. *Idolatry* is the worship of idols; figuratively it refers to any excessive devotion or reverence. *Immolation* refers to the act of sacrificing, to the state of being sacrificed, or to the thing or creature sacrificed (usually in a religious ceremony as an offering to the gods).

A *tithe* is a tenth of one's income paid to support a church. *Sacrilege* is a violation of something that is sacred. A *sepulcher* is a grave or tomb. *Apparition* usually refers to a ghost or phantom but can also refer to any unexpected or unexplained appearance. *Terrestrial* means worldly or earthly, as opposed to *celestial* (heavenly).

---

pontiff, curate, vestment, cassock, consecrate, apocalypse, idolatry, immolation, tithe, sacrilege, sepulcher, apparition, terrestrial

---

pontiff

(pon′tif) A high priest or chief religious figure, especially a bishop or the Pope. The bishop did not travel to Rome as a *pontiff* but rather as a pilgrim.

> The adjective *pontifical* can mean relating to a *pontiff* or having the dignity of such a person, but it more often means haughty or pompous. Similarly the verb *pontificate* can mean to act or speak as a *pontiff*, but it more often means to behave or speak pompously or with exaggerated authority.

Christmas Mass was celebrated by the pontiff. 4_____   That pompous man will pontificate on any subject. 7_____   The pontifical authority of the Pope extends throughout the Roman Catholic world. 5_____   Engineers were called in to build a pontiff across the stream. 8_____   The speaker displayed the pontifical air of a second-rate diplomat. 3_____   The pontiff was judged best of breed at the dog show. 1_____   A pontiff, as chief cleric, formulates religious policy. 9_____   My new stereo equipment produces a pontifical sound. 6_____   **Pontiff: 1** temporary bridge **2** breed of dog **3** echo **4** chief religious figure 2_____

YOUR SENTENCE: _____

_____

[1:w   2:4   3:r   4:r   5:r   6:w   7:r   8:w   9:r]

---

curate

(kūr′it) A member of the clergy who assists a vicar or rector.   The *curate* assisted the vicar at Mass.

> [Latin *curatus*, one in charge of the care of souls, from *cura*, care.] The same root appears in *cure*, *curious*, and *secure*. Do not confuse *curate* with *curator*, a person in charge of a museum or library.

When the rector fell ill, the curate took over his duties. 1_____   After she graduated from the seminary, she was given a curacy. 9_____   Her knowledge of curate helped her to subdue her attacker. 5_____   The priest had once been a curate in a small English village. 7_____   Mr. Fernandez was appointed curate in the community. 2_____   The rice was prepared with curate powder. 8_____   She loved her position as curate of the art museum. 3_____   The new building is an architectural curate. 6_____   **Curate: 1** one in charge **2** member of the clergy **3** oddity **4** seasoning 4_____

YOUR SENTENCE: _____

_____

[1:r   2:r   3:w   4:2   5:w   6:w   7:r   8:w   9:r]

150

vestment

(vest′ment) A ceremonial robe or gown, especially one worn by members of the clergy during religious services. The cardinal wore bright red *vestments* for the religious celebration.

[Latin *vestis*, garment.] In a broader sense *vestment* can occasionally refer to any covering or outer garment.

Only a small amount of light entered through the vestment window. 3 _____ The parishioners met in the vestment of the church. 2 _____ The stockbroker gave her some useful vestment advice. 7 _____ The queen donned her rich vestments in preparation for the coronation. 4 _____ After the rainfall there was no vestment of the forest trail. 5 _____ The vestmented clerics assembled for the conference. 8 _____ Green is the color chosen by nature for the vestment of the earth. 6 _____ Many religious leaders wear vestments appropriate to their office. 1 _____ **Vestment:** 1 entrance 2 ceremonial garment 3 hinged window 4 trace 9 _____

YOUR SENTENCE: _____

_____

[1:r 2:w 3:w 4:r 5:w 6:r 7:w 8:r 9:2]

cassock

(kas′ək) A long, close-fitting garment worn by members of the clergy as an outer garment or under other vestments. The priest donned a *cassock* just before the first morning service.

A *cassock* is often worn by members of a church choir as well as by the clergy. *Cassock* can occasionally refer to members of the clergy themselves.

A priest wears a black cassock, a bishop a purple one, and a cardinal a red one. 9 _____ The young cassock was appointed to a pulpit in Chicago. 8 _____ As the choir left the church, one little boy tripped on his cassock. 5 _____ The Cassock dancers excited my imagination. 1 _____ After a day on the waterfront the minister's cassock was spotted with mud. 4 _____ The minister was still wearing her cassock when she left the church to make calls. 3 _____ As we strolled past the church, we heard the cassock members singing. 6 _____ She loved to sit on the low cassock while she read. 2 _____ **Cassock:** 1 stool 2 Russian cavalry 3 clerical garment 4 choir 7 _____

YOUR SENTENCE: _____

_____

[1:w 2:w 3:r 4:r 5:r 6:w 7:3 8:r 9:r]

151

consecrate

(kon′sə·krāt) To make holy or to set apart as sacred; or to make someone a bishop, ruler, etc., in a religious or civil ceremony.   The rabbi *consecrated* the new synagogue.

> *Consecrate* can also mean to devote or dedicate, as in "He *consecrated* his life to art"; or to make memorable or significant, as in "Time has *consecrated* that principle."

He angrily consecrated against all religions. 8 _____   If you consecrate enough, you can solve any problem. 5 _____   Political parties are not mentioned in the Constitution; they have become consecrated by custom. 6 _____   In an impressive ceremony the prince was consecrated king. 1 _____   The tree suddenly began to consecrate sap. 9 _____   The criminal was refused burial in consecrated ground. 4 _____   Lincoln declared that the ground of Gettysburg had been consecrated by those who died in the battle. 3 _____   The minister's consecration was attended by representatives from many faiths. 2 _____   **Consecrate:** 1 yield 2 reject beliefs 3 focus upon 4 make holy 7 _____

YOUR SENTENCE: _____

_____

[1:r 2:r 3:r 4:r 5:w 6:r 7:4 8:w 9:w]

---

apocalypse

(ə·pok′ə·lips) A writing that claims to reveal the future, or any revelation.   The *Apocalypse* written by St. John records the visions that he saw on the Isle of Patmos.

> *Apocalypse* refers especially to the Jewish and early Christian writings from about 200 B.C. to about 150 A.D. that predicted the future of theological events by means of obscure symbolism. When *Apocalypse* is capitalized, it refers to the Book of Revelation in the New Testament.

The authenticity of many apocalyptic writings has been debated by religious scholars. 2 _____ According to the apocalypse, the line of emperors would end with Titus. 9 _____   I sent an apocalypse for being late. 5 _____   Not walking under ladders is a common apocalypse. 8 _____   The authorship of most apocalypses is unknown; many writers wrote them under assumed names. 7 _____ The Book of Enoch is one of the best known of the apocalypses. 1 _____   His story had the apocalyptic effect of making us cry. 6 _____   In an apocalyptic dream she foresaw a time of peace. 4 _____   **Apocalypse:** 1 unhappiness 2 excuse 3 superstition 4 prophecy or revelation 3 _____

YOUR SENTENCE: _____

_____

[1:r 2:r 3:4 4:r 5:w 6:w 7:r 8:w 9:r]

idolatry

(ī·dol'ə·tri) The worship of images, animals, spirits, physical objects, etc. Some religions frown on *idolatry.*

> *Idolatry* may also refer to an excessive devotion or reverence.

The ancient Egyptians practiced idolatry; they worshiped the spirits of the dead. 7＿＿＿＿   Francine is idolatrous and fights for what she believes in. 4＿＿＿＿   The Ten Commandments forbid idolatry of graven images. 2＿＿＿＿   The idolatry was secured with a padlock. 9＿＿＿＿   Because she idolatrized her brother, she could not see his shortcomings. 1＿＿＿＿   Carlotta had an idolatrous love of travel. 6＿＿＿＿   Greedy King Midas was an idolater of gold. 3＿＿＿＿   The judge explained the idolatry to the jury. 5＿＿＿＿   **Idolatry: 1** righteous **2** gate **3** law **4** worship of images or objects 8＿＿＿＿

YOUR SENTENCE: ＿＿

＿＿

[1:r   2:r   3:r   4:w   5:w   6:r   7:r   8:4   9:w]

immolation

(im'ə·lā'shən) A sacrificing or being sacrificed, or something sacrificed. At the Lord's command, Abraham prepared for the *immolation* of his only son, Isaac.

> Although *immolation* usually implies sacrifice by killing, it can occasionally refer to giving up of something for the sake of others, as in "He was willing to go through an *immolation* of his own desires in order to please his family."

A newborn infant has natural immolation against many diseases. 6＿＿＿＿   The minister conducted the wedding ceremony with all the dignity such an immolation requires. 1＿＿＿＿   The gods demanded the immolation of Agamemnon's daughter in return for favorable winds. 8＿＿＿＿   She was hired to make a small but precise immolation of the painting. 7＿＿＿＿   You should not immolate your needs except for a worthy cause. 9＿＿＿＿   Individuals occasionally immolate themselves as a cry against wars. 3＿＿＿＿   The energy of the lawyer was immolate; she never stopped working. 4＿＿＿＿   Before the altar of the gods, the immolator prepared the sacrificial victim. 2＿＿＿＿   **Immolation: 1** miniature copy **2** ceremony **3** sacrifice **4** protection 5＿＿＿＿

YOUR SENTENCE: ＿＿

＿＿

[1:w   2:r   3:r   4:w   5:3   6:w   7:w   8:w   9:r]

tithe

(tīᵗH) One tenth of one's income paid to support a church or clergy; or any small tax. In religious use a *tithe* came to mean any tax for the support of a church or its charities.

[Middle English *tethe*, tenth.] The same root appears in *ten* and *teen*. As a verb *tithe* means to pay a *tithe* or to collect a *tithe*. *Tithe* occasionally refers to a payment of a nonreligious nature; it can also mean a tenth part or any small part of something, as in "These are only a *tithe* of the valuable books she owns."

They are required to tithe a small portion of their income to the needy. 1_____ The tithe seems right for an Atlantic crossing. 2_____ A tithe of twelve makes the policy decisions in the organization. 7_____ All church members were urged to tithe their earnings. 6_____ Every citizen had to pay a tithe to support the army. 9_____ Tithing was a hardship for many peasants during medieval times. 8_____ With only a blunt tithe, he couldn't clear the pasture. 4_____ The income from one tenth of our tithable property was given to the church. 5_____ **Tithe: 1** forecast **2** council **3** tool **4** religious tax 3_____

YOUR SENTENCE: _____

_____

[1:r 2:w 3:4 4:w 5:r 6:r 7:w 8:r 9:r]

sacrilege

(sak′rə·lij) The act of violating something sacred, either by intentional injury or by disrespectful treatment. In the Middle Ages *sacrileges* against the church were often punishable by death.

[Latin *sacrilegus*, stealer of sacred things, from *sacri*–, sacred, and *legere*, to gather.] The root *sacri*– appears in *consecrate*, *sacred*, *sacrifice*, and *sacrament*. Although *sacrilege* usually has a religious connotation, it can also refer to disrespect for or violation of anything or anyone held in high esteem, as in "His argument against democracy was viewed as *sacrilege*."

The hikers carried sacrileges on their backs. 3_____ Every faith considers certain acts to be sacrilegious. 7_____ Polluting lakes and rivers is a modern-day sacrilege. 2_____ The minister was upset by the sacrilegious deed. 9_____ The professor spent her sacrilege studying Pacific Ocean currents. 1_____ Whoever stole the prayer books was guilty of sacrilege. 4_____ Harvesting the vegetable crop was a sacrilege last autumn. 6_____ Eating pork is a sacrilege to both Muslims and Orthodox Jews. 8_____ **Sacrilege: 1** celebration **2** violation of sacred things **3** heavy bag **4** time away from work 5_____

YOUR SENTENCE: _____

_____

[1:w 2:r 3:w 4:r 5:2 6:w 7:r 8:r 9:r]

sepulcher

(sep′əl·kər) A grave or tomb. In "Annabel Lee" Edgar Allan Poe talks of the heroine as lying "In the *sepulcher* there by the sea,/In her tomb by the sounding sea."

> [Latin *sepulchrum,* burial place.] *Sepulcher* can also refer to a place (like an altar) in which religious relics are stored or to any final end or resting place, as in "His failure at school was the *sepulcher* of his professional ambitions." The adjective *sepulchral* (sə·pul′krəl) means relating to burials or graves; however, it often has the additional meaning of dismal, gloomy, etc.

Notices of job openings were posted on the sepulcher. 4_____   The addition of sepulcher improved the paint. 5_____   After the body was cremated, the ashes were placed in a sepulchral urn. 3_____   A feeling of peace overcame her in the stillness of the sepulcher. 2_____   Rows of empty benches gave the room the aspect of a sepulcher. 7_____   The nun was sepulchered in the churchyard. 8_____   She was the sepulcher of the Legal Society. 1_____   The *Symphonie Pathétique* is sad, even sepulchral. 9_____   **Sepulcher:** 1 chemical additive 2 tomb 3 chief officer 4 bulletin board 6_____

YOUR SENTENCE: _____

_____

[1:w 2:r 3:r 4:w 5:w 6:2 7:r 8:r 9:r]

---

apparition

(ap′ə·rish′ən) A ghost or phantom, or something or someone who appears unexpectedly. "I think it is the weakness of mine eyes that shapes this monstrous *apparition*," said Brutus when he saw Caesar's ghost.

> *Apparition* applies especially to an appearance of someone dead or about to die that seems very real to the observer and yet impossible to explain.

The apparition of Hamlet's father appeared on the battlements at Elsinore. 5_____   After my illness I looked more like an apparition than like a human being! 6_____   The apparition between apartments was too thin to block out noise. 2_____   The sudden apparition at the window frightened the children. 3_____   At her retirement the doctor was praised for her faithful apparition to the hospital. 1_____   Do you remember the apparition—"Early to bed, Early to rise . . ."? 8_____ The house was said to be haunted by the apparition of a woman wrongfully murdered. 4_____   The poet William Wordsworth wrote of "A lovely apparition sent/To be a moment's ornament." 7_____   **Apparition:** 1 ghost 2 devotion 3 saying 4 division 9_____

YOUR SENTENCE: _____

_____

[1:w 2:w 3:r 4:r 5:r 6:r 7:r 8:w 9:1]

terrestrial

(tə·res′tri·əl) Worldly, earthly, or relating to the earth or its inhabitants. The priest had more interest in heavenly matters than in *terrestrial* matters.

> [Latin *terra*, earth, dry land.] The same root appears in *terrace, territory, Mediterranean,* and *terrier.*
> The opposite of *terrestrial* is *celestial*, heavenly, divine. *Terrestrial* can also mean consisting of land,
> living on land, or relating to land (as opposed to water).

Fishes need less body heat than terrestrial creatures. 5 _____   His terrestrial conduct alarmed all the members of his family. 6 _____   Both terrestrial and naval battles were recorded on the monument. 9 _____   The religious man had no interest in terrestrial power. 7 _____   Dogs and cats are terrestrial mammals, whereas whales are water mammals. 3 _____   Terrestrial publicity declared the accused guilty even before the trial began. 2 _____   Albert Einstein's vision was not merely terrestrial; it embraced the entire universe. 8 _____   Casting her eyes upward, she prayed to the terrestrial powers of heaven for guidance. 4 _____   **Terrestrial:** **1** spiritual **2** of wide extent **3** disrespectful **4** earthly 1 _____

YOUR SENTENCE: _____

_____

[1:4   2:w   3:r   4:w   5:r   6:w   7:r   8:r   9:r]

15 REVIEW EXERCISE

In each blank write a form of one of the words listed below. Use each word only once.

apocalypse   curate   pontiff   terrestrial
apparition   idolatry   sacrilege   tithe
cassock   immolation   sepulcher   vestment
consecrate

The servants claimed that the 3_____ of the dead knight returned to haunt the castle once a year.

The high point of her trip was an audience with the 8_____, Pope Paul VI.

A young girl was chosen as the victim for the 6_____ to the gods.

The 11_____ contained strange revelations worded in mysterious language.

Before he was made a rector, he had been a 9_____ for twenty years.

After the villagers had paid their yearly 2_____ to the church, they had barely enough money left to live on.

The pilgrims knelt before the ancient 12_____ of the saint.

She 7_____ her life to improving the lot of humanity.

His 1_____ of all material possessions prevented him from ever discarding anything.

Although he was a nonbeliever, he would never commit 5_____ against the church.

Those who knew her thought she was more like an angel than like a 10_____ being.

The priest set aside the appropriate 13_____ for the marriage ceremony.

Each member of the choir was given a black 4_____ to wear during the service.

1: *idolatry* 2: *tithe* 3: *apparition* 4: *cassock* 5: *sacrilege* 6: *immolation* 7: *consecrated* 8: *pontiff*
9: *curate* 10: *terrestrial* 11: *apocalypse* 12: *sepulcher* 13: *vestments*

FOR DICTIONARY STUDY

abbot

alb

amice

apotheosis

biretta

catacombs

chasuble

cleric

cope

crypt

deacon

dean

deify

empyrean

enshrine

fetch

friar

mausoleum

miter

mundane

ordination

papacy

phantom

preferment

prelate

primate

prior

profanation

rector

revenant

sacerdotal

sacrosanct

sanctity

secular

shade

sublunary

surplice

vicar

wraith

16 Biology, Health

The stitching used to close a wound or the seam so formed is called a *suture*. A *lancet* is a sharp surgical instrument used to make small incisions. To *cauterize* is to burn with a hot iron or a chemical in order to prevent infection or to destroy unwanted tissue such as a wart. In old books an *elixir* may refer to a cure-all (a remedy for all diseases) or to a substance supposed to change base metals into gold, but in modern pharmacy it refers to a sweetened medicine made from drugs mixed with alcohol.

A person who looks thin and weak from suffering may be described as *gaunt*. *Dyspepsia* is indigestion, and *grippe* is an old word that is still used occasionally for what is more commonly known as flu. *Hypochondriacs* are people who imagine that they are sick and worry excessively about their health. To *subsist* is to remain alive; to *subsist on* or *by* something is to live on or by means of that thing.

A *reflex* is a movement over which one has no control (such as sneezing) or one that is almost automatic (such as the movement of a boxer to avoid a punch). *Olfactory* means relating to the sense of smell. One common meaning of *diaphragm* is the body partition that separates the chest from the abdomen; other meanings are given in the headnote. *Bile* is a bitter fluid secreted by the liver; it can also refer to bad temper or bitterness, since *bile* was formerly thought to cause anger and sadness. The literal meaning of *astringent* is having the ability to shrink body tissue and body vessels; the figurative meaning is stern, severe, or harsh.

---

suture, lancet, cauterize, elixir, gaunt, dyspepsia, grippe, hypochondriac, subsist, reflex, olfactory, diaphragm, bile, astringent

---

suture

(sü′chər)   The seam formed in sewing up a wound; or the method, material, or stitch used in sewing up a wound.   The surgeon used stainless steel *sutures* to sew up the incision.

> [Latin *sutura*, surgical sewing, from *sutus*, sewn.] In a more general sense *suture* can refer to the seamlike line along which two things or parts have been joined or united, as in "*Sutures* occur in the skulls of many animals."

After his operation he was required to take things easy to prevent the opening of the sutures. 6_____   The sutures of recent wounds were visible on his arms and legs. 8_____   Simple cuts do not usually require any suturing. 7_____   Too great a pressure can suture the water pipes. 3_____   To ease her cough, Margaret took four doses of the cough suture daily. 4_____   Silk is a very widely used suture. 5_____   As soon as the doctor saw the length and depth of the wound, she knew she would have to suture it. 1_____   All visitors to the maternity ward were required to wear sterilized sutures. 2_____   **Suture: 1** medicine **2** surgical gown **3** break or burst **4** surgical sewing 9_____

YOUR SENTENCE: _____

_____

[1:r   2:w   3:w   4:w   5:r   6:r   7:r   8:r   9:4]

---

lancet

(lan′sit)   A sharp surgical instrument that is used to make small incisions.   Most *lancets* have two edges and are commonly used to make small cuts in veins, boils, etc.

> [Latin *lancea*, light spear.] A *lancet window* is a high and narrow window with a sharply pointed top; a *lancet arch* is a sharply pointed arch.

A large assortment of lancets and other surgical instruments lay gleaming on the doctor's table. 1_____   The infected lancet that had been growing on her neck had to be removed surgically. 4_____   He claimed that his face had been cut by a lancet. 7_____   The surgeon's nurse was in charge of sterilizing the lancets. 9_____   The ironworkers wore plastic lancets to protect their heads. 8_____   The surgeon used a lancet to cut open the abscess on my arm. 2_____   To the soft music of violins, the young couple danced a graceful lancet. 3_____   Because it had not healed, Dr. Richards decided to lance the boil. 6_____   **Lancet: 1** protective helmet **2** surgical instrument **3** abnormal growth **4** old-fashioned dance 5_____

YOUR SENTENCE: _____

_____

[1:r   2:r   3:w   4:w   5:2   6:r   7:r   8:w   9:r]

160

cauterize

(kô′tər·īz) To burn with a hot iron or with a chemical. To prevent the possibility of infection, the doctor *cauterized* her wound.

> *Cauterization* is used to prevent or stop bleeding and infection and to destroy living tissue such as warts and tumors. The instrument or substance used in the process is a *cauterant* or *cautery;* chemicals that burn or eat away living tissue can also be called *caustic* (kôs′tik) substances or *caustics.*

The nurse placed a cauterant on the deep cut in his hand. 7_____ Festering sores are often lanced and then cauterized. 8_____ The fullback's broken wrist did not cauterize in time for the important football game. 9_____ To remove the tumor, Dr. Hastings used a hot iron cautery. 2_____ Her heartbeat cauterized when she started to run. 3_____ The sick steer was cauterized from the herd. 5_____ In some cases of rabies, the wound is cauterized with nitric acid. 1_____ Dr. Jiménez used an electric needle to perform the cauterization. 4_____ **Cauterize: 1** speed up **2** separate **3** burn **4** mend 6_____

YOUR SENTENCE: _____

_____

[1:r   2:r   3:w   4:r   5:w   6:3   7:r   8:r   9:w]

elixir

(i·lik′sər) A remedy that is supposed to cure all ailments, or "cure-all"; or an imaginary substance once thought capable of changing base metals into gold or of prolonging life. To her, honey was the true *elixir.*

> *Elixir* also refers to a sweet, syrupy medicine made from drugs or herbs mixed with alcohol.

Medieval physicians believed they could prolong life indefinitely if they could find the elixir they sought. 7_____ Each day he took a spoonful of elixir to give himself energy. 5_____ The staff had a coiled elixir wound around its shaft. 4_____ The sound of music was like an elixir to his weary spirits. 3_____ Alchemists of the Middle Ages constantly sought the elixir that would turn lead or iron into gold. 8_____ My food tasted so peculiar that I wondered if it contained a toxic elixir. 2_____ He wore an elastic elixir to ease his backache. 1_____ She feels that a virtuous act is like an elixir: it can turn evil to good. 9_____ **Elixir: 1** strong poison **2** brace **3** cure-all **4** snake symbol 6_____

YOUR SENTENCE: _____

_____

[1:w   2:w   3:r   4:w   5:r   6:3   7:r   8:r   9:r]

gaunt

(gônt)   Haggard, or very thin and bony.   After her ordeal she looked *gaunt*.

> *Gaunt* suggests not only a bony thinness but also a starved and worn look, such as that caused by great hunger or suffering. As an extension of this meaning, *gaunt* can sometimes mean bare, grim, gloomy, or desolate, as in "The leafless trees looked *gaunt*."

To keep from being scratched by the falcon, he wore a gaunt on his left arm. 9_____   They were tall, gaunt people with watery eyes and graying hair. 2_____   Years of suffering had given him a look of intense gauntness. 5_____   After the long battle a few gaunt soldiers stumbled about on the battlefield. 1_____   You too would be gaunt if you ate such rich foods all the time. 4_____   At present we are surrounded by gaunt realities, but grim as they are we must face them squarely. 3_____   One of the symptoms of gaunt is a painful swelling of the big toe. 8_____   We were haunted by the image of the gaunt faces of the starving children. 7_____   **Gaunt: 1** overweight **2** thin and bony **3** protective glove **4** joint disease 6_____

YOUR SENTENCE: _____

_____

[1:r 2:r 3:r 4:w 5:r 6:2 7:r 8:w 9:w]

dyspepsia

(dis·pep′si·ə)   Indigestion or poor digestion.   Rapid eating and tension can lead to *dyspepsia*.

> [Greek *dys–*, bad, difficult, and *pepsis*, digestion, from *peptein*, to cook.] The word *dyspeptic* can mean causing or having *dyspepsia;* or gloomy, grouchy, or pessimistic (as a person with indigestion is apt to be). As a noun *dyspeptic* refers to a person suffering from *dyspepsia*.

Any disturbance of the functions of the stomach may be responsible for dyspepsia. 3_____   A French writer once called dyspepsia the "remorse of a guilty stomach." 9_____   The cheerleader was full of dyspepsia, vim, and vigor. 7_____   Because he has been a dyspeptic for years, he always eats slowly and cautiously. 2_____   Taking a dyspeptic view of the whole affair, Mary was sure that we would not succeed. 8_____   The patient showed decided dyspeptic symptoms. 4_____   Blood is carried from the heart to other parts of the body by blood vessels known as dyspepsias. 6_____   In many instances a change in diet is sufficient to relieve dyspepsia that is long continued; in other instances surgery or other treatment may be required. 5_____   **Dyspepsia: 1** alertness **2** indigestion **3** artery **4** anxiety 1_____

YOUR SENTENCE: _____

_____

[1:2 2:r 3:r 4:r 5:r 6:w 7:w 8:r 9:r]

grippe

(grip)   A contagious virus disease.   The symptoms of *grippe* are chills, fever, and aching limbs.

Influenza and *flu* are common synonyms of *grippe*.

The doctor removed the small grippe from her arm. 3_____   All the utensils in the grippe were thoroughly sterilized before the operation. 8_____   Although he had recovered quickly from grippe, he still felt somewhat weak. 2_____   Epidemics of grippe occur most frequently during the winter months. 4_____   The earliest recorded worldwide epidemic of grippe occurred in 1510. 6_____ The empire held many small nations in its grippe. 7_____   Pneumonia is a complication that can arise from grippe. 9_____   Although it has a short incubation period and a sudden onset, grippe can last for several weeks. 5_____   **Grippe:** **1** skin growth **2** virus disease **3** operating room **4** tight hold 1_____

YOUR SENTENCE: _____

_____

[1:2   2:r   3:w   4:r   5:r   6:r   7:w   8:w   9:r]

hypochondriac

(hī′pə·kon′dri·ak)   One who worries excessively about ill health and imagines that he or she has various diseases.   It is almost impossible to convince *hypochondriacs* that they are well.

The adjective form is either *hypochondriac* or *hypochondriacal* (hī′pə·kən·drī′ə·kəl). The state of excessive anxiety about one's health is called either *hypochondria* or *hypochondriasis* (hī′pə·kən·drī′ə·sis), although the latter term is usually reserved for the more extreme cases.

His complaints arise from his hypochondriacal imagination. 9_____   After receiving a hypochondriac, the patient was able to sleep. 3_____   Hypochondriacs usually watch for any unusual symptoms and then conclude that they are suffering from some disease. 4_____   The bite of a rabid dog will cause hypochondria. 8_____   The fear hypochondriacs go through can sometimes cause actual disturbances in their bodily functions. 7_____   The best treatment for those who are hypochondriacally disposed is to get them to stop thinking about their health. 6_____   The hypochondriac generates enough electricity to light a large city. 5_____   He is not really sick; he is merely suffering from hypochondria. 1_____   **Hypochondriac:** **1** drug that deadens pain **2** rabies **3** person overanxious about his health **4** power plant 2_____

YOUR SENTENCE: _____

_____

[1:r   2:3   3:w   4:r   5:w   6:r   7:r   8:w   9:r]

subsist

(səb·sist′) To continue to exist or to remain alive; or to have the necessities of life. For years he has *subsisted* on fish and fresh vegetables.

> Although *subsist* most often applies to people, it can occasionally apply to things or ideas, as in "Many superstitions *subsist* there." The noun *subsistence* can mean existence or a means of keeping alive; or it can mean the bare minimum necessary to support life, as in "The rocky soil provided no more than *subsistence*."

He earned his subsistence by selling old books. 6_____ She finally subsisted to the disease. 8_____ The townspeople subsisted by working in the one factory that was still operating. 1_____ When Edith was ill, her only subsistence was clear broth. 5_____ A large subsistence of fresh troops arrived to relieve the weary soldiers. 3_____ Alicia can subsist on a diet of good music and good books. 4_____ Is he strong enough to subsist this illness? 2_____ The prisoner subsisted on bread and water. 9_____ **Subsist:** **1** remain alive **2** yield **3** reinforce **4** fight against 7_____

YOUR SENTENCE: _____

_____

[1:r   2:w   3:w   4:r   5:r   6:r   7:1   8:w   9:r]

---

reflex

(rē′fleks) A largely automatic movement that results from stimulation of nerve cells. Sneezing and vomiting are very common *reflexes*.

> Another term for *reflex* is *reflex action*. *Reflex* can also refer to a habitual and predictable way of thinking or acting, as in "Avoiding emotional scenes was a *reflex* for him." In the plural *reflexes* often refers to the power of responding with adequate speed. Consult your dictionary for more technical meanings of *reflex*.

When his reflexes slowed down, he gave up his baseball career. 7_____ The heartbeat is reflexive; that is, we have no voluntary control over it. 6_____ She was engaged in research on the exact nature of reflexes. 2_____ Her broken reflex was set in a cast. 1_____ The traveler was sorely in need of rest to reflex his energy. 5_____ The sudden noise produced the expected reflex action: he jumped a foot. 8_____ Natural rubber has more reflex than synthetic rubber. 3_____ Telling the truth when she is asked a question is a reflex for her. 4_____ **Reflex:** **1** small bone **2** ability to move easily **3** automatic movement **4** restore 9_____

YOUR SENTENCE: _____

_____

[1:w   2:r   3:w   4:r   5:w   6:r   7:r   8:r   9:3]

olfactory

(ol·fak′tə·ri)   Relating to the sense of smell.   The nose is our *olfactory* organ.

Olfaction is the sense of smell or the act of smelling. Loss of the sense of smell is called *anosmia*.

The olfactory is even faster than the gazelle. 1_____   Olfactory cells are buried in the mucous membrane of the nose. 6_____   The sensation of smell is carried from the nose to the brain by the olfactory nerves. 2_____   Many fishes have an olfactory bulb for smelling. 9_____   The five common senses are sight, hearing, touch, olfaction, and gustation. 8_____   Olfaction is very keen in the bloodhound. 5_____   After the revolution they set up an olfactory form of government. 3_____   Olfaction of his nerve endings produced a feeling of numbness in his feet. 7_____

Olfactory: **1** swift animal **2** wasting away **3** relating to smell **4** relating to government by a few persons 4_____

YOUR SENTENCE: _____

_____

[1:w   2:r   3:w   4:3   5:r   6:r   7:w   8:r   9:r]

diaphragm

(dī′ə·fram)   The body partition of muscles and tendons that separates the chest cavity from the abdominal cavity in mammals.   The *diaphragm* is our chief muscle for breathing.

In optical instruments like the camera and telescope, the *diaphragm* is a device that regulates the opening of a lens and thus limits the amount of light admitted by the lens. The iris of the human eye performs the same function: by contracting, it regulates the intensity and quantity of light admitted. Consult your dictionary for other technical meanings of *diaphragm*.

Through the microscope he saw diaphragms swimming about. 3_____   By contracting and relaxing, the diaphragm varies the size and internal pressure of the chest and abdominal cavities. 1_____   Diaphragm is a substance that changes starch to sugar. 7_____   The diaphragm's muscles are attached to the breastbone. 5_____   The union leader delivered a violent diaphragm against the manufacturer. 6_____   Some diseases cause paralysis of the diaphragm; in such cases an artificial respirator is used to enable the patient to breathe. 8_____   In addition to the role the diaphragm plays in breathing, it gives added power to such explosive acts as sneezing, coughing, laughing, crying, and vomiting. 2_____   The hiccup is a diaphragmatic contraction. 4_____   **Diaphragm:** **1** body partition **2** microscopic animal **3** critical speech **4** chemical 9_____

YOUR SENTENCE: _____

_____

[1:r   2:r   3:w   4:r   5:r   6:w   7:w   8:r   9:1]

165

bile

(bīl) A bitter fluid secreted by the liver; or ill temper, anger, or bitterness of spirit. *Bile*, a greenish or yellowish-brown fluid, is stored in the gallbladder before it passes into the small intestine.

> The adjective *bilious* means relating to *bile;* having or resulting from a *bile* or liver ailment; or bitter, cross, or glum. Occasionally *bilious* can also mean very unpleasant (*bilious* weather).

Her illness left a bile on her arm. 4_____   When the ship struck a rock, the bile plates gave way.

1_____   Bile is secreted by the liver and discharged into the small intestine through the bile duct.

8_____   Bile aids digestion, absorbs fats, and prevents extreme decay within the intestine.

6_____   The bile ducts and gallbladder make up the biliary tract. 7_____   Because he was so bilious, he had few friends. 3_____   The pharmacist poured the medicine into a glass bile.

9_____   Blockage in the bile duct prevented the bile from reaching the small intestine.

2_____   **Bile: 1** part of a ship **2** liver secretion **3** skin disturbance **4** bottle for drugs 5_____

YOUR SENTENCE: _____

_____

[1:w 2:r 3:r 4:w 5:2 6:r 7:r 8:r 9:w]

---

astringent

(əs·trin′jənt) (1) Having the ability to shrink or contract body tissue and blood vessels. Alum is an *astringent* substance that reduces the flow of blood by shrinking the blood vessels. (2) Stern, severe, or harsh. Your *astringent* criticism hurt my feelings.

> [Latin *a–*, toward, and *stringens*, drawing tight.] The past participle of this root appears in *strict* and *restrict.*

The astringent was so powerful that it not only diminished the blood supply but killed the surrounding tissue. 9_____   Only an astringent person can lift that heavy desk. 8_____   She wore a brilliantly astringent pin. 5_____   Ann used astringents to cleanse the wound on the dog's leg. 4_____ Tannic acid, the chief ingredient of tea, is a strong astringent and is widely used in medical practice.

7_____   He was so astringent that he even saved pieces of wire and twine. 1_____   The military is known for its astringent insistence on obedience and loyalty. 2_____   The astringency of the green persimmons made my mouth pucker. 3_____   **Astringent** (choose two): **1** stern **2** glistening **3** powerful **4** miserly **5** causing contracting 6_____

YOUR SENTENCE: _____

_____

[1:w 2:r 3:r 4:r 5:w 6:1,5 7:r 8:w 9:r]

166

16 REVIEW EXERCISE

In each blank write a form of one of the words listed below. Use each word only once.

astringent	diaphragm	gaunt	lancet	subsist
bile	dyspepsia	grippe	olfactory	suture
cauterize	elixir	hypochondriac	reflex	

His agility was gone, and his 5_____ were no longer as swift as they had been.

Despite their search for hundreds of years, alchemists never found the magical 8_____ that would turn iron to gold.

Her 9_____ organ was so well developed that she could easily detect odors that no one else could detect.

After the doctor had thoroughly cleansed the wound, she sewed it up with silk 11_____.

Laughter is produced when a deep breath is followed by spasmodic contractions of the chest and 3_____.

A gallbladder disorder caused her body to store too much 10_____.

While he was lost in the woods, he 1_____ on wild roots and berries.

Because lemons are so 13_____, they cause a puckering of the mouth when they are eaten.

Using a sharp 12_____, the doctor pierced the boil on Mildred's cheek.

Dr. Phillips destroyed the wart by 6_____ it with an electric needle.

An epidemic of 14_____ swept through the country.

I took a dose of bicarbonate of soda to ease my attack of 4_____.

We all thought he was just a 2_____, but the truth was that he was actually quite ill.

One look at her 7_____ face told us of all the suffering she had been through.

1: *subsisted*   2: *hypochondriac*   3: *diaphragm*   4: *dyspepsia*   5: *reflexes*   6: *cauterizing*   7: *gaunt*
8: *elixir*   9: *olfactory*   10: *bile*   11: *sutures*   12: *lancet*   13: *astringent*   14: *grippe*

FOR DICTIONARY STUDY

anemia

asafetida

atrabilious

balm

cadaverous

constringent

emaciated

emetic

eupepsia

febrifuge

impairment

indisposition

infirmity

malady

medicament

melancholia

midriff

nostrum

pallid

panacea

restorative

robust

salubrious

salutary

scalpel

septic

styptic

valetudinarian

17 Government, Law, Business

A *despot* is a ruler with absolute power or any person who acts as though he or she had such power. A *reactionary* is an extreme conservative who favors a return to some former state of affairs. A *socialist* believes in national ownership and operation of principal industries and services on a nonprofit basis. An *edict* is an official order issued by some high authority. *Sedition* is talk, writing, or activity that seems likely to lead to rebellion. *Martial* means military or warlike.

A *tribunal* is a law court or any place of judgment. *Barrister* is the term used in England for a lawyer who pleads cases in court. To *filch* is to steal, usually by quick snatching of some small object. A *marauder* is one who plunders or makes raids in order to secure loot.

A *legacy* is money or property given in a will at the time of the owner's death. A *remittance* is the sending of money to a person or place, or the money so sent. A *franchise* is like a license: it is a right granted by a government or owner, usually to operate a business (including some professional sports); it can also refer to the right to vote.

Gratis means free, without any payment. *Liquidation* refers to the settling of a debt or to the winding up of the affairs of a company; it can also refer to the killing of a political enemy. *Pittance* means a very small allowance of money, usually an insufficient amount. *Collateral* means anything pledged as security for the payment of a loan; it can also mean secondary, indirect, or related but less important.

---

despot, reactionary, socialist, edict, sedition,
martial, tribunal, barrister, filch, marauder,
legacy, remittance, franchise, gratis, liquidation,
pittance, collateral

---

despot

(des'pət or des'pot) A tyrant or oppressor, or a ruler with absolute power. Louis XIV of France is among the best known of *despots*.

> [Greek *despotes*, master.] *Despot* can also refer to any domineering and oppressive person.

He applied for a despot that would free him of his debts. 4_____   In some families, one parent may exercise despotical control. 3_____   Despotism is a form of government inconsistent with majority rule. 5_____   Since I was late in arriving at the despot, I missed my train. 1_____   A band of revolutionists attempted a despot against the regime. 7_____   Many peasants suffered under the despotism of the Russian czars. 9_____   By the eighteenth century many European rulers had become less tyrannical and came to be known as benevolent or enlightened despots. 8_____   Can an elected leader govern despotically? 6_____   **Despot: 1** rebellion **2** court order **3** tyrant **4** train station 2_____

YOUR SENTENCE: _____

_____

[1:w 2:3 3:r 4:w 5:r 6:r 7:w 8:r 9:r]

---

reactionary

(ri·ak'shən·er'i) An extreme conservative, or one who favors a movement back to a former or less advanced stage, especially in politics, economics, etc. Conservatives want to preserve established traditions, whereas *reactionaries* want to return to a former set of traditions.

> As an adjective *reactionary* means supporting or characterized by a backward movement in politics. It is almost always used in a derogatory manner.

Reactionary people often see only the bad in the present and only the good in the past. 5_____   If his reactionary ideas were followed, it would be like living in the Middle Ages. 3_____   His economic theory is too reactionary to work in the modern world. 6_____   Marlene is so reactionary that she always faces facts squarely. 9_____   The prisoner was too reactionary to obey the guards. 7_____   When she praised our ancestors' way of life, she was accused of being a reactionary. 2_____   "Things have been getting worse for years" is a sentiment typical of a reactionary. 1_____   The liberals expressed their modern, reactionary ideas for improvements in government. 8_____   **Reactionary: 1** practical person **2** forward-looking person **3** stubbornly defiant **4** extreme conservative 4_____

YOUR SENTENCE: _____

_____

[1:r 2:r 3:r 4:4 5:r 6:r 7:w 8:w 9:w]

170

socialist

(sō'shəl·ist) A believer in national ownership and operation of principal industries and services on a nonprofit basis. *Socialists* believe in compensating owners for property that is nationalized.

As an adjective *socialist* means operating on the principles of *socialism.* In Communist doctrine, *socialism* is the stage of society between the capitalist and communist stages.

Socialists play important roles in the politics of many European countries, including, in some, heading the government. 5 _____ Some socialists believe that only a few industries should be nationalized. 4 _____ The king stamped the royal socialist on the treaty. 8 _____ The socialists tried to get the government to take over the oil industry. 3 _____ Because he himself was outgoing, he sought only socialist people for friends. 2 _____ Institutions that would be little changed by socialism are the post office and the public schools. 7 _____ Socialism is contrasted to the free enterprise system of capitalism. 1 _____ Socialism is the study of the history and development of social groups. 6 _____ **Socialist: 1** one fond of companionship **2** believer in government ownership **3** formal seal **4** one who studies social groups 9 _____

YOUR SENTENCE: _____

_____

[1:r 2:w 3:r 4:r 5:r 6:w 7:r 8:w 9:2]

edict

(ē'dikt) A decree, or an official public proclamation or order. The premier fastened the king's newest *edict* on the palace gate.

[Latin *edictum,* decree, from *e–*, out, and *dicere,* to say.] *Edicts* are usually proclaimed by the highest authority—either a ruler, a high church official, or a superior court.

His edict of the winner of the match was mistaken. 6 _____ The ruler's new edict was resented by the citizens. 4 _____ The religious council posted public edicts on the church door. 1 _____ In the Edict of Nantes of 1598, Henry IV of France granted a large measure of religious freedom to French Protestants. 2 _____ The landlord edicted the tenants for nonpayment of rent. 7 _____ The dictator issued an edict that banned private ownership of business. 3 _____ It was clear that everyone would have to obey the edict proclaimed by the court. 9 _____ The edict of the school newspaper has received the journalism prize. 8 _____ **Edict: 1** prediction **2** public proclamation **3** cast out **4** head of a newspaper 5 _____

YOUR SENTENCE: _____

_____

[1:r 2:r 3:r 4:r 5:2 6:w 7:w 8:w 9:r]

sedition

(si · dish′ən) Speech or action that causes discontent or rebellion against a government. He was accused of preaching *sedition* against the nation's ruler.

> *Sedition* is milder than *treason*: *sedition* applies to anything that stirs up resistance against a government, whereas *treason* implies an open act that violates one's allegiance to one's country, such as waging war against it or giving aid to its enemies.

The patient felt better after taking a sedition for his pain. 4_____   The sedition to the problem was not at first evident. 7_____   The rebel spread seditious rumors about corrupt government. 6_____   In early English law the scope of sedition was broad and permitted prosecution for a remark that insulted the king. 5_____   In some countries a soldier who joins a seditious movement can be put to death. 8_____   Only citizens can sign the sedition for nomination. 9_____   Extreme poverty and discontent are among the causes of sedition. 1_____   Drinking wine at meals was a daily sedition with them. 3_____   **Sedition:** **1** drug that lessens pain **2** rebellious language or conduct **3** formal request **4** established custom 2_____

YOUR SENTENCE: _____

_____

[1:r 2:2 3:w 4:w 5:r 6:r 7:w 8:r 9:w]

---

martial

(mär′shəl) Warlike, or relating to military life. The soldier was stirred by the *martial* music.

> [Latin *Mars*, god of war.] A *court-martial* is a military court that tries offenses against military law. *Martial law* is temporary rule of civilians by the military, either in time of war or when civil authority has broken down. The opposite of *martial* is *civil*. Do not confuse *martial* with *marital*, relating to marriage.

The general dreamed about martial glory. 3_____   The troops marched by, their martial strides echoing on the pavement. 2_____   She tried to shield her child from the martial atmosphere of the army town. 4_____   At the earliest opportunity the deserter was court-martialed. 8_____   They had many martial problems during their first year of marriage. 9_____   The martial music brought back memories of past victories. 5_____   A weird figure martialized out of the fog. 7_____   When the army of occupation moved in, the town was placed under martial law. 1_____   **Martial:** **1** relating to marriage **2** warlike **3** appearing **4** gather together 6_____

YOUR SENTENCE: _____

_____

[1:r 2:r 3:r 4:r 5:r 6:2 7:w 8:r 9:w]

tribunal

(tri·bū′nəl or trī·bū′nəl) A court of justice or a place of judgment. The highest *tribunal* of our country is the United States Supreme Court.

[Latin *tribunus,* magistrate.] *Tribunal* can also refer to the bench on which judges sit or figuratively to any seat of judgment, as in "The *tribunal* of public opinion was against him."

She has been appointed judge on the civil tribunal. 7_____ The soldier suffered many miserable tribunals in the cold and wet foxhole. 5_____ The queen was brought before the revolutionary tribunal for judgment. 1_____ Many Nazis were brought before the tribunal at Nuremberg to stand trial for war crimes. 4_____ The tribunal requested that he be excused from the case. 8_____ Although the ruler wished to have his own way, he realized that the tribunal of popular sentiment would condemn him. 6_____ Many tribunals fed into the mighty river. 3_____ Francesca declared that the most important tribunal was her own conscience. 9_____ **Tribunal: 1** small stream **2** distress **3** court of justice **4** lawyer 2_____

YOUR SENTENCE: _____

_____

[1:r 2:3 3:w 4:r 5:w 6:r 7:r 8:w 9:r]

barrister

(bar′is·tər) In England, a lawyer who presents and pleads cases in court. The new *barristers* were urged to present their cases according to established traditions.

The American equivalent of *barrister* is *counselor;* the Scottish is *advocate.* Distinguish *barrister* from *solicitor* (an *attorney* in America), a lawyer who does not plead cases in court but who acts on behalf of the client in such matters as settling property and drawing up contracts and wills.

There are few more highly paid professions in England than that of a barrister. 4_____ On his bedside table was a barrister filled with hot water. 1_____ The hardworking barrister was rewarded by being appointed a judge. 2_____ People who live in barristers have less freedom than people who live in democracies. 5_____ To become a barrister, one must pass a public examination. 6_____ Barristers are permitted to speak before all the higher courts of England. 9_____ A stone barrister surrounded the castle. 3_____ Until 1919 women were not permitted to practice as barristers. 8_____ **Barrister: 1** English lawyer **2** protective wall **3** form of government **4** basin 7_____

YOUR SENTENCE: _____

_____

[1:w 2:r 3:w 4:r 5:w 6:r 7:1 8:r 9:r]

filch

(filch) To pilfer or steal by snatching small objects. He emerged from the barnyard hiding a chicken that he had *filched*.

> In the language of the underworld, *filch* once meant a hooked stick that thieves used to steal articles; but it now means to steal petty objects in a secretive manner.

In former times prisoners were often filched with whips for having committed even minor crimes. 9_____   When the filcher was caught, he was ordered to return all the items he had taken. 7_____   Daniel was accused of filching a record from the music store. 5_____   When the owner's back was turned, someone filched a few pieces of candy from the counter. 3_____   The general ordered the army to filch the enemy territory completely. 4_____   After looking around to make sure no one could see him, he filched a flower from the garden. 1_____   The sharp blow on his arm caused him to filch with pain. 6_____   The members of the band of thieves were very skillful in filching trinkets. 2_____   **Filch: 1** steal **2** survey **3** whip **4** wince 8_____

YOUR SENTENCE: _____

_____

[1:r   2:r   3:r   4:w   5:r   6:w   7:r   8:1   9:w]

---

marauder

(mə·rôd′ər) One who plunders or makes raids for booty or loot. The roving band of *marauders* consisted of thieves from several nations.

> [French *marauder,* to raid and plunder, from *maraud,* tomcat, vagabond.]

His fiery speech marauded a riot. 3_____   The main grievance of the strikers was marauder and unconcern on the part of management. 2_____   Marauding bands roamed the countryside in search of food and weapons. 7_____   Throughout the ninth and tenth centuries, the Vikings continued to maraud England's shores. 4_____   The small settlement was marauded by a group of robbers. 1_____   A cup of hot marauder tastes good on a cold day. 6_____   The marauders hovered around the settlers like vultures around a wounded man. 8_____   At night they tried to keep the cattle safe from marauders. 5_____   **Marauder: 1** neglect **2** instigator **3** plunderer **4** rum drink 9_____

YOUR SENTENCE: _____

_____

[1:r   2:w   3:w   4:r   5:r   6:w   7:r   8:r   9:3]

legacy

(leg′ə·si)   Money or other personal property given to another in a will; or anything handed down to a descendant or to future generations.   The peasants were left *legacies* by their feudal lord.

One who receives a *legacy* is known as a *legatee*. A common synonym of *legacy* is *bequest*.

When a person dies, any debts must be paid before the legacies can be distributed. 7_____   The legacy from her aunt consisted of a Monet painting. 8_____   Nine magnificent symphonies are only a part of the legacy that Beethoven left to the world. 4_____   The neighbors were involved in legacy over where the property line was located. 2_____   My lawyer questioned the legacy of the business transaction. 1_____   The generous work the group did created a legacy of goodwill. 9_____ They left a legacy of a million dollars to the medical school. 5_____   Ideas are perhaps the greatest legacies that genius leaves to humankind. 3_____   **Legacy: 1** lawfulness **2** court case **3** punishment   **4** gift by will 6_____

YOUR SENTENCE: _____

_____

[1:w   2:w   3:r   4:r   5:r   6:4   7:r   8:r   9:r]

remittance

(ri·mit′əns)   The sending of money to another person or place, or the sum of money so sent.   When notified that my account was overdrawn, I sent a *remittance* to my bank.

[Latin *re*–, back, and *mittens*, sending.] The same root appears in *permit, commit, admit,* and *transmit*. The verb *remit* can mean to send or pay money; or it can mean to pardon (*remit* sins), to decrease (*remit* pain), to refrain from demanding (*remit* a fine), or to submit for judgment (*remit* a question to a special committee).

"Enclosed is a remittance of three dollars," the letter stated. 5_____   The restless patient was given a narcotic in order to remit sleep. 1_____   Because he did not remit payment for his bill, his telephone service was canceled. 3_____   The company asked that remittance be made by check or money order. 2_____   A remittance of six officers was called in to judge the case. 7_____   After the war a remittance was set up to govern the territory. 6_____   Prompt remittance of all sums owed was requested by the credit company. 9_____   Only after she had sent a remittance did the mail-order house forward the book she had ordered. 4_____   **Remittance: 1** group of military judges **2** cause or bring on **3** ruling council **4** sending of money 8_____

YOUR SENTENCE: _____

_____

[1:w   2:r   3:r   4:r   5:r   6:w   7:w   8:4   9:r]

franchise

(fran′chīz) A right or privilege granted by a government to an individual or a group. Local governments give companies *franchises* to supply utilities or other necessary services.

> *Franchise* can also refer to the exclusive right granted by a manufacturer to a dealer to market a product in a specified area. Another common meaning of *franchise* is the right to vote; when one is given this right, one is said to be *enfranchised.* Consult your dictionary for more technical meanings of *franchise.*

The Constitution states that no citizen can be denied the franchise because of race, color, or sex. 8 _____ Franchise and honesty are two admirable qualities. 9 _____ An independent telephone company was given a twenty-five-year franchise to provide telephone service in the town. 4 _____ The company applied to the local government for a franchise to operate buses in the city. 6 _____ Most corporations that hold franchises pay franchise taxes to the government that has granted them the privilege. 5 _____ He was found guilty of franchise against the government. 7 _____ There is no franchised foreign-car dealer in our town. 3 _____ The lawyer exerted all possible franchise to win the case. 1 _____ **Franchise: 1** sincere effort **2** act of spying **3** right or privilege **4** generosity 2 _____

YOUR SENTENCE: _____

_____

[1:w 2:3 3:r 4:r 5:r 6:r 7:w 8:r 9:w]

---

gratis

(grat′is or grā′tis) Free or without payment or charge. Refusing to take money, she declared that she would provide legal advice *gratis.*

> [Latin *gratiis,* graciously, freely, from *gratia,* gratitude.] The same root appears in *grace, ingratiate,* and *congratulate. Gratis* may be used either as an adjective or as an adverb.

Asparagus au gratis was the most appetizing vegetable on the menu. 9 _____ The captain offered to take him to Lisbon gratis. 8 _____ The poor members of the community appreciated Dr. Todd's giving them medicine gratis. 2 _____ He had to pay a traffic gratis of ten dollars. 4 _____ Hoping for a gratis, we performed our jobs with extraordinary care. 5 _____ No one will pay for what can be obtained gratis. 6 _____ Children were allowed to enter the fairground gratis. 7 _____ "Nothing is gratis anymore," he grumbled as he paid admission to the museum. 1 _____ **Gratis: 1** free **2** cheese sauce **3** gift of money **4** fine 3 _____

YOUR SENTENCE: _____

_____

[1:r 2:r 3:1 4:w 5:w 6:r 7:r 8:r 9:w]

liquidation

(lik'wə·dā'shən) The clearing off or settling of a debt, or the process of winding up the affairs of a company. The revenue received from income taxes aids in the *liquidation* of the national debt.

> *Liquidation* can also mean the converting of assets into cash. *To go into liquidation* means to gather up one's assets and pay one's debts in order to close one's business. *Liquidation* can also refer to a killing, especially of a political enemy.

When the company went into bankruptcy, it was forced to liquidate its assets to pay off whatever debts it could. 9＿＿＿＿   As the business declined, she realized that the firm would have to go into liquidation. 8＿＿＿＿   I shall try to liquidate my debts by the end of the year! 6＿＿＿＿   The tax assessor's job is to liquidate all houses in the town. 3＿＿＿＿   Under Stalin's regime many supposed political enemies were liquidated. 5＿＿＿＿   Hilary's estate was applied to the liquidation of his debts. 4＿＿＿＿   The patient was placed on a liquidation diet. 1＿＿＿＿   He was jailed for having liquidated his debts. 2＿＿＿＿   **Liquidation:** 1 collecting of taxes 2 settling of a debt 3 fluids 4 illegal business activity 7＿＿＿＿

YOUR SENTENCE: ＿＿＿

＿＿＿

[1:w   2:w   3:w   4:r   5:r   6:r   7:2   8:r   9:r]

pittance

(pit'əns) A small allowance of money that is regarded as insufficient. His wages were only a *pittance*.

> *Pittance* can also refer to a small charitable gift of money, food, clothing, etc. By extension it can also mean any small amount, as in "She had only a *pittance* of musical instruction."

You can't expect to keep employees if you pay them such a pittance. 3＿＿＿＿   Each night he ate just a pittance of supper. 7＿＿＿＿   The monthly pittance the community workers received was barely enough to pay for their food. 6＿＿＿＿   Only a pittance of truth can be found in his statements. 5＿＿＿＿   The mountain climber could not have reached the top without steel pittances. 4＿＿＿＿ He exerted great pittance of influence on the committee. 2＿＿＿＿   What some people consider a mere pittance, others consider a large fortune. 9＿＿＿＿   Feeling pittance for the kitten, the child fed it some milk. 1＿＿＿＿   **Pittance:** 1 small amount of money 2 large amount 3 climbing tool 4 sympathy 8＿＿＿＿

YOUR SENTENCE: ＿＿＿

[1:w   2:w   3:r   4:w   5:r   6:r   7:r   8:1   9:r]

collateral

(kə·lat′ər·əl) (1) Anything given or pledged as security for payment of a loan. He used his stocks and bonds as *collateral* for the loan. (2) Secondary, indirect, or related but less important. Many *collateral* questions arose after the main question had been posed.

> *Collateral* can also mean parallel or side by side; in this sense it is often applied to lines of descent in a family. *Collateral* relatives are those descended from the same ancestors but not in a direct line: cousins or brothers or sisters are *collateral* relatives, whereas a father and son, for example, are *lineal* relatives. Consult your dictionary for other meanings of *collateral*.

Since Sir John had no children, a collateral relative inherited his estate. 3＿＿＿＿ Because she could offer no collateral, she was refused the loan she had requested. 1＿＿＿＿ If a borrower defaults on a loan, the collateral is sold and applied toward the payment of the debt. 2＿＿＿＿ Instead of discussing all the collateral issues, let us concentrate on the chief issue. 5＿＿＿＿ After the war they were imprisoned for having been collateral with the enemy. 4＿＿＿＿ Although I could find no direct evidence, I did find some collateral evidence to support my views. 8＿＿＿＿ To keep out the wind, button the collateral around your neck. 7＿＿＿＿ Holding the deed to her house as collateral, the finance company gave her a loan. 6＿＿＿＿ **Collateral** (choose two): **1** one who cooperates with the enemy **2** fellow worker **3** goods pledged as security **4** secondary or indirect **5** stiff collar 9＿＿＿＿

YOUR SENTENCE: ＿＿＿＿＿＿＿＿＿＿＿＿＿＿＿＿＿＿＿＿＿＿＿＿＿＿＿＿＿＿＿＿＿＿＿＿

＿＿＿

[1:r 2:r 3:r 4:w 5:r 6:r 7:w 8:r 9:3,4]

17 REVIEW EXERCISE

In each blank write a form of one of the words listed below. Use each word only once.

barrister	franchise	marauder	remittance
collateral	gratis	martial	sedition
despot	legacy	pittance	socialist
edict	liquidation	reactionary	tribunal
filch			

A salary that was considered magnificent fifty years ago may now be viewed as being a mere 4_____ .

He chose to 9_____ his assets into cash in order to pay off his debts.

Outsiders had to pay admission to the concert, but it was 6_____ to all students and faculty members.

Leonardo da Vinci left the world a 2_____ of masterful paintings.

The farmers were never really safe from the band of 14_____ who roamed about the country-side in search of plunder.

The small boy 12_____ eggs from the robin's nest.

It is unsafe to send cash 1_____ through the mail.

When she applied for a loan, all she could offer as 3_____ was her automobile.

Rebecca, an American law student, visited a group of 16_____ in England last summer.

The government granted the company a 5_____ to provide electricity for the city.

The 8_____ looked forward to the day when private ownership would be abolished.

The 15_____ of the group argued for a return to the old political system.

The emperor issued a royal 7_____ that prohibited dancing or merrymaking.

To the strains of 13_____ music, the soldiers charged into battle.

All the judges at the 10_____ declared the new law to be constitutional.

The citizens yearned to be free from the 17_____ rule of the harsh tyrant.

He was accused of sowing 11_____ seeds of discontent against the government.

1: *remittances*   2: *legacy*   3: *collateral*   4: *pittance*   5: *franchise*   6: *gratis*   7: *edict*   8: *socialist*
9: *liquidate*   10: *tribunal*   11: *seditious*   12: filched   13: *martial*   14: *marauders*   15: *reactionary*
16: *barristers*   17: *despotic*

FOR DICTIONARY STUDY

absolutism

autocracy

bellicose

belligerent

birthright

buccaneer

collectivism

defalcate

despoil

devise

fiat

footpad

forum

gratuitous

highwayman

insurgent

jurist

magistrate

mandate

oligarchy

ordinance

peculate

pilfer

pillage

potentate

promulgate

republic

rifle

sack

solvent

spoliate

statute

suffrage

testator

totalitarian

unrecompensed

unremunerated

writ

SECTION 1 ANALOGIES

Directions: For each of the following items, choose the lettered pair of words that expresses a relationship that is most similar to the relationship between the pair of capitalized words. Write the letter of your answer on the line provided before the number of the item. For answers, see the next page.

_____ 1. BENEVOLENCE : GOODWILL ::
A. complexity : solution
B. individual : humanity
C. generosity : trait
D. anger : insanity
E. consideration : thoughtfulness

_____ 2. EXEMPLARY : SAINT ::
A. liberal : politician
B. unlawful : criminal
C. private : censor
D. haughty : princess
E. seasick : mariner

_____ 3. GENTILITY : DISCOURTEOUS ::
A. rudeness : impolite
B. blurriness : cloudy
C. impurity : clean
D. hospitality : gracious
E. vagabond : mobile

_____ 4. PUNCTILIOUS : CARELESS ::
A. important : essential
B. athletic : muscular
C. ridiculous : unreasonable
D. logical : absurd
E. passed : past

_____ 5. CANDID : FRANK ::
A. conscious : awake
B. miniature : microscopic
C. genuine : artificial
D. distracted : feeble
E. charitable : miserly

_____ 6. SOLACE : GRIEF ::
A. reward : honor
B. despair : torture
C. fortune-teller : fortune
D. envy : jealousy
E. nourishment : hunger

_____ 7. ELATION : SORROW ::
A. wealth : poverty
B. boredom : sleepiness
C. desire : greed
D. weight : obesity
E. liberty : freedom

_____ 8. MORALE : MENTAL ::
A. exercise : physical
B. fantasy : realistic
C. observation : truthful
D. sincerity : false
E. illness : fatal

_____ 9. VERACITY : TRUTHFULNESS ::
A. culture : agriculture
B. prairie : grassland
C. curse : prayer
D. fuzz : peach
E. lizard : reptile

_____ 10. FEASIBLE : ACCOMPLISH ::
A. impossible : achieve
B. adaptable : adjust
C. uncontrollable : tame
D. decorative : create
E. complete : begin

[**Section 17:** 1:C 2:B 3:D 4:E 5:A 6:E 7:B 8:C 9:C 10:D]

SECTION 2 ANALOGIES

Directions: For each of the following items, choose the lettered pair of words that expresses a relationship that is most similar to the relationship between the pair of capitalized words. Write the letter of your answer on the line provided before the number of the item. For answers, see the next page.

_____ 1. DESPONDENT : THRILLED ::
  A. eager : energetic
  B. mildewed : moldy
  C. transparent : delicate
  D. insulted : humiliated
  E. dismayed : delighted

_____ 2. AUSTERE : SEVERE ::
  A. plush : extravagant
  B. muddled : organized
  C. trustworthy : corrupt
  D. lighthearted : youthful
  E. lucky : optimistic

_____ 3. PRIVATION : SUFFERING ::
  A. poverty : abundance
  B. warfare : peace
  C. doubt : certainty
  D. study : mastery
  E. cowardice : forgiveness

_____ 4. RUE : MISTAKE ::
  A. deserve : glory
  B. avoid : attraction
  C. triumph : ecstasy
  D. confine : confinement
  E. appreciate : compliment

_____ 5. RECOIL : SHRINK ::
  A. flinch : balk
  B. attack : surrender
  C. remember : mention
  D. predict : repeat
  E. deprive : spoil

_____ 6. LANGUID : VIGOR ::
  A. absurd : pointless
  B. awkward : grace
  C. sensitive : emotion
  D. romantic : romance
  E. unfair : injustice

_____ 7. MELEE : CONFUSION ::
  A. system : order
  B. law : protest
  C. neutron : proton
  D. investigation : trial
  E. tent : palace

_____ 8. ABASH : EMBARRASS ::
  A. employ : dismiss
  B. enchant : insult
  C. demolish : destroy
  D. rhyme : reason
  E. mangle : scream

_____ 9. DERANGE : ORDER ::
  A. build : construction
  B. segregate : integration
  C. prohibit : request
  D. pledge : promise
  E. overflow : flood

_____ 10. HARASS : TORMENT ::
  A. flirt : sparkle
  B. scrimp : share
  C. mutter : view
  D. bother : irritate
  E. pursue : escape

[**Section 1:** 1:E 2:B 3:C 4:D 5:A 6:E 7:A 8:E 9:B 10:B]

SECTION 3 ANALOGIES

Directions: For each of the following items, choose the lettered pair of words that expresses a relationship that is most similar to the relationship between the pair of capitalized words. Write the letter of your answer on the line provided before the number of the item. For answers, see the next page.

_____ 1. COVET : WEALTH ::
- A. expect : shock
- B. return : supplies
- C. thirst : water
- D. throw : toss
- E. record : handwriting

_____ 2. PLAUDITS : APPLAUSE ::
- A. sneezes : pneumonia
- B. drawbacks : advantages
- C. milk : tomcats
- D. pitchers : catchers
- E. smirks : snickers

_____ 3. CREDENCE : DOUBT ::
- A. reliability : undependability
- B. beef : steer
- C. option : choice
- D. sting : itchiness
- E. irritant : annoyance

_____ 4. LIAISON : CONNECTION ::
- A. venison : chicken
- B. cleaver : butcher
- C. requirement : necessity
- D. gratitude : bitterness
- E. gypsy : dancer

_____ 5. FIDELITY : MARRIAGE ::
- A. devotion : duty
- B. addition : subtraction
- C. peninsula : island
- D. penitentiary : prison
- E. suggestion : command

_____ 6. SOLIDARITY : ALONENESS ::
- A. refreshment : lemonade
- B. woodpecker : woodpile
- C. passion : rage
- D. unity : division
- E. author : novelist

_____ 7. ASSENT : AGREE ::
- A. humble : glorify
- B. predict : choose
- C. fight : battle
- D. conceal : acknowledge
- E. whisper : shout

_____ 8. CONCORD : DISCORD ::
- A. elbow : knee
- B. agreement : disagreement
- C. fee : ransom
- D. shape : contour
- E. troll : goblin

_____ 9. PALAVER : CONFERENCE ::
- A. brass : copper
- B. silence : outcry
- C. mermaid : fairy
- D. democrat : democracy
- E. conversation : discussion

_____ 10. ACCOST : SHUN ::
- A. increase : magnify
- B. inquire : require
- C. ignite : douse
- D. encase : envelop
- E. scoot : scamper

[**Section 2:** 1:E 2:A 3:D 4:E 5:A 6:B 7:A 8:C 9:B 10:D]

183

SECTION 4 ANALOGIES

Directions: For each of the following items, choose the lettered pair of words that expresses a relationship that is most similar to the relationship between the pair of capitalized words. Write the letter of your answer on the line provided before the number of the item. For answers, see the next page.

____ 1. DERIDE : MOCK ::
- A. vanish : reappear
- B. shame : tease
- C. worsen : improve
- D. shrivel : starve
- E. employ : resign

____ 2. DEROGATORY : FLATTERING ::
- A. rotten : disgusting
- B. serious : amusing
- C. odoriferous : odorous
- D. humorous : silly
- E. fundamental : simple

____ 3. CULL : SEPARATE ::
- A. invent : copy
- B. hasten : drag
- C. maul : massage
- D. scram : intrude
- E. gossip : gab

____ 4. MALEDICTION : BLESSING ::
- A. tenant : landlord
- B. belfry : bat
- C. mustard : seasoning
- D. nightfall : nightmare
- E. praise : tribute

____ 5. CHASTEN : MISBEHAVIOR ::
- A. shiver : flu
- B. tease : mischief
- C. outlaw : menace
- D. punish : misconduct
- E. celebrate : misfortune

____ 6. TAUNT : RIDICULING ::
- A. pledge : loyal
- B. travel : worldly
- C. unwind : tightened
- D. rejoin : welcomed
- E. harmonize : contradictory

____ 7. IMPRECATION : CURSE ::
- A. snort : snore
- B. guardhouse : guilt
- C. veto : rejection
- D. astronaut : sailor
- E. skyline : skyscraper

____ 8. DISSENT : DISSENTER ::
- A. follow : disciple
- B. seat : minister
- C. write : addressee
- D. sneak : rodent
- E. abandon : protector

____ 9. REPUDIATE : REJECT ::
- A. push : wrestle
- B. impress : disgrace
- C. proclaim : declare
- D. overwhelm : bore
- E. toil : loiter

____ 10. HARANGUE : QUIET ::
- A. defeat : surrender
- B. cuckoo : warbler
- C. sod : turf
- D. cyclone : tornado
- E. tragedy : comedy

[**Section 3:** 1:C 2:E 3:A 4:C 5:A 6:D 7:C 8:B 9:E 10:C]

SECTION 5 ANALOGIES

Directions: For each of the following items, choose the lettered pair of words that expresses a relationship that is most similar to the relationship between the pair of capitalized words. Write the letter of your answer on the line provided before the number of the item. For answers, see the next page.

_____ 1. SUFFERANCE : TOLERANCE ::
    A. pity : sympathy
    B. patience : impatience
    C. platter : portion
    D. prefix : suffix
    E. action : consequence

_____ 2. ASSUAGE : RELAXED ::
    A. swim : dived
    B. crawl : prowled
    C. save : economized
    D. feast : famished
    E. determine : witnessed

_____ 3. MOLLIFY : SOFTEN ::
    A. toughen : harden
    B. ignore : observe
    C. sing : dance
    D. speak : influence
    E. blind : blindfold

_____ 4. INCANTATION : WITCH ::
    A. lumber : lumberjack
    B. menu : restaurant
    C. advice : adviser
    D. poison : rattler
    E. freedom : redeemer

_____ 5. CONDUCE : PREVENT ::
    A. recall : respond
    B. gather : scatter
    C. displease : infuriate
    D. prolong : lengthen
    E. stagger : collapse

_____ 6. INGRATIATE : FAVORED ::
    A. inherit : disfavored
    B. inhabit : nomadic
    C. restrain : restricted
    D. accuse : guilty
    E. scare : scarce

_____ 7. CONTRIVE : SCHEME ::
    A. purchase : return
    B. regret : repent
    C. overshadow : dwarf
    D. wander : roam
    E. anticipate : dread

_____ 8. PROVOCATION : INCITEMENT ::
    A. bedspring : bedspread
    B. channel : straw
    C. cathedral : pew
    D. scraps : waste
    E. tardiness : lateness

_____ 9. ARBITRARY : RULE ::
    A. silent : rumor
    B. honest : cheater
    C. correct : error
    D. speechless : chatterbox
    E. absolute : authority

_____ 10. OMNIPOTENT : POWERLESS ::
    A. listless : lifeless
    B. sturdy : frail
    C. sluggish : weary
    D. dazzling : blinding
    E. stationary : permanent

[Section 4: 1:B 2:B 3:E 4:A 5:D 6:A 7:C 8:A 9:C 10:E]

SECTION 6 ANALOGIES

Directions: For each of the following items, choose the lettered pair of words that expresses a relationship that is most similar to the relationship between the pair of capitalized words. Write the letter of your answer on the line provided before the number of the item. For answers, see the next page.

_____ 1. FOOLHARDY : DAREDEVIL ::
   A. intelligent : moron
   B. lost : guide
   C. stern : president
   D. poised : ballerina
   E. confused : expert

_____ 2. IDIOSYNCRASY : PECULIARITY ::
   A. assistant : trainer
   B. funeral : burial
   C. freshman : senior
   D. lullaby : dream
   E. purpose : aim

_____ 3. ENCROACH : TRESPASS ::
   A. march : retreat
   B. minimize : maximize
   C. count : multiply
   D. assign : ask
   E. envelop : surround

_____ 4. FRIVOLOUS : NECESSARY ::
   A. frilly : ornamental
   B. sarcastic : polite
   C. stained : filthy
   D. tall : huge
   E. northern : western

_____ 5. POMPOUS : PEACOCK ::
   A. wise : owl
   B. gigantic : elephant
   C. handsome : king
   D. towering : giraffe
   E. noisy : racket

_____ 6. GLIB : SMOOTH ::
   A. messy : sloppy
   B. velvety : deep
   C. naked : skeletal
   D. arctic : blue
   E. electric : yellow

_____ 7. LETHARGY : UNCONSCIOUS ::
   A. moisture : evaporated
   B. offense : safe
   C. recognition : famous
   D. work : busy
   E. debt : rich

_____ 8. LUDICROUS : SUPERB ::
   A. casual : formal
   B. stubborn : headstrong
   C. cranky : cruel
   D. inhuman : wild
   E. pretty : beautiful

_____ 9. INTERLOPER : MEDDLES ::
   A. aviator : zooms
   B. copycat : imitates
   C. promoter : follows
   D. convict : escapes
   E. sparrow : chirps

_____ 10. ECCENTRIC : STRANGE ::
   A. uneasy : unreliable
   B. slim : tall
   C. upsetting : settling
   D. common : ordinary
   E. happy : joyless

[**Section 5:** 1:A 2:C 3:A 4:C 5:B 6:C 7:D 8:E 9:E 10:B]

SECTION 7 ANALOGIES

Directions: For each of the following items, choose the lettered pair of words that expresses a relationship that is most similar to the relationship between the pair of capitalized words. Write the letter of your answer on the line provided before the number of the item. For answers, see the next page.

_____ 1. MALEFACTOR : CRIME ::
  A. inspector : pipes
  B. revolutionist : uprising
  C. passenger : plane
  D. playwright : television
  E. lieutenant : uniform

_____ 2. BOGUS : MONEY ::
  A. artificial : teeth
  B. polished : silver
  C. gorgeous : darling
  D. rightful : cause
  E. cowardly : lion

_____ 3. INSIDIOUS : SINCERE ::
  A. abandoned : forsaken
  B. unjust : fair
  C. flabby : fat
  D. bad : disgusting
  E. hope : wishful

_____ 4. FLAGRANT : OUTRAGEOUS ::
  A. different : opposite
  B. primary : secondary
  C. usable : functional
  D. better : best
  E. pitiless : pitiful

_____ 5. WANTON : VICIOUS ::
  A. faithful : disloyal
  B. cool : steamy
  C. positive : negative
  D. horrible : terrible
  E. odd : normal

_____ 6. DIABOLIC : ANGELIC ::
  A. difficult : easy
  B. amusing : entertaining
  C. distasteful : unpleasant
  D. grimy : greasy
  E. airy : earthy

_____ 7. REPUGNANT : UGLY ::
  A. hilarious : funny
  B. dependent : possessive
  C. fishy : scaly
  D. larger : smaller
  E. pure : diluted

_____ 8. EERIE : GHOST ::
  A. protected : child
  B. gallant : warrior
  C. colossal : midget
  D. fashionable : designer
  E. nutritious : candy

_____ 9. INIQUITY : INJUSTICE ::
  A. apprentice : master
  B. mockery : praise
  C. stamp : collection
  D. kindness : meanness
  E. dissatisfaction : discontentment

_____ 10. FEIGN : DEATH ::
  A. declare : bankruptcy
  B. save : money
  C. carry : weight
  D. imitate : life
  E. assume : nothing

[**Section 6:** 1:D 2:E 3:E 4:B 5:A 6:A 7:C 8:A 9:B 10:D]

SECTION 8 ANALOGIES

Directions: For each of the following items, choose the lettered pair of words that expresses a relationship that is most similar to the relationship between the pair of capitalized words. Write the letter of your answer on the line provided before the number of the item. For answers, see the next page.

_____ 1. EXORBITANT : COSTS ::
  A. extended : credit
  B. expensive : clothes
  C. excessive : prices
  D. missed : payments
  E. bounced : checks

_____ 2. COPIOUS : HARVEST ::
  A. abundant : yield
  B. colorful : fruit
  C. reaped : wheat
  D. failing : crops
  E. planted : seeds

_____ 3. PIECEMEAL : PLAN ::
  A. hopeless : case
  B. installment : loan
  C. preliminary : sketch
  D. hidden : view
  E. approved : schedule

_____ 4. SUNDRY : MISCELLANEOUS ::
  A. creative : overflowing
  B. alone : lonely
  C. steady : upset
  D. magnetic : hypnotic
  E. varied : assorted

_____ 5. ULTIMATE : GREATEST ::
  A. best : finest
  B. dignified : splendid
  C. sickly : healthy
  D. powerful : remarkable
  E. authentic : falsified

_____ 6. PAROCHIAL : BROAD-MINDED ::
  A. festive : funny
  B. greeted : welcomed
  C. shallow : deep
  D. breathless : airless
  E. operable : workable

_____ 7. TEEM : DIMINISH ::
  A. pronounce : translate
  B. team : divide
  C. meet : know
  D. overflow : decrease
  E. coach : exercise

_____ 8. PREVALENT : SCARCE ::
  A. marked : branded
  B. long : wide
  C. visible : unclear
  D. widespread : scanty
  E. powdery : dusty

_____ 9. FINITE : ENDLESS ::
  A. numerous : plentiful
  B. mysterious : revealing
  C. marked : stained
  D. legal : constitutional
  E. concerned : crazy

_____ 10. CONSUMMATE : SUPREME ::
  A. ideal : perfect
  B. worst : best
  C. revised : efficient
  D. worthless : precious
  E. worthwhile : costly

[Section 7: 1:B 2:A 3:B 4:C 5:D 6:A 7:A 8:B 9:E 10:D]

SECTION 9 ANALOGIES

Directions: For each of the following items, choose the lettered pair of words that expresses a relationship that is most similar to the relationship between the pair of capitalized words. Write the letter of your answer on the line provided before the number of the item. For answers, see the next page.

_____ 1. PROXIMITY : NEARNESS ::
   A. distance : fondness
   B. bride : party
   C. sea : river
   D. kinship : family
   E. physical : spiritual

_____ 2. CLEFT : CHIN ::
   A. freckle : face
   B. bump : nose
   C. mole : thigh
   D. dimple : cheek
   E. wrinkle : wrist

_____ 3. PINNACLE : MOUNTAIN ::
   A. top : hill
   B. bottom : barrel
   C. middle : day
   D. pinworm : intestine
   E. side : personality

_____ 4. TAUT : LOOSE ::
   A. chilly : frozen
   B. tight : slack
   C. forward : backward
   D. lifeless : dead
   E. tied : chained

_____ 5. FACET : GEM ::
   A. phase : moon
   B. mining : rock
   C. rocket : universe
   D. glass : diamond
   E. empire : soldier

_____ 6. ASUNDER : TOGETHER ::
   A. unfit : unsuitable
   B. apart : single
   C. separate : united
   D. crowded : individualistic
   E. inexpressible : unspeakable

_____ 7. PROTUBERANCE : SWELLING ::
   A. soreness : blister
   B. bubble : pimple
   C. bulge : puffiness
   D. gash : bandage
   E. lump : throat

_____ 8. LABYRINTH : MAZE ::
   A. riddle : jester
   B. lantern : plug
   C. hail : cyclone
   D. question : answer
   E. jigsaw : puzzle

_____ 9. LITHE : BALLERINA ::
   A. savage : poodle
   B. flexible : gymnast
   C. stinging : bee
   D. limp : rag
   E. snappy : lobster

_____ 10. PALPITATE : HEART ::
   A. hang : neck
   B. burp : belch
   C. gargle : mouth
   D. scratch : back
   E. cramp : muscle

[**Section 8:** 1:C 2:A 3:B 4:E 5:A 6:C 7:D 8:D 9:B 10:A]

189

SECTION 10 ANALOGIES

Directions: For each of the following items, choose the lettered pair of words that expresses a relationship that is most similar to the relationship between the pair of capitalized words. Write the letter of your answer on the line provided before the number of the item. For answers, see the next page.

_____ 1. RECANT : WITHDRAW ::
  A. distribute : grab
  B. wax : mop
  C. skyjack : skyrocket
  D. elect : recall
  E. manufacture : make

_____ 2. DEBAR : BAR ::
  A. exclude : prohibit
  B. combine : match
  C. form : remake
  D. bring : take
  E. act : audition

_____ 3. GENESIS : END ::
  A. limit : boundary
  B. task : goal
  C. period : sentence
  D. introduction : conclusion
  E. heel : forehead

_____ 4. CESSATION : FIGHTING ::
  A. starting : warfare
  B. stopping : combat
  C. planning : revolt
  D. splashing : water
  E. winning : argument

_____ 5. RAZE : HOUSE ::
  A. lift : building
  B. build : home
  C. light : hearth
  D. destroy : hopes
  E. demolish : dwelling

_____ 6. DETER : ENCOURAGE ::
  A. sleep : dream
  B. endure : survive
  C. capture : arrest
  D. discourage : inspire
  E. pamper : spoil

_____ 7. BREACH : CONTRACT ::
  A. cross : bridge
  B. sign : treaty
  C. break : law
  D. present : proposal
  E. advertise : product

_____ 8. RESCIND : STOP ::
  A. pause : yawn
  B. treasure : boast
  C. move : settle
  D. cancel : cease
  E. marry : divorce

_____ 9. OBLIVION : NOTHINGNESS ::
  A. storm : calmness
  B. forgetfulness : memory
  C. nowhere : blankness
  D. acceptance : denial
  E. talent : intelligence

_____ 10. NOVICE : BEGINNER ::
  A. slave : prisoner
  B. trainee : apprentice
  C. private : sergeant
  D. student : observer
  E. customer : clerk

[Section 9:   1:D   2:D   3:A   4:B   5:A   6:C   7:C   8:E   9:B   10:E]

190

SECTION 11 ANALOGIES

Directions: For each of the following items, choose the lettered pair of words that expresses a relationship that is most similar to the relationship between the pair of capitalized words. Write the letter of your answer on the line provided before the number of the item. For answers, see the next page.

_____ 1. REJUVENATE : AGE ::
   A. mature : ripen
   B. renew : wilt
   C. resist : oppose
   D. examine : operate
   E. touch : grasp

_____ 2. SATIATE : APPETITE ::
   A. deny : desire
   B. moisten : stamp
   C. fill : cupboard
   D. shake : habit
   E. satisfy : craving

_____ 3. RAMIFICATION : RESULT ::
   A. consequence : outcome
   B. arm : limb
   C. series : sequel
   D. speedway : road
   E. chance : peril

_____ 4. ASSIMILATE : ABSORB ::
   A. stroke : tickle
   B. mourn : pout
   C. view : understand
   D. thaw : defrost
   E. cluster : sort

_____ 5. ENHANCE : REPUTATION ::
   A. improve : relationship
   B. provide : encouragement
   C. demand : fame
   D. increase : speed
   E. analyze : situation

_____ 6. ADULTERATE : FOOD ::
   A. blacken : eye
   B. tarnish : silver
   C. infect : wound
   D. burn : dinner
   E. soil : laundry

_____ 7. REVERBERATE : RESOUND ::
   A. peel : dice
   B. restate : echo
   C. reduce : save
   D. tranquilize : doze
   E. lure : chase

_____ 8. REGRESS : PROGRESS ::
   A. surface : emerge
   B. seize : snatch
   C. descend : ascend
   D. submerse : submerge
   E. waterlog : sink

_____ 9. PARTITION : COUNTRY ::
   A. knot : tie
   B. separation : powers
   C. welding : metal
   D. mingling : cultures
   E. division : nation

_____ 10. GARNER : FLOWERS ::
   A. prune : roses
   B. garden : hose
   C. gather : blossoms
   D. garble : nonsense
   E. throw : rice

[**Section 10:** 1:E 2:A 3:D 4:B 5:E 6:D 7:C 8:D 9:C 10:B]

191

SECTION 12 ANALOGIES

Directions: For each of the following items, choose the lettered pair of words that expresses a relationship that is most similar to the relationship between the pair of capitalized words. Write the letter of your answer on the line provided before the number of the item. For answers, see the next page.

_____ 1. ACCESSORY : PURSE ::
    A. wrench : pliers
    B. centerpiece : flowers
    C. nail : hammer
    D. French : accent
    E. pencil : paper

_____ 2. MOMENTOUS : OCCASION ::
    A. special : occurrence
    B. unfortunate : soul
    C. boundless : energy
    D. perfect : timing
    E. wishful : thinking

_____ 3. PREFATORY : FINAL ::
    A. barren : productive
    B. sleazy : sloppy
    C. begun : finished
    D. secure : locked
    E. cheezy : mousy

_____ 4. EPOCH : PERIOD ::
    A. while : hour
    B. minute : year
    C. twinkling : eye
    D. moment : instant
    E. flash : 'fire

_____ 5. EXTEMPORE : PLANNED ::
    A. vital : urgent
    B. scared : terrified
    C. fused : wiry
    D. unskillful : clumsy
    E. unrehearsed : practiced

_____ 6. TEMPORAL : LASTING ::
    A. momentary : eternal
    B. temporary : perishable
    C. evergreen : tree
    D. enduring : immortal
    E. endless : ceaseless

_____ 7. TERMINAL : INTRODUCTORY ::
    A. uneven : balanced
    B. postmarked : delivered
    C. harmful : helpful
    D. last : first
    E. enclosed : attached

_____ 8. NOCTURNAL : STARS ::
    A. daytime : sun
    B. wiggly : eel
    C. heavenly : earth
    D. comical : clown
    E. clever : fox

_____ 9. BELATED : WISHES ::
    A. tardy : attendance
    B. late : greetings
    C. slow : progress
    D. rapid : order
    E. immediate : satisfaction

_____ 10. INTERIM : MEANTIME ::
    A. century : year
    B. ten : decade
    C. now : present
    D. time : past
    E. season : summer

[**Section 11:**   1:B   2:E   3:A   4:D   5:A   6:D   7:B   8:C   9:E   10:C]

SECTION 13 ANALOGIES

Directions: For each of the following items, choose the lettered pair of words that expresses a relationship that is most similar to the relationship between the pair of capitalized words. Write the letter of your answer on the line provided before the number of the item. For answers, see the next page.

_____ 1. MISSIVE : ORAL ::
   A. penmanship : spoken
   B. music : heard
   C. painting : visual
   D. sculpture : displayed
   E. broadcast : rapid

_____ 2. EUPHONY : CLAMOR ::
   A. nursery : rhyme
   B. shriek : howl
   C. shrill : pitch
   D. yelp : holler
   E. lullaby : uproar

_____ 3. EPIGRAM : SAYING ::
   A. quotation : reporting
   B. poem : verse
   C. appendix : preface
   D. chorus : orchestra
   E. apostrophe : pronoun

_____ 4. PARODY : IMITATES ::
   A. copyright : protects
   B. plot : performs
   C. movement : idles
   D. charade : inactivates
   E. theater : opens

_____ 5. ALLITERATION : REPETITION ::
   A. ballad : prestige
   B. narration : impersonalization
   C. analogy : comparison
   D. epitaph : engraving
   E. usage : spelling

_____ 6. ARIA : MELODY ::
   A. tune : praise
   B. legend : myth
   C. book : hymn
   D. grammar : science
   E. biography : autobiography

_____ 7. DISSERTATION : OUTLINE ::
   A. profile : silhouette
   B. envelope : address
   C. sketch : layout
   D. report : draft
   E. sermon : lecture

_____ 8. FARCE : HUMOR ::
   A. joke : literature
   B. journalism : news
   C. drama : mask
   D. dialog : journals
   E. slang : scholar

_____ 9. PLATITUDE : DULL ::
   A. screech : gentle
   B. speech : clever
   C. exclamation : excited
   D. utterance : deafening
   E. wisecrack : kindhearted

_____ 10. FLORID : ELABORATE ::
   A. colorful : fashionable
   B. frilly : fluffy
   C. tropical : feathery
   D. adorned : decorated
   E. shiny : silky

[**Section 12:** 1:B 2:A 3:C 4:D 5:E 6:A 7:D 8:A 9:B 10:C]

193

SECTION 14 ANALOGIES

Directions: For each of the following items, choose the lettered pair of words that expresses a relationship that is most similar to the relationship between the pair of capitalized words. Write the letter of your answer on the line provided before the number of the item. For answers, see the next page.

_____ 1. TENET : PRINCIPLE ::
    A. register : visitors
    B. recipe : cookery
    C. belief : knowledge
    D. record : employment
    E. regulation : law

_____ 2. SUBJECTIVE : PERSONAL ::
    A. ambitious : artificial
    B. confidential : secret
    C. gaping : closed
    D. bruised : clubbed
    E. stolen : enriched

_____ 3. PITH : CANTALOUPE ::
    A. heart : lettuce
    B. peel : banana
    C. leaves : celery
    D. pistachio : nut
    E. core : apple

_____ 4. SCRUTINY : CAREFUL ::
    A. encounter : forgetful
    B. examination : reckless
    C. inspection : thorough
    D. attitude : carefree
    E. pessimism : glad

_____ 5. DEFINITIVE : INCOMPLETE ::
    A. admired : idolized
    B. improper : indecent
    C. defined : illogical
    D. complete : unfinished
    E. branded : identified

_____ 6. LITERAL : ACTUAL ::
    A. precise : exact
    B. close : clear
    C. sprayed : liquefied
    D. started : finished
    E. imaginary : brainless

_____ 7. EPITOME : HEALTH ::
    A. achievement : vigor
    B. muscle : well-being
    C. ideal : fitness
    D. cure : infection
    E. power : hardiness

_____ 8. RECAPITULATE : INCIDENT ::
    A. request : favor
    B. summarize : experience
    C. oppose : enemy
    D. paint : masterpiece
    E. lug : barrel

_____ 9. INEXPLICABLE : EXPLAINABLE ::
    A. translated : interpreted
    B. doubtful : questionable
    C. synthetic : plastic
    D. helpless : self-reliant
    E. plentiful : considerable

_____ 10. SEMBLANCE : HAPPINESS ::
    A. appearance : joy
    B. assembly : parts
    C. desire : peace
    D. attempt : perfection
    E. sense : purpose

[**Section 13:**   1:A   2:E   3:B   4:A   5:C   6:B   7:D   8:B   9:C   10:D]

SECTION 15 ANALOGIES

Directions: For each of the following items, choose the lettered pair of words that expresses a relationship that is most similar to the relationship between the pair of capitalized words. Write the letter of your answer on the line provided before the number of the item. For answers, see the next page.

_____ 1. CONSECRATE : EVIL ::
  A. smack : harmful
  B. curse : sacred
  C. discover : solved
  D. pack : loaded
  E. daydream : relaxed

_____ 2. PONTIFF : POPE ::
  A. chief : president
  B. assistant : manager
  C. captain : sailor
  D. waiter : customer
  E. bishop : minister

_____ 3. SEPULCHER : TOMB ::
  A. date : tombstone
  B. spirit : grave
  C. cemetery : burial
  D. flowers : funeral
  E. coffin : casket

_____ 4. SACRILEGE : VIOLATE ::
  A. sin : forgive
  B. holiness : injure
  C. hostility : avoid
  D. cursing : abuse
  E. luggage : unpack

_____ 5. TERRESTRIAL : WORLD ::
  A. muddy : water
  B. foggy : heaven
  C. earthly : soil
  D. scientific : humanities
  E. heavyweight : champion

_____ 6. APPARITION : GHOST ::
  A. goblin : ghoul
  B. fossil : fuel
  C. gloss : enamel
  D. whale : hippopotamus
  E. demon : gentleness

_____ 7. VESTMENT : CLERGY ::
  A. medicine : nurse
  B. badge : police
  C. hose : firefighter
  D. computer : clerk
  E. animals : veterinarian

_____ 8. CASSOCK : PRIEST ::
  A. hat : attorney
  B. gown : prom
  C. tuxedo : penguin
  D. collar : cat
  E. uniform : soldier

_____ 9. TITHE : TENTH ::
  A. foot : inch
  B. mice : three
  C. pound : ounce
  D. dozen : twelve
  E. luck : thirteen

_____ 10. APOCALYPSE : FUTURE ::
  A. bookcase : book
  B. conversation : present
  C. history : past
  D. time : alarm
  E. lightning : thunder

[**Section 14:** 1:E 2:B 3:E 4:C 5:D 6:A 7:C 8:B 9:D 10:A]

SECTION 16 ANALOGIES

Directions: For each of the following items, choose the lettered pair of words that expresses a relationship that is most similar to the relationship between the pair of capitalized words. Write the letter of your answer on the line provided before the number of the item. For answers, see the next page.

_____ 1. ELIXIR : REMEDY ::
   A. medicine : cure
   B. drug : drugstore
   C. licorice : sugar
   D. fruit : watermelon
   E. headache : aspirin

_____ 2. SUTURE : SEW ::
   A. broom : wash
   B. hobby : stitch
   C. pants : pleat
   D. airplane : glue
   E. incision : cut

_____ 3. GAUNT : OVERWEIGHT ::
   A. plump : chubby
   B. muscular : strong
   C. miniature : large
   D. massive : bulky
   E. rich : buttery

_____ 4. CAUTERIZE : BURN ::
   A. disinfect : sterilize
   B. slice : peel
   C. stab : murder
   D. dab : clean
   E. clang : tingle

_____ 5. LANCET : KNIFE ::
   A. fork : spoon
   B. shield : sword
   C. pencil : switchblade
   D. hatchet : ax
   E. axle : wheel

_____ 6. GRIPPE : DISEASE ::
   A. wound : healing
   B. flu : illness
   C. cold : pneumonia
   D. stress : relaxation
   E. grip : handcuff

_____ 7. HYPOCHONDRIAC : WELLNESS ::
   A. laborer : factory
   B. alcoholic : soberness
   C. bagpiper : Scotland
   D. worrier : problems
   E. breadwinner : bread

_____ 8. DIAPHRAGM : BREATHING ::
   A. ears : hearing
   B. nose : smelling
   C. intestines : digestion
   D. skin : perspiration
   E. lung : respiration

_____ 9. ASTRINGENT : SHRINKAGE ::
   A. automobile : exhaustion
   B. milk : evaporation
   C. heat : expansion
   D. word : contraction
   E. smoke : inhalation

_____ 10. BILE : LIVER ::
   A. ribs : chest
   B. stones : kidney
   C. oxygen : breath
   D. saliva : mouth
   E. mucus : membrane

[**Section 15:**   1:B   2:A   3:E   4:D   5:C   6:A   7:B   8:E   9:D   10:C]

SECTION 17 ANALOGIES

Directions: For each of the following items, choose the lettered pair of words that expresses a relationship that is most similar to the relationship between the pair of capitalized words. Write the letter of your answer on the line provided before the number of the item. For answers, see page 181.

_____ 1. DESPOT : RULER ::
A. depot : railway
B. prince : king
C. dictator : leader
D. symphony : conductor
E. mayor : governor

_____ 2. SEDITION : REBELLIOUS ::
A. promotion : sluggish
B. slander : hurtful
C. sermon : lengthy
D. liberation : enslaving
E. conversation : wordless

_____ 3. TRIBUNAL : JUSTICE ::
A. firetrap : safety
B. life : fairness
C. battlefield : neutrality
D. court : lawfulness
E. beachhead : peace

_____ 4. SOCIALIST : NATIONAL ::
A. commentator : private
B. democrat : free
C. optimist : crabby
D. librarian : conservative
E. capitalist : individual

_____ 5. COLLATERAL : LOAN ::
A. bond : bail
B. banking : withdrawal
C. gold : mine
D. mortgage : garage
E. insurance : earthquake

_____ 6. GRATIS : COUNSEL ::
A. public : trial
B. gathered : attendance
C. city : council
D. guilty : verdict
E. free : advice

_____ 7. REMITTANCE : MONEY ::
A. payment : debt
B. telegram : message
C. snowflake : storm
D. microphone : mike
E. monkey : ape

_____ 8. PITTANCE : SMALL ::
A. love : hateful
B. microscope : tiny
C. million : large
D. wages : high
E. temperature : low

_____ 9. MARAUDER : LOOT ::
A. pianist : orchestra
B. kidnapper : police
C. thief : money
D. plumber : sewer
E. guard : royalty

_____ 10. LIQUIDATION : SETTLEMENT ::
A. prediction : memory
B. education : income
C. emotion : logic
D. assassination : slaying
E. sharpness : speech

[**Section 16:** 1:A 2:E 3:C 4:A 5:D 6:B 7:B 8:E 9:C 10:D]

197

Index

The entry words in *Vocabulary for College A* are listed alphabetically in this index with the page numbers on which they appear as entry words. Also listed are variant forms or related words that are treated in the exercises.

B 9
C 0
D 1
E 2
F 3
G 4
H 5
I 6
J 7